AMERICAN WOMEN

EDITED BY *Margaret Mead* AND *Frances Balgley Kaplan*
WITH AN INTRODUCTION AND AN EPILOGUE BY *Margaret Mead*

Illustrated with charts

AMERICAN WOMEN

The Report of the President's Commission
on the Status of Women and
Other Publications of the Commission

CHARLES SCRIBNER'S SONS · NEW YORK

Contents

CONTENTS

CONTENTS

List of Charts

List of Tables

INTRODUCTION

Introduction

by MARGARET MEAD

In the United States, progress toward the realization of ideals, which we first profess and then work to achieve, is marked by various democratic devices. First, there are conferences and commissions, platforms and declarations. Then, organs of the federal government are established to implement activities embodying the newly enunciated principles. The growth of the movement to give American women more freedom can be traced in such steps through the first modern congress on women's rights, the Seneca Falls Convention of 1848; the Women-in-Industry Service, created in 1918 to deal with the labor problems of the millions of women who went to work during World War I; the ratification of the Woman Suffrage Amendment in 1920; and the establishment of the Women's Bureau by an Act of Congress, approved by President Woodrow Wilson on June 5, 1920, as a continuing service within the Department of Labor, an advance that marked the recognition by the federal government that the conditions under which women work are a matter of lasting national concern.

In 1920, there were $8\frac{1}{4}$ million working women. Since then, their numbers in the labor force have almost tripled, but no definite federal action on their behalf was taken until the establishment of a Commission on the Status of Women by President John F. Kennedy in 1961. Between the two world wars, many barriers of custom broke down, and there was progress on many fronts. Women won the vote, and more and more of them went to work. In contrast to World War I, when they were only admitted to the Navy as yeomen, women were allowed a variety of roles in the armed services in World War II.

In spite of progress, there also was a profound and growing unease among those who felt an important part of American democracy to be the freedom of women to contribute to our society not only as mothers, but also as individuals. Especially after World War II, women seemed to be retreating from active participation in the wider society. Early marriage, more children, wives who left school and college to support their husbands' education, a smaller proportion of women in graduate schools—all these seemed to be symptoms of a diminution of women's earlier drive for a chance to be persons in their own right, with work and interests of their own.

As in earlier years, when the movement for woman suffrage was linked with other reforms—in race relations, labor relations, education, and so on— national needs in the 1960's have refocused attention on women. One of these contemporary demands is for more well-educated workers to meet the new technological advances. But the interest in new kinds of science education, which is in part a response to this demand, has revealed a widening gap in the educational and career expectations for boys and for girls. At the same time, our growing national awareness of the $\frac{1}{10}$ of the nation who, because of physical dissimilarities from the majority, are dispossessed of civil rights and of the $\frac{2}{5}$ who are educationally and economically deprived is echoed in an awakened sense that great numbers of our women are being wasted. Statistics on changes in life expectancy emphasize how many more years married women will have after their grown children have left the home. Statistics on juvenile delinquency have led to new questions about the adequacy of homes in which women must be simultaneously mothers and breadwinners. From around the world, as an effect of the United Nations Commission on Human Rights and the voices of women newly emerging into public life, the pressure of other peoples' opinion is being exerted on the United States. The great gains of American women in health, literacy, education, and opportunity have been compared with the relatively few positions held by American women in government and industry—a puzzling contrast between our claim to freedom of opportunity and our actual accomplishments.

The time was ripe for a new stocktaking. It was highly appropriate that President Kennedy should ask Mrs. Eleanor Roosevelt, with her world orientation, to chair the Commission that would work toward bringing the status of American women up to date. It was appropriate, too, that this should be Mrs. Roosevelt's final service to the women of America, to whom she had so long been an inspiration. The present outcome of the Commission's work, its Report, *American Women,* is a complete document. It stands by and for itself as it was presented to President Kennedy on October 11, 1963.

This volume presents, along with the Report, an account of the work of the various Committees and consultations supplementary to the basic document, so that the reader will have the background information upon which the Commission drew. However, it is important to distinguish between the Committee writings, each of which is more limited in scope but fuller in detail, and the final, authoritative Report, written after the Commission had carried out its task of deciding among various alternative solutions to the problems that had been considered.

American Women marks where we now stand. Some of the suggestions made may open up new possibilities for the future, but the work of the Committees and the Commission is finished. Even before this first phase was completed, the second phase, action on the federal level to implement the Report, had begun.

On November 1, 1963, an Executive order established an Interdepartmental Committee on the Status of Women and a Citizens' Advisory Council to ensure that the work begun by the Commission would be continued. Then, in the winter of 1963–64, President Lyndon B. Johnson introduced another form of implementation by stimulating the search for highly competent women for responsible posts filled by presidential appointment. By June 1964, 56 such appointments had been made.

In the same period, the third phase also was initiated. In June 1964, representatives of the 32 State Commissions on the Status of Women that then existed met in Washington. There is still much unfinished business on the federal level, some of which will take years to complete, but the third phase belongs to the states, the national voluntary organizations, and the local committees. At this stage regional, state, and local differences in history, wealth, and degree of industrialization must be dealt with imaginatively and patiently, community by community.

Like all documents directed toward removing legal restrictions and altering formal usage, the Commission's Report can only lay the foundation on which men and women may build. They are freer to act because of the recommendations that have been made, but the document itself is permissive, not coercive. If women regard these greater possibilities as essentially threatening to their sense of themselves as persons, they will be unable to take advantage of the legal support given to their greater freedom. And to the extent that men believe they achieve a sense of their intrinsic masculinity only in those situations in which women know less, earn less,

5

achieve less, and win less recognition than they do, efforts to put the recommendations of the Commission into practice will be effectively, even though often unconsciously, sabotaged.

It is also the case that, to the extent that the present education of and expectations for girls and women are scrutinized and revision is attempted, these tasks will change the educators themselves. The mother who can give her daughter confidence in her ability to understand mathematics will herself be more ready to use her own gifts in middle age. The father who is equally committed to his daughter's and to his son's education will find himself a less skeptical and a more sympathetic employer and colleague of women. In the United States, change comes through a change of educational style. Opening new kinds of educational opportunity for women is a way of saying most definitely that women can and should, as individuals, contribute more to society as trained and responsible participants.

Historically, no women's movement has worked for women alone. In each generation the leaders have taken to heart the plight of those who in greater measure shared their disabilities—the slave, the child working in a factory, the landless sharecropper, the homeless migratory worker, the urban worker who has lost his tools, the starving and the helpless millions who have died for causes they neither understood nor espoused.

Greater freedom for women today has rightly been linked in the Commission's Report with a conscious recognition of the American women who are caught in the grip of poverty, racial discrimination, and cultural deprivation, the women who are members of minority groups, and the more than 4½ million women who are the heads of households.

This Report deals with women in America, but it is crucial to emphasize that all over the world they are looked to as models to emulate or to fear. In many of the new countries, women want to have the status of American women, not that of their own men. Where American women succeed, others can hope that they, too, will be successful. But where they see us fail, either in the perennial tasks of women as homemakers or in the exercise of the freedom of which we have made too little use, the hands of the clock are turned back for them.

SECTION I

AMERICAN WOMEN

The Report of the President's Commission
on the Status of Women

1917–1963

We are at the beginning of an era when the inroads of poverty, hunger, and disease will be lessened and when men and women everywhere will have it within their power to develop their potential capacities to the maximum.

JOHN F. KENNEDY
Denver, Colorado
October 14, 1960

Letter of Transmittal

Washington, D. C., October 11, 1963.

Dear Mr. President:

In presenting to you the report of your Commission on the Status of Women, we are mindful first of all that we transmit it bereft of our Chairman. Today is Eleanor Roosevelt's birthday. In handing you the results of work started with her active participation, we wish once again to pay tribute to a great woman. Her devotion to fuller realization of the abilities of women in all walks of life and in all countries raised the status of women everywhere in the world.

Accepting your invitation to do so, we have assessed the position of women and the functions they perform in the home, in the economy, in the society. In so vast a field, selection of points of concentration was unavoidable. In any case, certain priorities were established for us by your Executive order that brought the Commission into being.[*]

At every stage, we have drawn upon the wisdom, experience, and technical competence of varied groups beyond the Commission's membership. Seven Committees, composed of knowledgeable men and women in addition to members of the Commission, explored in depth the following areas: education; home and community services; private employment, in particular that under federal contracts; employment in the federal government; labor standards; federal social insurance and taxes as they affect women; and the legal treatment of women in respect to civil and political rights. These

[* The Executive order, Appendix I, appears on pages 207–209. All bracketed footnotes to the Commission Report are by the Editors of this new edition.]

9

Committees authorized the preparation of special papers on matters under consideration, invited presentations by advocates of various points of view and spokesmen for various organizations, and sponsored two special consultations: one examining private employment opportunities for women, attended by representatives of management, labor, and professional organizations; and one exploring new patterns in volunteer work.[*]

The Commission itself arranged two consultations, with appropriate participation, to assess the portrayal of women by the mass media and to consider problems of Negro women.[†]

Realizing that women's opportunities expand or contract with the economic well-being of the nation as a whole, the Commission has been gravely troubled about the relation between population growth and economic growth over the next decades. In your State of the Union message this year, you pointed out that "32 million Americans . . . still live in the outskirts of poverty." We note that the American population, 189 million in 1963, is estimated to reach 226 million by 1975 and 333 million by the year 2000. Americans have been marrying younger—nearly a quarter of a million boys between 14 and 19, married in their teens, are now out of school and at work. Young couples in the 1950's and 1960's have been having more children than their parents did, and lowered rates of infant mortality are enabling more of these children to reach maturity than in earlier years of this century. Unemployment among youth is a serious problem now, and unless the economy grows much more rapidly in the future than it has during the past decade, today's youngsters will feel the sharp pinch of declining ratios of new employment opportunities to persons seeking work.

Current lack of fuller employment bears specifically on many women in low-income families unable to offer their children opportunities that better-off citizens take for granted as part of the American standard of living. Substandard homes and stunted lives are individually tragic; the existence of handicapped groups retards the whole society.

Adoption of programs for more complete realization of the potentialities of all of the American people becomes increasingly difficult in times of financial stringency. A rapidly growing economy is, therefore, a prior condition of the achievement of many of the changes that we recommend.

[* See Section II, pages 97–177, for a review of this work. The names of Committee members, Commission members, and other acknowledgments and references appear on pages 254–267.]

[† See Appendix III, pages 214–228.]

But a society cannot claim greatness solely because a majority of its members are well housed, well clothed, well fed. In a great society, talents are evoked and realized, creative minds probe the frontiers of knowledge, expectations of excellence are widely shared. Higher quality in American life was a specific concern of this Commission, both because of the potential contribution of outstanding women to it and because women in their families are transmitters of the central values of the culture.

The quality of women's exercise of their capacities and responsibilities will be higher as American institutions become more suitable to contemporary life. We have considered the basic framework of the education and training of girls and women, the counseling through which they become aware of opportunities, the conditions of their life in the home and outside it in the years of their maturity. Our signed report conveys our major recommendations.

When you announced the appointment of our Commission in December 1961, you suggested the appropriateness of recounting the story of women's progress in a free, democratic society, noting gains already achieved and advances still to be made. Appended to our report is a summary of changes in the position of American women in the course of the twentieth century that we believe will give perspective to our proposals.

The last section of our document credits the intensive and sustained work of the Committees, through which much of the Commission's assessment was made, and that of the participants in our various consultations. Their reports and other material, providing substantiation at length for the recommendations here presented, are available to interested individuals and groups carrying on special work in particular areas.

We note with satisfaction that even while the Commission was engaged in its inquiry, a number of its recommendations were put into effect. Employment opportunities for women in federal public service were notably widened by changes in policy and procedure following your directive to executive agencies of July 1962. Among administration measures submitted to Congress, several have contained provisions which we had endorsed or recommended, outstandingly the bill that became the Equal Pay Act of 1963.

On behalf of the Commission, Mr. President, we are honored to submit to you this unanimous report. In inviting action on its recommendations, we count on a widely varied initiative, both private and public, in all parts of the country. May we express again our appreciation of your special interest in our work and of the cooperation that we have enjoyed in the

11

course of our deliberations from both the Congress and the federal executive agencies. We wish also to thank the public officials of state and local governments and the many private citizens and organizations engaged in a broad range of activities who have given us generously of their time and been of great assistance in the formation of our policies.

Sincerely yours,

Executive Vice Chairman.

Vice Chairman.

1884–1962

Because I anticipate success in achieving full employment and full use of America's magnificent potential, I feel confident that in the years ahead many of the remaining outmoded barriers to women's aspirations will disappear. Within a rapidly growing economy, with appropriate manpower planning, all Americans will have a better chance to develop their individual capacities, to earn a good livelihood, and to strengthen family life.

ELEANOR ROOSEVELT
Hyde Park
June 15, 1962

Invitation to Action

This report is an invitation to action. When President John F. Kennedy appointed our Commission, he said: ". . . we have by no means done enough to strengthen family life and at the same time encourage women to make their full contribution as citizens. . . . It is appropriate at this time . . . to review recent accomplishments, and to acknowledge frankly the further steps that must be taken. This is a task for the entire nation."

The 96 million American women and girls include a range from infant to octogenarian, from migrant farm mother to suburban homemaker, from file clerk to research scientist, from Olympic athlete to college president. Greater development of women's potential and fuller use of their present abilities can greatly enhance the quality of American life. We have made recommendations to this end.

We invite response to our recommendations by citizen initiative exercised in many ways—through individual inventiveness, voluntary agencies, community cooperation, commercial enterprise, corporate policy, foundation support, governmental action at various levels. In making our proposals, we have had in mind the well-being of the entire society; their adoption would in many cases be of direct benefit to men as well as women.

Certain tenets have guided our thinking. Respect for the worth and dignity of every individual and conviction that every American should have a chance to achieve the best of which he—or she—is capable are basic to the meaning of both freedom and equality in this democracy. They have been, and now are, great levers for constructive social change, here and around the world. We have not hesitated to measure the present shape of things against our convictions regarding a good society and to note discrepancies between American life as it is in 1963 and as it might become through informed and intelligent action.

The human and national costs of social lag are heavy; for the most part, they are also avoidable. That is why we urge changes, many of them long overdue, in the conditions of women's opportunity in the United States.

RESPONSIBLE CHOICE

We believe that one of the greatest freedoms of the individual in a democratic society is the freedom to choose among different life patterns. Innumerable private solutions found by different individuals in search of the good life provide society with basic strength far beyond the possibilities of a dictated plan.

Illumined by values transmitted through home and school and church, society and heritage, and informed by present and past experience, each woman must arrive at her contemporary expression of purpose, whether as a center of home and family, a participant in the community, a contributor to the economy, a creative artist or thinker or scientist, a citizen engaged in politics and public service. Part and parcel of this freedom is the obligation to assume corresponding responsibility.

Yet there are social as well as individual determinants of freedom of choice; for example, the city slum and the poor rural crossroad frustrate natural gifts and innate human powers. It is a bitter fact that for millions of men and women economic stringency all but eliminates choice among alternatives.

In a progress report to the President in August 1962, the Commission's Chairman, Eleanor Roosevelt, said: "A rapidly rising national output is the strongest weapon against substandard jobs, poverty-stricken homes, and barren lives."

In the same vein, Secretary of Labor W. Willard Wirtz has warned: "There is not going to be much in the way of expanding opportunities for women unless we are ready and able to assure the jobs which the economy as a whole requires."

GROWTH AND OPPORTUNITY

Unless the economy grows at a substantially faster rate than at present, oncoming generations will not find work commensurate with their skills. The number of new entrants of all ages into the labor force was about 2 million a year in 1960. By 1970, it will be 3 million.

Much of the work offered by a modern economy demands types of skill requiring levels of education that only a nation with abundant resources can supply; if such skills, when acquired, are not used because the economy is lagging, the resulting human frustrations and material waste are very costly indeed.

Economic expansion is of particular significance to women. One of the ironies of history is that war has brought American women their greatest economic opportunities. In establishing this Commission, the President noted: "In every period of national emergency, women have served with distinction in widely varied capacities but thereafter have been subject to treatment as a marginal group whose skills have been inadequately utilized."

Comparable opportunity—and far more varied choice—could be provided by full employment in a period without war.

The Council of Economic Advisers has estimated that between 1958 and 1962 the country's productive capacity exceeded its actual output by some $170 billion, or almost $1,000 per person in the United States. Had this potential been realized, lower rates of unemployment and an impressive supply of additional goods and services would have contributed to national well-being. The currently unused resources of the American economy include much work that could be done by women.

BIRTHS RISE, DEATHS DROP, POPULATION GROWS

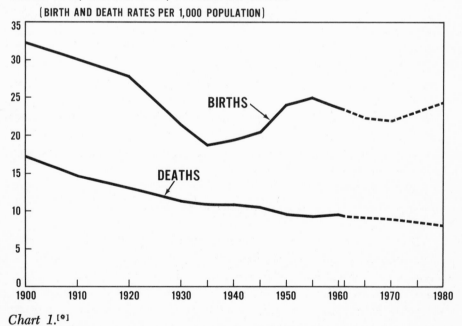

(BIRTH AND DEATH RATES PER 1,000 POPULATION)

Chart 1.[*]

[* For all chart sources, see Appendix V, pages 265–267.]

HIGHER EXPECTATIONS

But while freedom of choice for many American women, as for men, is limited by economic considerations, one of the most pervasive limitations is the social climate in which women choose what they prepare themselves to do. Too many plans recommended to young women reaching maturity are only partially suited to the second half of the twentieth century. Such advice is correspondingly confusing to them.

Even the role most generally approved by counselors, parents, and friends—the making of a home, the rearing of children, and the transmission to them in their earliest years of the values of the American heritage—is frequently presented as it is thought to have been in an earlier and simpler society. Women's ancient function of providing love and nurture stands. But for entry into modern life, today's children need a preparation far more diversified than that of their predecessors.

Similarly, women's participation in such traditional occupations as teaching, nursing, and social work is generally approved, with current shortages underscoring the nation's need for such personnel. But means for keeping up to date the skills of women who continue in such professions are few. So, too, are those for bringing up to date the skills of women who withdraw in order to raise families but return after their families are grown.

Commendation of women's entry into certain other occupations is less general, even though some of them are equally in need of trained people. Girls hearing that most women find mathematics and science difficult, or that engineering and architecture are unusual occupations for a woman, are not led to test their interest by activity in these fields.

Because too little is expected of them, many girls who graduate from high school intellectually able to do good college work do not go to college. Both they as individuals and the nation as a society are thereby made losers.

The subtle limitations imposed by custom are, upon occasion, reinforced by specific barriers. In the course of the twentieth century many bars against women that were firmly in place in 1900 have been lowered or dropped. But certain restrictions remain.

DISCRIMINATIONS AND DISADVANTAGES

Some of these discriminatory provisions are contained in the common law. Some are written into statute. Some are upheld by court decisions. Others take the form of practices of industrial, labor, professional, or governmental organizations that discriminate against women in apprenticeship, training, hiring, wages, and promotion. We have identified a number of outmoded and prejudicial attitudes and practices.

Throughout its deliberations, the Commission has kept in mind certain women who have special disadvantages. Among heads of families in the United States, 1 in 10 is a woman. At least half of them are carrying responsibility for both earning the family's living and making the family's home. Their problems are correspondingly greater; their resources are usually less.

Seven million nonwhite women and girls belong to minority racial groups. Discrimination based on color is morally wrong and a source of national weakness. Such discrimination currently places an oppressive dual burden on millions of Negro women. The consultation held by the Commission on the situation of Negro women emphasized that in too many families lack of opportunity for men as well as women, linked to racial discrimination, has forced the women to assume too large a share of the family responsibility. Such women are twice as likely as other women to have to seek employment while they have preschool children at home; they are just beginning to gain entrance to the expanding fields of clerical and commercial employment; except for the few who can qualify as teachers or other professionals, they are forced into low-paid service occupations.

FAMILY INCOMES VARY BY COLOR, REGION, MEMBERS WORKING
(MEDIAN INCOME, 1961)

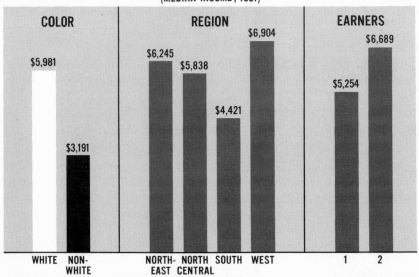

Chart 2.

Hundreds of thousands of other women face somewhat similar situations: American Indians, for instance, and Spanish-Americans, many of whom live in urban centers but are new to urban life and burdened with language problems.

While there are highly skilled members of all these groups, in many of the families of these women the unbroken cycle of deprivation and retardation repeats itself from generation to generation, compounding its individual cost in human indignity and unhappiness and its social cost in incapacity and delinquency. This cycle must be broken, swiftly and at as many points as possible. The Commission strongly urges that in the carrying out of its recommendations, special attention be given to difficulties that are wholly or largely the products of this kind of discrimination.

LENGTHENING LIFE SPANS

The Commission has also been impressed with the extent to which lengthening life spans are causing changes in women's occupations and preoccupations from decade to decade of their adult experience. The life expectancy of a girl baby is now 73 years; it was 48 years in 1900. In comparison with her own grandmother, today's young woman has a quarter century of additional life with abundant new choices to plan for. It is essential that the counseling of girls enable them to foresee the later as well as the earlier phases of their adulthood.

Eight out of 10 women are in paid employment outside the home at some time during their lives, and many of these, and others as well, engage in unpaid work as volunteers.

The population contains 13 million single girls and women 14 and over. A 20-year-old girl, if she remains single, will spend some 40 years in the labor force. If after working for a few years, she marries and has a family, and then goes back into the labor force at 30, she is likely to work for some 23 more years. Particularly during the years when her children are in school but have not yet left home permanently, the work she seeks is apt to be part-time. Inflexibility with regard to part-time employment in most current hiring systems, alike in government and in private enterprise, excludes the use of much able and available trained womanpower; practices should be altered to permit it.

Women's greater longevity as compared with men makes them the predominant group in the final age brackets. There are almost 800,000 more women than men 75 and over. The number of such women grew from slightly over 2 million in 1950 to more than 3 million in 1960. To most, this

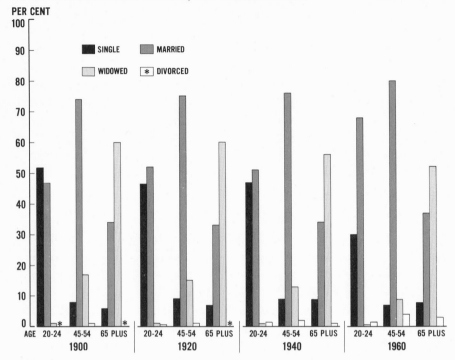

TODAY'S WOMEN MARRY EARLIER, ARE WIDOWED LATER

PER CENT

Chart 3.

is a period of economic dependency which often ends in a need for terminal care.

AREAS OF SPECIAL ATTENTION

With such facts in view, the Commission has considered developments in American institutions which might usefully be coupled to the long series of historic changes that have increased women's opportunities and security. We were directed to review progress and make recommendations as needed for constructive action in six areas:

- Employment policies and practices, including those on wages, under federal contracts.

- Federal social-insurance and tax laws as they affect the net earnings and other income of women.

22

- Federal and state labor laws dealing with such matters as hours, night work, and wages, to determine whether they are accomplishing the purposes for which they were established and whether they should be adapted to changing technological, economic, and social conditions.

- Differences in legal treatment of men and women in regard to political and civil rights, property rights, and family relations.

- New and expanded services that may be required for women as wives, mothers, and workers, including education, counseling, training, home services, and arrangements for care of children during the working day.

- The employment policies and practices of the Government of the United States with reference to additional affirmative steps which should be taken through legislation, executive, or administrative action to assure nondiscrimination on the basis of sex and to enhance constructive employment opportunities for women.

As our work progressed, we became convinced that greater public understanding of the value of continuing education for all mature Americans is perhaps the highest priority item on the American agenda. And it is one of particular importance to women.

In the past, Americans have regarded education as something for the young. It is true that over recent decades the age at which a person's education was generally held to be completed has moved up. When a majority of the population went to work at 14, much used to be made of closing exercises for the eighth grade. Such ceremonies are now commonly reserved for high school graduation; to a rising proportion of the population, commencement means the award of college diplomas. But even so, education continues to be thought of as a preparation for life that ends when adult life begins. Recognition of the necessity of education during adult life has still to be established.

Yet today, abilities must be constantly sharpened, knowledge and skills kept up to date. Continuing opportunities to do this must be widely available and broad enough to include both the person who did not finish elementary school and the highly gifted specialist who must follow the frontiers of learning as they move; both the person whose skill has been superseded by automation and the person (usually a woman) who has been out of the labor market for a time but can, with preparation, go back in and make effective use of her talents. Formal and informal adult education can enable women of all ages both to fit themselves for what they do next and to experience the satisfactions that come from learning for its own sake. We start, therefore, with our recommendations in the field of education.

Education and Counseling

The Commission has given great weight to educational needs of mature women, but nothing it can recommend to meet the special needs of women is of greater importance than improvement in the quality of early education available to all of the nation's youth. Good basic instruction—adequate facilities and able, dedicated teachers—must be within the reach of all children from the time they start school.

We wholeheartedly advocate measures, undertaken by localities, by states, and, when needed, by the federal Congress, to provide financial support for the improvement of primary, secondary, and higher education through better plant and equipment, teacher training, increased salaries for teachers, experiment and research on curricula and teaching methods, adequate counseling, and better vocational programs.

We also support expansion, in numbers and scope, of private, federal, and other public scholarship and loan programs.

But improvement in American education as it has been in the past is not enough. Its framework must be enlarged to include adult education as an integral part of the structure.

In its widest context, adult education is now a major undertaking, with 30 to 40 million individuals involved. Between 2½ and 3 million adults, with some 82,000 teachers and administrators, take courses in public schools. But it is too often thought of as a diversion on the fringes of adult life. So far, neither in monetary allocations nor in quality of instruction have formal educational institutions, foundations, or indeed the individuals concerned caused it to receive the attention it merits in a rapidly moving industrial society.

The new range of opportunities must be diversified, comprehensive, and flexible; it must have counseling at its center. In an evolving culture, education and vocation are inextricably combined. Each contributes to the other to an extent only slowly becoming understood. The proportion of time that an individual gives to education and to other activities at any given moment depends on many factors, among them age, capacity, and current responsibilities. But flexible opportunities to pursue lines of interest to higher levels, or to branch out into new lines, should be at hand.

EDUCATION FOR THE MATURE WOMAN

Men and women are equally in need of continuing education, but at present women's opportunities are more limited than men's. In part, this is because neither the substantial arrangements for advanced training provided by businesses for their executives nor the educational and training programs of the armed services are open to many women. In part, it is because counseling and training are of particular importance at times when new choices are likely to be made, and women's lives are less likely than men's to follow continuous patterns.

The woman who marries and is raising a family has urgent educational needs that have so far been badly neglected. During her intensive home-making years, she should be encouraged to prepare for at least 3 decades of life after 40 when she will be relatively free to use her abilities and will wish to use them as constructively and as interestingly as possible. She also needs to continue her education in one form or another in order to provide the assistance, companionship, and stimulation needed by her husband and by her children as they develop.

The education required by mature women is at all levels. While illiteracy and near-illiteracy grow less year by year, almost 4 million adult women, alive in 1960, had had less than 5 years of schooling. In a society in which literacy is essential, they cannot follow a simple written instruction or fill out a simple form. In a time when automation is displacing workers far more qualified than they, their chances in the job market are slim indeed. Those with young children cannot help prepare them adequately for entry into today's world.

Similarly, over 11½ million adult women have started, but failed to finish high school; less than half of all women 25 and over are high school graduates. Completion of high school would lift many out of the congested competition for declining jobs in unskilled employment.

Most single women work for a large part of their lives. Many young widows and married women from low-income families work outside the home even when they have young children. In 1963, more than half of all

PER CENT OF WOMEN WORKERS OVER 45 IS RISING

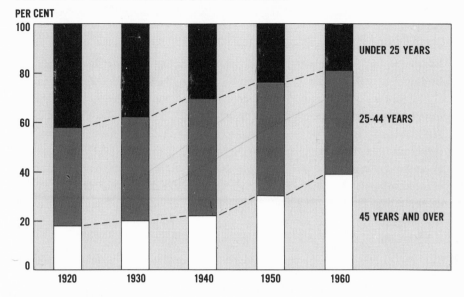

Chart 4.

women in the 45- to 54-year age bracket were in paid employment. In the schools and out of the schools, a realistic, many-sided vocational program can reduce the tendency for women returning to the labor market, or entering it for the first time, to take the first job that comes along and remain in it. Their capabilities may be well above the level of competence which this job requires. Technical training for clerical, manual, and other skills is especially important to women of minority groups. During their school years they were not trained for fields that are now being opened to them.

Until recently, up to the college level, more young women than young men have stayed in school: in 1962, the median number of years of school completed was 12 for women as against 11.6 for men. Even in 1962, 872,000 in the nation's high school graduating classes were boys as against 966,000 girls.

But once the college level is reached, the girls begin to fall behind. The 437,000 women who enrolled in college in 1962 constituted only about 42 per cent of the entering class. Women are earning only 1 in 3 of the B.A.'s and M.A.'s awarded by American institutions of higher learning, and only 1 in 10 of the Ph.D.'s. Today's ratios, moreover, represent a loss of ground as compared with the 1930's, when 2 out of 5 B.A.'s and M.A.'s and 1 out of 7 Ph.D.'s were earned by women.

27

Presentation of higher education in the form in which women with family responsibilities can take advantage of it quite clearly requires new adaptations.

To be usable by the large numbers of young women who marry in their late teens and early twenties, and by the mature woman in general, continuing education must be geographically available where the woman is. If she breaks away from school or college to marry, she is less likely to return after a gap than if practicable means of continued study are immediately at hand. Higher education at a local junior college offers an immediate opportunity. Community colleges are now being founded at the rate of one every two weeks. Restyled correspondence courses and programed learning can be pursued at home. By 1971, the National Educational Television network is expected to provide credit-carrying courses equivalent to about half an undergraduate program.

The importance of vocational training to parallel academic courses is attested by the fact that increasing numbers of women are going to college and that almost 70 per cent of women college graduates work for part of the second half of their adult lives. Many high schools offer vocational

WOMEN AT ALL AGES NEED MORE EDUCATION

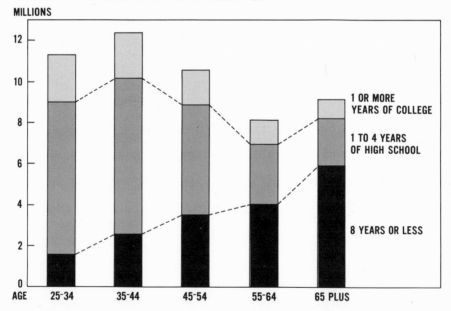

Chart 5.

28

courses suitable for use by their graduates. Four-fifths of the larger junior and community colleges provide technical training under the National Defense Education Act (NDEA). The opportunity to attain advanced skills to match national scarcities is clear from the very names of the courses: electronics, plastics, nucleonics.

For mature women using educational facilities at any level, part-time study is a likely pattern. Its legitimacy must be recognized both by institutions of higher education in accepting plans of study projected on this basis and by academic and other bodies determining eligibility for fellowships, scholarships, and loans.

Many current rigidities in regard to admission, academic prerequisites, residence, and the like, as well as scheduling, will have to yield to greater flexibility. For instance, proficiency testing should be widely available as a means of obtaining credit for knowledge acquired outside regular academic courses.

Means of acquiring or continuing education must be available to every adult at whatever point he or she broke off traditional formal schooling. The structure of adult education must be drastically revised. It must provide practicable and accessible opportunities, developed with regard for the needs of women, to complete elementary and secondary school and to continue education beyond high school. Vocational training, adapted to the nation's growing requirement for skilled and highly educated manpower, should be included at all of these educational levels. Where needed and appropriate, financial support should be provided by local, state, and federal governments and by private groups and foundations.[*]

Existing studies of education take too little account of sex differences—averages that include performance by men and women often obscure the facts about both. Research agencies should be encouraged to analyze more data by sex. Too little is known about factors affecting motivation in girls, about the effects of economic, ethnic, religious, and regional backgrounds on their aspirations and their learning processes. Much thinking is now being done about the need to teach problem-solving ability and broadly

[* Several new developments in federal aid to education will expand educational opportunities. Information about these and other significant developments affecting the status of women that have occurred since the publication of *American Women* appears in "Accomplishments through Continuing Leadership," pages 161–177.

The sections printed in bold-face type throughout the report are the formal recommendations of the Commission. These have been gathered together in Appendix II, pages 210–213.]

29

JOBS WOMEN HOLD REFLECT TRAINING THEY HAVE HAD

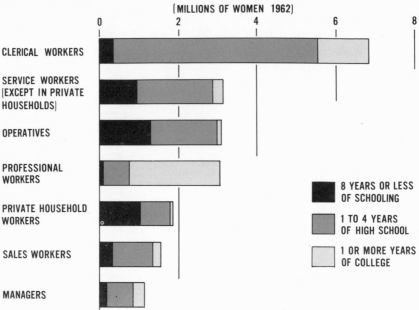

(MILLIONS OF WOMEN 1962)

Chart 6.

based fundamentals that will survive technological change. Such training has special relevance for married women, who can be expected to interrupt and then resume a field of study or a job.

We believe that a federal program should be established to survey, summarize, and disseminate research and statistics on women's education, fostering inclusion in new studies of separate data on males and females.

COUNSELING FOR CHOICE

In a democracy offering broad and everchanging choices, where ultimate decisions are made by individuals, skilled counseling becomes an inseparable part of education. Properly timed awareness of alternatives can be decisive in securing a student's maximum use of abilities without great waste of human and material resources.

Because of differences in life patterns of women as contrasted with men, the counseling of girls and women is a specialized form of the counseling profession. From infancy, roles held up to girls deflect talents into narrow channels. Among women of all levels of skill there is need for encourage-

30

ment to develop broader ranges of aptitudes and carry them into higher education. Imaginative counseling can lift aspirations beyond stubbornly persistent assumptions about "women's roles" and "women's interests" and result in choices that have inner authenticity for their makers.

Individuals should be helped to find out what alternatives exist, aided to reach judgments about them, and encouraged to make plans and take appropriate steps to execute them.

Lack of parental stimulation often conditions grade school youngsters from low-income families to settle for less education than their abilities warrant even before they reach high school. Daughters of families that are well able to pay for higher education too often see no reason for going as far as they could. In both cases, counselors can supply missing motivation.

Negro girls and women especially can be helped by counselors who are able to stimulate confidence to enter new fields and are aware of changing trends in marketable skills and newly opening job opportunities.

With imaginative guidance, employed women approaching retirement and mature women with grown families can find uses for their new leisure that are rewarding alike to them and to their communities.

Expanded counseling facilities have recently been urged by two presidential advisory groups—the President's Committee on Youth Employment and the Panel of Consultants on Vocational Education. The National Defense Education Act of 1958 provided training for secondary school guidance counselors and grants to the states for guidance, counseling, and testing services for secondary school students. Since enactment of this law, some 12,000 counselors have received training. The proposed National Education Improvement Act would extend and expand the NDEA guidance services. We regard such expansion as urgent.

Public and private schools and colleges increasingly assign full-time staff as counselors. In addition, the public employment offices counsel ⅔ of each year's high school seniors who seek employment. They also counsel some ¾ million women job seekers annually.

Yet, in quantity as well as quality, counseling is at present wholly inadequate. The recommended ratio of full-time guidance staff to secondary school students is 1 to 300; the actual ratio is 1 to 550, with great variation among regions and shortages greatest in low-income areas. Many counselors do not meet recommended standards of either the United States Employment Service or the professional associations in the field. Far too few have had supervised practice in counseling women. Counseling based on obsolete assumptions is routine at best; at worst, it is dangerous.

With up-to-date guidance for young and old accepted as a regular part

31

of the educational framework, programs for raising the competence of counselors should not be looked on as emergency measures. Cooperative relationships linking the public employment service, educational institutions, and employers are essential as opportunities shift and adult education increases.

Directories of existing vocational and educational counseling facilities in communities and states and occupational literature geared to the age groups using it can call attention to the rapidly changing requirements for jobs and to opportunities for intellectual development and maintenance of professional ability.

In a democracy offering broad and everchanging choices, where ultimate decisions are made by individuals, skilled counseling is an essential part of education. Public and private agencies should join in strengthening counseling resources. States and school districts should raise their standards for state employment service counselors and school guidance counselors. Institutions offering counseling education should provide both course content and ample supervised experience in the counseling of females as well as males, adults as well as adolescents.

Public and private-nonprofit employment counseling organizations should be adequately staffed to provide comprehensive and imaginative counseling services to:

- High school girls, not only as seniors but in their earlier years, and women engaged in higher education and continuing education;

- Women workers either entering the labor market, displaced from their jobs by economic changes, staying in on a part-time basis, or re-entering;

- Women wishing to make constructive use of their leisure, whether outside working hours, at times of lessened home responsibilities, or after retirement.

PREPARATION FOR FAMILY LIFE

Widening the choices for women beyond their doorstep does not imply neglect of their education for responsibilities in the home. Modern family life is demanding, and most of the time and attention given to it comes from women. At various stages, girls and women of all economic back-

8 OF EVERY 10 GIRLS WILL WORK IN PAID EMPLOYMENT

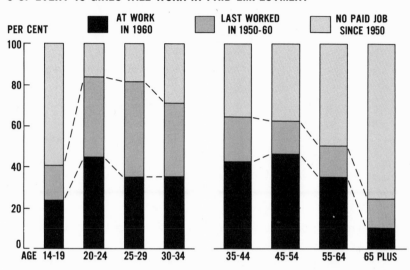

Chart 7.

grounds should receive education in respect to physical and mental health, child care and development, human relations within the family.

The teaching of home management should treat the subject with breadth that includes not only nutrition, textiles and clothing, housing and furnishings, but also the handling of family finances, the purchase of consumer goods, the uses of family leisure, and the relation of individuals and families to society.

Too little is currently known about effective instruction in homemaking skills, particularly about its timing. Neither home economics nor health education can be taught once and for all or at only one level; these subjects gain relevance at the time when a girl or woman finds them an answer to a felt need. For many high school youngsters, discussions on management of money, selection of food and clothing, and care of younger brothers and sisters can start from responsibilities that they already exercise at home.

Girls who drop out of school are likely to do so because they must assume responsibilities beyond their years either in the homes from which they come or in homes of their own. School-age mothers who drop out because of pregnancy are an extreme case of those for whom special instruction is necessary.

Experiments in schools, ranging all the way from the elementary grades

33

through junior college, and by private organizations working with youth and young married couples are developing new and effective patterns. The extent to which education for family responsibility can best be done outside of school through media such as television needs further exploration.

In the last years of high school, many students are looking forward to marriage in the near future. Courses in the social and economic responsibilities involved in establishing a home are sometimes advantageously studied by boys and girls together, contributing to their knowledge of each other's interests and concerns. Even women's colleges have given remarkably little serious thought to the better preparation of their students for the homemaking most of them will do.

Women should have opportunity for education about sex and human reproduction in the context of education for family responsibility.

The education of girls and women for their responsibilities in home and community should be thoroughly re-examined with a view to discovering more effective approaches, with experimentation in content and timing, and under auspices including school systems, private organizations, and the mass media.

Home and Community

The Commission recognizes the fundamental responsibility of mothers and homemakers and society's stake in strong family life. Demands upon women in the economic world, the community, and the home mean that women often simultaneously carry on several different kinds of activity. If the family is to continue to be the core institution of society as it has been for many centuries, new and expanded community services are necessary. Women can do a far more effective job as mothers and homemakers when communities provide appropriate resources and when they know how to use such resources for health, education, safety, recreation, child care, and counseling.

Of the 68 million women and girls 14 years and over in the United States today, 44 million are married and keeping house. Few twentieth-century changes have been more striking than those in the composition of American households.

Not so long ago, and not only in rural areas, family tasks were shared by members of two or more generations—by grandmothers, mothers or mothers-in-law, and maiden aunts, as well as by women with young children. Sisters and sisters-in-law often lived under the same roof or closeby.

Now, though fathers often take a larger share in the performance of household tasks than they used to and the older children help in many ways, in most families the mother is the only grown person present to assume day-to-day responsibility in the home. And the family is more than likely to be an anonymous newcomer among strange neighbors in an urban or suburban setting. These simultaneous changes in the composition of families and communities have altered the very nature of family life.

CHILD-CARE AND FAMILY SERVICES

Child-care services are needed in all communities, for children of all kinds of families who may require day care, after-school care, or intermittent care. In putting major emphasis on this need, the Commission affirms that child-care facilities are essential for women in many different circumstances, whether they work outside the home or not. It is regrettable when women with children are forced by economic necessity or by the regulations of welfare agencies to seek employment while their children are young. On the other hand, those who decide to work should have child-care services available.

The gross inadequacy of present child-care facilities is apparent. Across the country, licensed day care is available to some 185,000 children only. In nearly half a million families with children under 6 years, the mother is frequently the sole support. There are 117,000 families with children under 6 with only a father in the home. Almost 3 million mothers of children under 6 work outside the home although there is a husband present. Other mothers, though not at work, may be ill, living in overcrowded slum conditions with no play opportunities for children, responsible for mentally

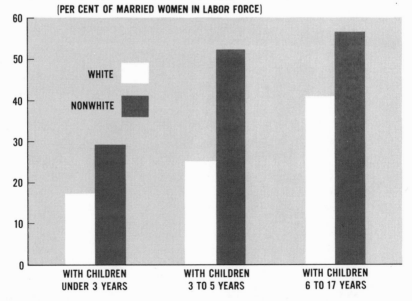

Chart 8.

36

TOO MANY CHILDREN LACK GOOD DAY CARE

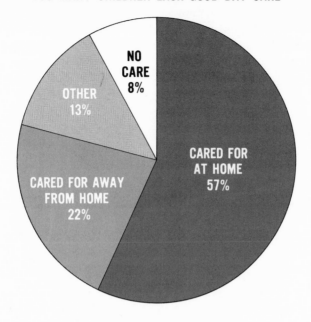

Chart 9.

retarded or emotionally handicapped children, or confronting family crises. Migrant families have no fixed homes.

In the absence of adequate child-care facilities, many of these mothers are forced to resort to makeshift arrangements or to leave their children without care. A 1958 survey disclosed no less than 400,000 children under 12 whose mothers worked full time and for whose supervision no arrangements whatsoever had been made. Suitable after-school supervision is especially crucial for children whom discrimination in housing forces into crowded neighborhoods.

Plans for housing developments, community centers, urban renewal projects, and migratory labor camps should provide space for child-care centers under licensing procedures insuring adequate standards.

Localities should institute after-school and vacation activities, in properly supervised places, for school-age children whose mothers must be away from home during hours when children are not in school.

Failure to assure such services reflects primarily a lack of community awareness of the realities of modern life. Recent federal legislation offering assistance to communities establishing day care is a first step in raising its provision to the level of national policy. As a number of localities have

37

discovered, child care can be provided in many ways as long as proper standards are assured: cooperatively by groups of parents; by public or private agencies with fees on a sliding scale according to ability to pay; or as a public undertaking.

Where group programs serve children from a cross section of a city, they provide training grounds for democratic social development. Their educational possibilities range from preparing underprivileged children for school, to providing constructive activities for normal youngsters, to offering especially gifted children additional means of development.

For the benefit of children, mothers, and society, child-care services should be available for children of families at all economic levels. Proper standards of child care must be maintained, whether services are in homes or in centers. Costs should be met by fees scaled to parents' ability to pay, contributions from voluntary agencies, and public appropriations.

Since passage of the Revenue Act of 1954, the financing of child care by working mothers has been aided by the allowance of deductions from federal income-tax liability to help cover care of children and disabled dependents of women workers. Such deductions have been available to couples with the joint income of man and wife not exceeding $5,100 a year.

Advantage from this act still accrues to some families of moderate income and to low-income families, but the limit above which deductions are not allowed has become unrealistic. In 1954, the median income of families with husband working and wife in the labor force was approximately $5,336; by 1961, it had risen to $7,188. The majority of working couples are therefore ineligible for deductions.

In calculating tax deductions for child care, moreover, no account has been taken of the number of children that must be cared for.

Tax deductions for child-care expenses of working mothers should be kept commensurate with the median income of couples when both husband and wife are engaged in substantial employment. The present limitation on their joint income, above which deductions are not allowable, should be raised. Additional deductions, of lesser amounts, should be allowed for children beyond the first. The 11-year age limit for child-care deductions should be raised.

No deduction has been allowed for child care in families where the wife is incapacitated. An allowance should be permitted immediately in cases where the wife is in an institution; study should be given to the feasibility of extending the deduction to cases where an incapacitated wife is not institutionalized.

The emphasis which we place on child care does not mean that we are unaware of the importance of other services to strengthen family life. Population growth, with increasing proportions of very young and very old; urbanization; and mobility resulting in separation from traditional family resources are intensifying pressures on many services already inadequate in scope, variety, and quality.

Family counseling by professionally trained social workers should be available to families disrupted by separation and desertion, unmarried parents, children who lack protection or have special problems, and young people who need guidance to prevent delinquency. Contact with resources that may be available in the community can often resolve problems menacing the stability or security of such persons and aid in their rehabilitation. Among very low-income families and those without income, skilled services can help develop potential for self-support, establishing self-respect and capacity to act as self-directing and useful citizens.

In most communities, skilled homemakers available to assume responsibility in times of family emergency or stress are very rare. Yet the services of a trained and able woman, professional or volunteer, to keep a home running for an interim period can be the deciding factor preventing the disintegration of a family. Such a resource should be at hand when mothers are incapacitated or require emergency short-term child care, or when the presence of a skilled person for an interval can help teach mothers who have difficulty in managing their homes and children how to do their homemaking job effectively.

Many women live alone beyond the age at which they can manage the mechanics of a household. For them, for chronically ill or disabled persons, for convalescents coming out of general or mental hospitals, the availability of a visiting nurse or home nursing, home-delivered meals, or homemaker services, often required only on a part-time basis, can mean the difference between continued life at home as a member of a community and removal to an institution. Counseling on special problems—social, legal, or financial as well as health—is frequently needed by older persons.

Family services under public and private auspices to help families avoid or overcome breakdown or dependency and establish a soundly based homelife, and professionally supervised homemaker services to meet

emergency or other special needs should be strengthened, extended, or established where lacking.

The provision of preventive, curative, and rehabilitative health services is a community responsibility which should be planned on a community-wide basis, including out-of-hospital as well as hospital programs. Many women are unaware of existing facilities for prenatal, infant, and preschool services and adult preventive and diagnostic services. Many others do not have such services accessible where they live or work. The decline in infant mortality rates has been one of the great gains of this century, but in some disadvantaged groups the rates are still almost twice as high as in the general population. Education in the care of families in health and in illness and expanded health services which reach women in lower-income and minority groups are necessary if these rates are to be changed. If women in general are to avoid the high prevalence of chronic illness now found in older age groups, such services must be available to and used by them during their formative and early adult years.

More than 1.3 million women living outside institutions have chronic conditions which make them unable to carry on their major activity—going to school or to work or keeping house. Over 5 million women of working age have chronic conditions limiting their activity. The combined efforts of public and voluntary programs reach only a very small portion of those who need rehabilitation services; additional investment could restore many of them to satisfying and productive lives.

Large numbers of physically and mentally disabled women in this country need rehabilitation services to fit them either for work or for self-care and independence in the activities of daily living.

Community programs under public and private auspices should make comprehensive provisions for health and rehabilitation services, including easily accessible maternal and child health services, accompanied by education to encourage their use.

Staffing such services as these requires considerable womanpower, and serious shortages already exist in the pertinent fields of social work, education, home economics, and health. But most communities could meet the need for personnel by tapping their resources of women with skills that could be rapidly upgraded or retrained and are not now fully used, particularly mature women whose children are grown. The pool of available skills could be greatly expanded if, in addition to recruiting women to enter the shortage professions, subprofessional categories of jobs were developed with appropriate training.

Such trained and qualified assistants could free the professionals to concentrate on that part of their work that demands highest training. So far, nursing has been particularly successful in developing such division of labor; various parts of the nurse's job are now regularly handled by competent aides. Other professions may well follow suit in this regard.

The reorganization of ordinary home-maintenance service is long overdue. That many of the women employed in household work remain in it only because they have no alternative became apparent when other opportunities opened up during World War II. In 1940, almost 18 per cent of all employed women were household workers; by 1950, the percentage had gone down to 8. Slightly more than $2\frac{1}{4}$ million women are employed in household work at present.

Household workers have, historically, been low paid, without standards of hours and working conditions, without collective bargaining, without most of the protections accorded by legislation and accepted as normal for other workers, and without means and opportunity adequately to maintain their own homes.

Few families can now afford to employ such workers full time at decent wages, but many families can pay rates in line with modern labor standards for special services as they need them. Privately run placement organizations to market such special services can operate to the mutual benefit of employer and employee, and are doing so in some communities. They can conduct training programs and insure standards of job performance, and they can monitor conditions of work and wages paid. The public employment offices should review their treatment of household service, encouraging the development of specialties and conducting placement on that basis.

In the days when the majority of Americans lived on farms or in rural areas, the Home Demonstration Service was established to aid farm women to improve their homemaking skills. Today, about two-thirds of the nation's people live in city or suburban areas; but currently, the urban homemaker's chief sources of suggestions on household management are the mass media.

Recently, the Home Demonstration Service has been conducting pilot operations in urban areas; and we believe that the guidance which its agents provided for substantial numbers of American families when the majority of the population lived on farms can be useful to equally substantial numbers of families who now live in cities. Most of the buying done by American families as consumers is done by women. Buying is particularly heavy by young married women at the time of setting up their households and supplying their young families. Yet few girls, at any income level, receive training to develop sound judgment in budgeting, in the wise use of credit, and in selection among bewildering varieties of goods. Low-income families are in especial need of counseling on how to stretch their earnings to get maximum value per dollar spent.

Continuing programs of evaluation and research should determine how well the services currently provided meet the needs of a given community, appraise new needs, and plan for the utilization of new knowledge as it becomes available.

COMMUNITY PLANNING

Community planning is essential for the orderly, balanced development of constructive environments for family living. Communities throughout the country are exerting themselves to eliminate slums, cope with traffic, and guide metropolitan growth. Many federal and state programs are contributing to community development through urban renewal, highway construction, housing projects, hospitals. But these efforts will not result in neighborhoods that are conducive to democratic living if they are guided by physical and economic considerations alone, without relation to the social needs and conditions of the community, nor will they benefit families in all segments of the community if they displace some families while accommodating others.

The location of schools, hospitals, and child-care and health facilities should be planned with participation by the parts of the population that are directly affected. The establishment of well-informed and well-co-ordinated information centers should be considered, where families can obtain advice on home management, education, employment, and housing. Particularly in the case of families from minority groups and of newcomers from rural to urban areas, such centers could transcend local barriers and make known the existence of facilities to whose benefits these groups are entitled but which might otherwise be denied them through indifference on the part of the larger community.

Local leadership should be encouraged to assure the needed range of community services through all appropriate means—by commercial or co-operative enterprises, voluntary agencies, or public programs. This type of community planning is producing promising pilot projects on the part of both government bodies and private agencies.

VOLUNTARY ACTIVITIES

Responsible citizenship in a democracy implies unremunerated activity on behalf of the community and participation in the institutions through which it carries on its life. Many of the services just discussed have in the past been made possible by voluntary activity. As communities have changed, the basis of voluntary activity has changed with them, both in respect to what needs to be done and in respect to the womanpower available to do it.

Pilot projects geared to current conditions, initiated under the auspices of citizens organizations or voluntary agencies or directly undertaken by volunteers, are developing widely adaptable new models in many fields. Among them are after-school centers for cultural enrichment and occupation of teenagers, community centers for health education and information, counseling and employment services for older persons, especially women, training and retraining programs, aids to homemakers and older persons, care of children, and services to enable newcomers moved by the currents of American mobility to find their way in the anonymity of urban life. Once their value is demonstrated on a pilot basis, projects initiated by volunteers are frequently adopted for wider application by private, commercial, or public bodies.

Voluntary organizations are attracting new sources of personnel: in addition to business organizations and service clubs, community activities are officially sponsored by the AFL–CIO, and individual unions have pioneered in housing and medical care through mutual self-help. In large measure, however, women of minority groups and low-income families have in the past been left out of this form of activity. Special attention should be given to assuring their active participation.

Where a cross section of the community takes part in policy decisions, the shift from planning for to planning with the persons to be served permits new assumptions of responsibility, brings new insights to bear, and widens the range of persons to be drawn on by organizations and agencies using the services of volunteers. Programs designed to prevent juvenile delinquency, for instance, have gained strength and acceptability as youngsters themselves acquired commitment to their purposes.

Volunteer activity can be carried on at all levels, depending on the qualifications of the interested individual and the jobs to be done. Where accompanied by training, such service can upgrade participants' skills. Volunteer work, under the auspices of voluntary agencies, communities, or educational institutions, can become a substantive part of the preparation

43

for citizenship of today's young girls and enable them to test at first hand various possibilities for subsequent careers. At the same time, professional men and women who have reached retirement age can contribute highly trained skills on a volunteer basis.

Increased stress on standards and increased specialization by voluntary agencies in many fields—social work, recreation, health—call for high levels of volunteer performance. Where pursued in a disciplined fashion and in accordance with standards comparable to those of employed persons, volunteer activity constitutes valid work experience that merits recognition if and when the individual performing it seeks paid employment. Voluntary agencies should keep records of such work and make them available on request.

As in the case of subprofessional assistants, volunteers trained and qualified for specific tasks can augment the supply of skills in occupations where there are shortages of professionals, supplementing the professionals' work and enabling them to use their capacities to best advantage.

Volunteers' services should be made more effective through coordinated and imaginative planning among agencies and organizations for recruitment, training, placement, and supervision, and their numbers augmented through tapping the large reservoir of additional potential among youth, retired people, members of minority groups, and women not now in volunteer activities.

Women in Employment

American women work both in their homes, unpaid, and outside their homes, on a wage or salary basis. Among the great majority of women, as among the great majority of men, the motive for paid employment is to earn money. For some, work has additional—or even primary—value as self-fulfillment.

When America was an agricultural country, most of both man's and woman's work was an unpaid contribution to family subsistence. As production developed in factory and city centers, many women began to do outside, for pay, what they had formerly done, unpaid, in their homes— making textiles or garments, processing food, nursing the sick, teaching children. Women's participation in paid employment importantly increases the nation's labor force: 1 worker in 3 is a woman.

In any average month in 1962, there were some 23 million women at work; the forecast is for 30 million in 1970. Approximately 3 out of 5 women workers are married. Among married women, 1 in 3 is working; among nonwhites, almost 1 in 2. Many of these women, nearly a third, work part time; ⅗ of all part-time work is done by married women. Some 17 million women, in an average month, are full-time workers.

Their occupations range widely: the 1960 census recorded 431 geologists and geophysicists and 18,632 bus drivers. The largest concentration—7 million—is in the clerical field. Three other main groupings—service workers (waitresses, beauticians, hospital attendants), factory operatives, and professional and technical employees (teachers, nurses, accountants, librarians) —number between 3 and 3¾ million each.

Though women are represented in the highly paid professions, in industry, in business, and in government, most jobs that women hold are in

45

EVERY THIRD WORKER IS A WOMAN
(PER CENT OF ALL WORKERS)

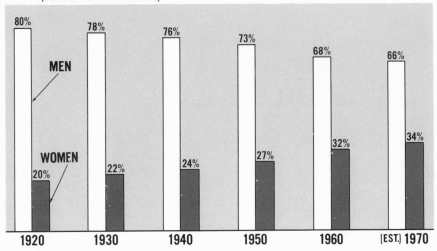

Chart 10.

low-paid categories. Some occupations—nursing and household work, for instance—are almost entirely staffed by women. The difference in occupational distribution of men and women is largely responsible for the fact that in 1961 the earnings of women working full time averaged only about 60 per cent of those of men working full time. But in various occupations where both sexes were employed, the levels of women's earnings were likewise demonstrably lower than those of men.

The existence of differentials in pay between men and women for the same kind of work has been substantiated by studies from numerous sources: an analysis of 1,900 companies, for example, showed that 1 out of 3 had dual pay scales in effect for similar office jobs.

The Commission attempted to gather informed views as to the extent to which access to jobs, rates of pay, and opportunities for training and advancement are based on the qualifications of the women who apply for or hold them, and the extent to which discriminations are made against them in these regards solely because they are women.

The reasons given by employers for differential treatment cover a considerable range. Frequently, they say they prefer male employees because the nonwage costs of employing women are higher. They say that the employment pattern of younger women is in and out of the labor force,

MOST WOMEN WHO WORK ARE MARRIED

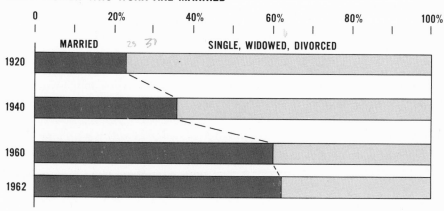

Chart 11.

working for a time before marriage and thereafter putting family obligations first until their children are grown. They say that women's rates of sickness, absenteeism, and turnover are higher than men's; that the hiring of married women introduces one more element into the turnover rate because the residence of a married couple is normally determined by the occupation of the man. They say that though attendance rates of older women are often better than those of men, insurance and pensions for older workers are expensive, and that compliance with protective labor legislation applying to women is sometimes disruptive of schedules. They say that men object to working under women supervisors.

Because many personnel officers believe that women are less likely than men to want to make a career in industry, equally well-prepared young women are passed over in favor of men for posts that lead into management training programs and subsequent exercise of major executive responsibility.

Actually, situations vary far too much to make generalizations applicable, and more information is needed on rates of quits, layoffs, absenteeism, and illness among women workers and on the qualifications of women for responsible supervisory or executive positions. However, already available statistics on absenteeism and turnover indicate that the level of skill of the job, the worker's age, length of service with the employer, and record of job stability all are much more relevant than the fact that the worker is a man or a woman.

47

Reluctance to consider women applicants on their merits results in underutilization of capacities that the economy needs and stunts the development of higher skills.

EQUALITY IN PRIVATE EMPLOYMENT

Various means of causing employers to consider actualities rather than rely on conventional assumptions were considered by the Commission.

The long-time policy of the United States Employment Service is to refer people for jobs on the basis of their qualifications. But at the request of the Commission, the USES issued a further directive to public employment offices in the states, instructing their staffs to refer applicants on the basis of qualifications regardless of sex and requesting employers using these offices to avoid job orders specifying sex except where genuinely warranted.

Private employers of all kinds can be urged to examine individual qualifications rather than accept general attitudes when hiring women, as they have begun to do when hiring young persons, older workers, the physically handicapped, and members of minority groups. In the case of private employers holding government contracts, their performance in respect to employment of women can be made a factor in contract awards.

At the federal level, the Commission concluded that the most feasible tool for directing employers' attention to the importance of equal treatment for women workers would be an Executive order.

Equal opportunity for women in hiring, training, and promotion should be the governing principle in private employment. An Executive order should state this principle and advance its application to work done under federal contracts.

The Commission estimates that no more than 20 per cent of all women workers would be covered by an Executive order regarding government contracts. Action should be undertaken to encourage employers who do not have government contracts to comply with the federal policy of non-discrimination.

Executive Order 10925 now forbids discrimination based on race, creed, color, or national origin in employment under federal contracts. The President's Committee on Equal Employment Opportunities is charged with surveillance of this program, and the various procurement agencies with its specific application. We are aware that this order could be expanded to forbid discrimination based on sex. But discrimination based on sex, the Commission believes, involves problems sufficiently different from discrimination based on the other factors listed to make separate treatment preferable.

Experience is needed in determining what constitutes unjustified discrimination in the treatment of women workers. For instance, expenditures for on-the-job training are now divided about $\frac{1}{10}$ for women workers and $\frac{9}{10}$ for men workers, whereas women workers constitute $\frac{1}{3}$ of the work force. Is it discrimination, when providing such training, to limit it to men on the assumption that women will not be in the labor force continually?

The program under the Executive order that we propose obviously ought to be interrelated with already existing programs to encourage wider employment opportunities in a coordinated approach to private employers. Interpretation and periodic review of the results of the proposed order should become a guide to future action.

FEDERAL SERVICE AS A SHOWCASE

Where the federal government is itself the employer, its hiring and promotion practices can become a showcase for equal employment opportunity without discrimination of any kind. Recognizing that merit is a well-established principle in federal employment policy, the Commission sought to bring practice into closer accord with principle throughout the federal service, civilian and military. Here, action on our recommendations took place so rapidly during the life of the Commission that our report becomes for the most part an account of progress already achieved.

One of our remaining concerns has to do with part-time employment.

At present, federal systems of manpower utilization discourage part-time employment. Many able women, including highly trained professionals, who are not free for full-time employment, can work part time. The Civil Service Commission and the Bureau of the Budget should facilitate the imaginative and prudent use of such personnel throughout the government service.

In the Commission's canvass of federal civilian employment, no significant differences were found in the treatment of either sex in terms and conditions of employment such as pay, premium pay, leave, insurance, retirement, and appellate rights and procedures. But policies and practices

MOST WOMEN IN FEDERAL SERVICE ARE IN LOWER GRADES

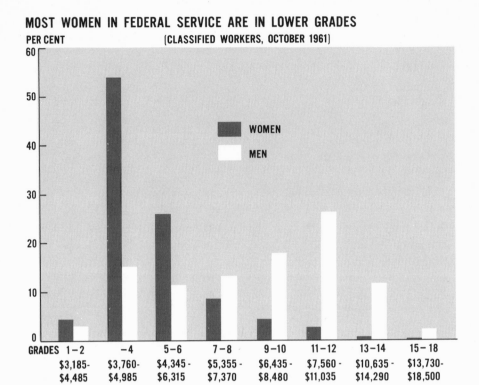

PER CENT   (CLASSIFIED WORKERS, OCTOBER 1961)

WOMEN

MEN

GRADES 1–2	–4	5–6	7–8	9–10	11–12	13–14	15–18
$3,185- $4,485	$3,760- $4,985	$4,345 - $6,315	$5,355 - $7,370	$6,435 - $8,480	$7,560 - $11,035	$10,635 - $14,290	$13,730- $18,500

Chart 12.

concerning appointment and advancement were such as to demand immediate action. The distribution of employment revealed similarities to the private sector: heavy concentration of women in the lower-grade office positions, and heavy concentration of men in the professions (other than nurses) and in middle and upper administrative and managerial posts. Less than 2 per cent of higher-level positions were found to be filled by women.

Based upon interpretation of an old law predating the Civil Service Act of 1883, and reaffirmed by an Attorney General's ruling in 1934, discretion had traditionally been exercised by appointing officials to specify men only or women only, as they chose, for any position regardless of duties. Civil-service examinations have over the years been opened to both men and women, but this prerogative of officials in charge of appointments had resulted in specification of sex in a high percentage of requests for names of eligibles from examination lists.

The Commission requested review of the legal basis for this practice. In June 1962, the Attorney General issued an opinion reversing the prior interpretation. In July 1962, by presidential directive, federal agencies were instructed to make all selections for appointments, advancement, and training in the federal service without regard to sex, except in unusual circumstances found justified by the Civil Service Commission. Revised civil-service regulations amplifying this directive became effective September 1, 1962; there are now very few positions for which sex can be specified in requests for candidates.

Even before issuance of the new regulations, the Civil Service Commission began to require agencies to give reasons for specifying sex. The requirement had prompt effect. Comparison of the requests from Washington agencies for eligibles from the Federal Service Entrance Examination (the examination taken by many college students) during the two periods November 13–December 8, 1961, and February 4–March 3, 1962, shows that in the earlier period, there were 33 requests for women, 205 requests for men, 216 requests with no sex specified; in the latter, 1 request for women, 11 for men, and 682 with no sex specified. Appointments of women from this register have been rising: between October 1960 and October 1961, 14.9 per cent of those appointed were women; in the calendar year 1962, 17.3 per cent.

Information as to state practices similar to those current until recently in the federal government became available when the Public Personnel Association, at the invitation of the Commission, instituted an inquiry into equality of opportunity for women in public employment at state and municipal levels and released the responses of 43 states and 32 cities. In the light of these findings, the Commission recommended that when the standards for state merit systems in connection with various grants-in-aid from the Departments of Health, Education, and Welfare, Labor, and Defense were revised, the existing provision against discrimination be rewritten to prohibit discrimination on the basis of any nonmerit factor. This was done in January 1963.

Similarly at the request of the Commission, comprehensive studies of employment profiles and advancement patterns in civilian federal employment and in the Foreign Service Officers Corps were conducted by the Civil Service Commission and the Department of State. Their results now make it possible, for the first time, to substitute facts for conjecture with respect to separation rates and their causes, grade levels reached, and attitudes affecting promotions, with data given by sex.

There are 307 women Foreign Service Officers. Study of separation rates among persons appointed in the 1956 class showed that some 47 per cent of the women had resigned at the end of 2½ years as contrasted with 6 per cent of the men. The frequent changes in assignment required by a diplomatic career discourage marriage for women; only 17 of the women career officers are married. No differences were found in the women's advancement rate as compared with the men's in this service.

In the Civil Service Commission study, women's voluntary quits, over-all, were found to be between 2½ and 3 times those of men. This is because women predominate in younger age groups and low-paid occupations, where turnover is higher for both men and women. When comparisons were made by age groups, salary levels, and occupations, it appeared that women's rates, while still higher, are much closer to men's: the loss of employees by turnover decreases significantly with increasing grade level. Women in the middle-age ranges are a more stable group than either men or women under 25; women who enter the labor market in their forties show very low turnover rates compared with other women.

Almost half of the women who leave federal agencies give reasons related to family responsibilities. The reasons of single women for leaving are similar to those of men. Nearly 1 woman in 4 leaves for the same reasons as are given by almost half of the men—to receive broader experience or better pay elsewhere, or because of dissatisfaction with their working situation. The next ranking cause of women's quits is health or voluntary retirement.

While the advancement rate of men and women differs considerably according to occupation, the over-all difference in median grade in white-collar occupations is about 5 grades. Some ¾ of the men are in grades reached by only ¼ of the women. Differences are less sharp in such highly professional groups as attorneys, but in most cases women with comparable education and years of service are at lower grades than men. The women in the higher grades are somewhat older than the men; more of them have college degrees. Typically, they are not married; those who are, have smaller families than men in the same grade. The advancement of single women is noticeably, but not strikingly greater than that of married women. Women in the upper grades are quite as involved in their careers as men; they engage more frequently than men in professional activities related to their jobs.

A very large proportion of men at all grade levels believe that men are better supervisors than women, and a somewhat smaller number that men do better in nonsupervisory posts as well, though actual experience working with women as supervisors or co-workers modified the strength of such views. The majority of women thought there was no difference in performance of men and women. The extent of negative attitudes among men as to the ability of women emphasizes the need for research on the sources of such views and attitudes and the adoption of positive policies to diminish prejudice where it exists and to improve women's performance where grievances are found to be justified.

These studies of the federal service, offering the first firm data on many phases of women's employment, place ascertained facts at the disposal of the personnel policymakers of the nation's largest employer. The Commission believes that they will be of interest to large private employers as well. In the government service, this new knowledge can become the basis of policies extending women's opportunities to new levels. While the President's directive, by requiring equal consideration of men and women for promotions, will improve the promotion rate of women, the Civil Service Commission and top management of the individual agencies must give continuing attention to insuring that advancement is based solely on merit.

The uniformed services have done much commendable pioneering in training and utilizing women in positions traditionally reserved for men. Statutory restrictions on the numbers of top officers in the women's components, however, dating from their formation 21 years ago, still set specific limits on the numbers of Marine, Army, and Air Force colonels and lieutenant colonels and Navy commanders and lieutenant commanders. The Commission proposed that these restrictions be eliminated, with the number of such officers left to the discretion of the Secretary of each service, within the over-all limits provided for all officers. The Commission also proposed that the services re-examine their estimates of requirements for top officers in the Nurse Corps and the Medical Specialists Corps in light of the need for staff cadres capable of fast expansion in an emergency. In July 1962, the Secretary of Defense stated that these recommendations had been adopted; the bill for revision of career management of officer personnel, sent to the Congress in 1963, included the change with respect to women officers.

Labor Standards

Many of the lowest-paid jobs in industry and the service occupations have historically been filled by women; driven by economic necessity, they have taken whatever jobs they could find even though conditions were damaging to health and family life. They have labored—and been exploited—as textile and needle trades workers, as laundresses and waitresses, as doers of industrial homework. Among the lowest-paid workers, many have been women from minority groups.

When the formation of trade unions helped raise wages and improve working conditions through collective bargaining, some of these occupations proved—and have remained—hard to organize. Even now, nearly 30 years after the right to organize and bargain collectively was given federal recognition in the Wagner Act, only a little over 3⅓ million out of 24 million women in the labor force are union members.

Little by little, first in some of the states and then at the federal level, legislation has put floors under wages and ceilings on hours. But such laws are far from uniform from state to state and are still far from adequate. At both federal and state levels, research and regular reporting on the operation and protective labor laws would point the way to desirable future changes.

MINIMUM WAGES

In 1938, the federal Fair Labor Standards Act (FLSA) put a floor under wages for both men and women engaged in a large number of occupations related to interstate commerce. It set minimum wages, and its requirement of premium pay for hours worked above 40 a week helped control excessive hours. But the FLSA exempts most workers, many of them women, in

54

hotels, motels, restaurants, laundries, nonprofit organizations, and certain retail establishments.

At the same time, an estimated 6 million women are employed in intrastate work not covered by minimum-wage legislation. Twenty-one states are either without minimum-wage statutes or without such statutes in operation. There and elsewhere, several million women earn less than $1 an hour. Most of them are in the service trades, retailing, or domestic service.

The federal Fair Labor Standards Act, including premium pay for overtime, should be extended to employment subject to federal jurisdiction but now uncovered, such as work in hotels, motels, restaurants, and laundries, in additional retail establishments, in agriculture, and in nonprofit organizations.

State legislation, applicable to both men and women, should be enacted, or strengthened and extended to all types of employment, to provide minimum-wage levels approximating the minimum under federal law and to require premium pay at the rate of at least time and a half for overtime.

MAXIMUM HOURS

In the past, minimum-wage and maximum-hour legislation for women has been a lever for eliminating substandard conditions for both men and women, yet the benefits to be derived from such labor standards remain to be achieved for many workers. The existing range of legal working hours for women, applicable to one or more types of employment, becomes clear when the maximum-hour laws of the states are compared. Seven states and Puerto Rico set no legal maximum; 4, a maximum of 60 hours a week for women workers; 14, within a range under 60 but over 48; 24 states and the District of Columbia place a ceiling at 48; the remaining state specifies a top limit of a 44-hour week and an 8-hour day.

In private employment excluding agriculture and household service, the hours actually worked in early 1963 averaged around 40 a week. Nearly 3 workers in 4—71 per cent—work 40 hours or less; but 13.5 per cent work 49 hours or more. The effectiveness over the past 25 years of the Fair Labor Standards Act in providing a deterrent in the form of premium pay designed to reduce the scheduling of excessive hours recommends this as the most practicable method of achieving future protection under normal circumstances. But while events press toward this goal, the welfare of all workers requires that where special hour protection for women represents the best so far attained it should be maintained and strengthened.

The normal workday and workweek at this moment of history should be not more than 8 hours a day and 40 hours a week. The best way to discourage excessive hours for all workers is by broad and effective minimum-wage coverage, both federal and state, providing overtime of at least time and a half the regular rate for all hours in excess of 8 a day or 40 a week.

Until such time as this goal is attained, state legislation limiting maximum hours of work for women should be maintained, strengthened, and expanded. Provisions for flexibility under proper safeguards should allow additional hours of work when there is a demonstrated need. During this interim period, efforts should continuously and simultaneously be made to require premium rates of pay for all hours in excess of 8 a day or 40 a week.

There is one group of workers, however, for whom exemption from existing maximum-hour laws is desirable. Executive, administrative, and professional women frequently find that limitations on hours adversely affect their opportunities for employment and advancement. Exemptions for such occupations should be carefully drawn so as to insure against evasion of

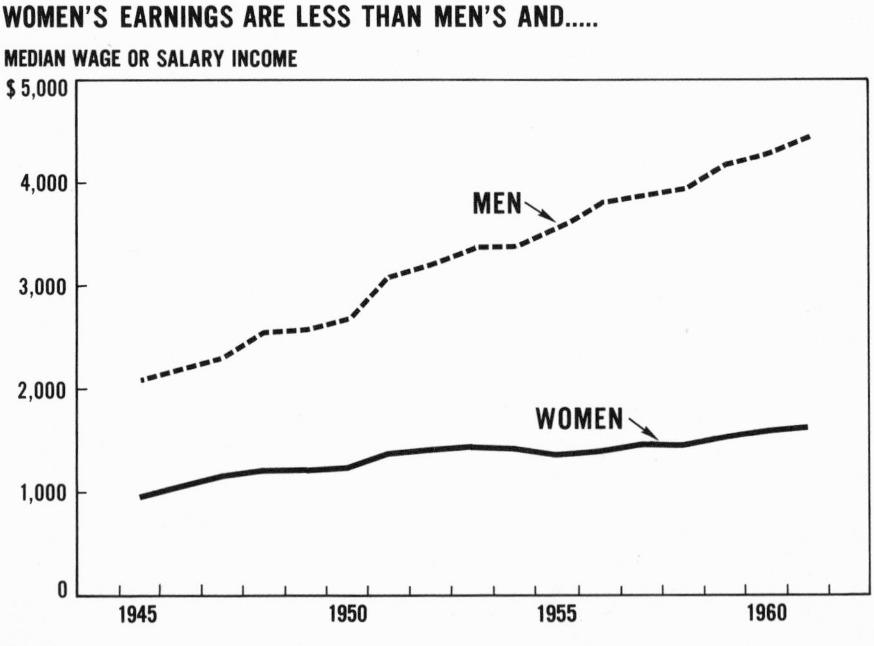
WOMEN'S EARNINGS ARE LESS THAN MEN'S AND.....
MEDIAN WAGE OR SALARY INCOME
$ 5,000
4,000
3,000
2,000
1,000
0
MEN
WOMEN
1945
1950
1955
1960

Chart 13.

normally applicable hour laws in the case of workers who genuinely need their protection.

EQUAL PAY

In 1919, the first equal-pay laws in the states were enacted; 24 states now require that women who do the same or comparable work as men in the same establishment be paid at the same rates. Lower-pay rates for women doing the same work as men are not uncommon. For instance, studies made in 1960 showed area averages of women bank note-tellers with less than 5 years of experience running typically $5–$15 a week less than the averages of men with the same years of experience, and differences of 9 to 49 cents an hour between the averages of men and women in the same power laundry occupations in a number of metropolitan areas.

In February 1962, the Commission endorsed the policy of equal pay for comparable work. A bill embodying this principle cleared both houses of

HOURLY PAY IN RETAIL TRADE ILLUSTRATES WHY

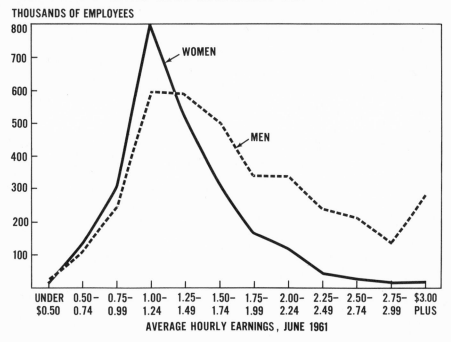

Chart 14.

Congress in 1962 but failed to reach conference before adjournment. Reintroduced in 1963, it passed and was signed by President Kennedy on June 10. The act amends the Fair Labor Standards Act of 1938 to require equal pay for equal work; it covers some 27.5 million men and women.

State laws should establish the principle of equal pay for comparable work.

GREATER FLEXIBILITY

In the case of a few state statutes, none of which currently affects large numbers of workers, the Commission believes that revision in the interest of greater flexibility is desirable. These measures, originally intended to protect women workers, have sometimes proved impracticable in their actual operation.

Restrictions that set fixed maximum limits upon weights women are allowed to lift do not take account of individual differences, are sometimes unrealistic, and always rigid. They should be replaced by flexible regulations, applicable to both men and women and set by appropriate regulatory bodies.

Night work, especially on the graveyard shift, is undesirable for most people, and should be discouraged for both men and women. Overly rigid prohibitions, however, may work to the disadvantage of women in some circumstances. Strict regulations to prevent abuse are therefore normally preferable to prohibitions.

Prohibitions of exploitative industrial homework should remain in force. Gaps in protection should be closed, and resourcefulness exercised to arrest the development of new types of undesirable homework. However, many women who withdraw from the labor force to raise families have clerical skills; these—and editorial and research skills also—lend themselves to part-time work during years of intensive homemaking; their use is subject to exploitation and should be monitored, but it should not be made impossible by legal inflexibility.

Handicapped women, homebound for physical or psychological reasons or because of their location, should likewise not be blocked from undertaking suitable gainful employment. Offers of employment to the homebound, however, need to be carefully policed by public agencies to protect against swindles and rackets.

The women who are now without the protection of adequate federal or state laws or collective-bargaining contracts are highly vulnerable elements in the labor force. Many are women of minority groups. As labor standards have been raised, those who remain unprotected are increasingly those who suffer multiple handicaps and disabilities. This gives special urgency to completion of the task of assuring decent standards for all people who work.

THE RIGHT TO ORGANIZE

The effectiveness of unions in achieving improved working conditions, increased dignity, and essential protections has long been amply demonstrated, and the right of workers to organize and bargain collectively has been established under federal law. In places of work solely under state jurisdiction, the difficulty of organizing women, especially those in low-paid work who are least able to risk possible loss of earnings, is augmented when employers are under no legal obligation to bargain collectively or to refrain from antiunion practices, including discharge of union members.

State laws should protect the right of all workers to join unions of their own choosing and to bargain collectively.

Security of Basic Income

Security of basic income for the men and women who produce the country's goods and services was greatly enlarged in the mid-thirties by measures to assure to workers and their dependents a minimum income on which they could rely when their earnings were interrupted by unemployment or halted by retirement. The Social Security Act, first passed in 1935, instituted the federal system of old-age, survivors, and disability insurance and the cooperative federal-state program for unemployment compensation. Over the years, these programs have been successively widened in their coverage. But some important gaps remain, and for many workers, state unemployment-insurance benefits lag so far behind current earnings levels as to undercut the intent of the legislation.

Because increases in general benefits under old-age, survivors, and disability insurance and unemployment insurance would be applicable to the entire population, the Commission did not consider them. Similarly, it did not consider current proposals to add hospitalization for elderly persons to the old-age benefit system, even though in this case women would be the major beneficiaries, since in the upper age groups they outnumber men and outlive them. The improvements proposed are limited to inequities directly affecting women.

WIDOWS' BENEFITS

Among provisions of the old-age benefit system, the Commission gave special attention to the benefits of aged widows. The number of such beneficiaries is now almost 2 million and will rise rapidly over the next decade.

The law calculates the benefit of a dependent as a percentage of the pri-

60

MILLIONS OF ELDERLY WOMEN DEPEND ON SOCIAL-SECURITY BENEFITS

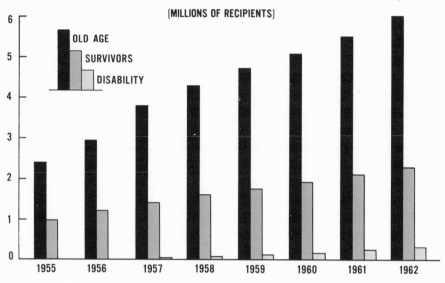

Chart 15.

mary benefit based on a worker's earnings. A widow now becomes eligible at age 62 to receive a benefit equal to 82½ per cent of her husband's primary benefit. Currently, the primary benefits of retired workers average $76 a month; those of widows, $66. An aged widow should not have to live on less than her husband would receive if he survived her. We are aware of the cost of such a program—its full realization would require an increase of 0.25 per cent of taxable payrolls—but this much additional basic security would mitigate existing dependency.

A widow's benefit under the federal old-age insurance system should be equal to the amount that her husband would have received at the same age had he lived. This objective should be approached as rapidly as may be financially feasible.

The situation of two smaller, special groups of widows now unprovided for should likewise be considered. A divorced wife, if she has not remarried and if her marriage continued for a substantial period, such as 10 years, or a divorced widow should become eligible at 62 to a wife's or widow's

61

benefit based on her former husband's wage record. Similarly, a widow who is disabled at the time of her husband's death, or becomes so after cessation of her benefits as a mother but before she has had a reasonable period in which to acquire insured status in her own right, should have a disabled widow's benefit. The estimated cost of the first program would be 0.02 per cent of taxable payrolls; that of the second, 0.04 per cent.

DEPENDENTS OF SINGLE WOMEN

Many single women who are primary workers have relatives other than parents who are as dependent on their earnings as wives and children are on the earnings of husbands or fathers. Many single workers, for instance, have dependent sisters who keep house for them. Yet on their death, parents alone are eligible for benefits. A broader definition of dependents of single workers, men and women alike, would meet a genuine social need. The cost—in the neighborhood of 0.01 per cent of taxable payrolls—would not be significant in relation to the gains it would bring.

UNEMPLOYMENT INSURANCE

Women for the most part receive the same protection as men under the federal-state system of unemployment insurance. But all except one of the major groups still left uncovered are substantially, if not predominantly, composed of women workers. These groups are employees of small firms, nonprofit organizations, and state and local governments; household workers, and agricultural laborers. Both the federal government and the states should work toward broader inclusion.

The coverage of the unemployment-insurance system should be extended. Small establishments and nonprofit organizations should be covered now through federal action, and state and local government employees through state action. Practicable means of covering at least some household workers and agricultural workers should be actively explored.

Furthermore, statutory, administrative, and judicial limitations have, over the years, restricted the protection of women against loss of income that this program was originally intended to cover. The restrictive decisions seem to assume that all women are secondary workers, loosely attached to the job market, who work only to supply the household with extras. In this view, men are considered the primary workers, and concentrated attention is given to preventing women from drawing unemployment benefits on the ground that they work sporadically without seriously looking for continuous employment.

The analysis of the employment experience of persons drawing benefits under the Temporary Extended Unemployment Compensation Act of 1961 showed that 61 per cent of women claimants had been in the labor market continuously for the preceding 36 months, and only 10 per cent for less than 24 of the 36 months. We believe that benefits should be afforded women on the same basis as men, with adoption of realistic measurements of attachment to the labor market which would prevent benefit payments to persons of either sex who seek work only sporadically.

In all states, workers unable or unwilling to work are disqualified from the receipt of unemployment compensation. But in 36 states, disqualification of women for specified periods during pregnancy and maternity is additionally stipulated. Wide variations among types of jobs and physical capacities of individuals suggest the desirability of flexible means of determining the period during which a woman is in fact unable to work.

The overwhelming majority of workers who quit because of marital obligations, such as following a spouse to another locality, are women. In the majority of states they are eligible for benefits if they seek to continue in employment. In 22 states, however, laws specify periods after leaving a job, or periods after re-employment on a new job, which must elapse before such persons again become eligible for unemployment compensation.

The income gap thus caused is by no means inconsiderable. Accordingly, we believe that unemployment compensation should be available to persons seeking work who are temporarily jobless because of a family move, but recommend that such compensation be drawn from the general unemployment fund of the state rather than charged against the account of the former employer.

MATERNITY BENEFITS

The general federal system of social security makes no provision for compensating a working wife for loss of income due to childbearing. Forty-six of the 50 states also ignore it. Yet in about 70 other countries, governmental action has provided for such protection, mostly as part of broader programs of insurance against income loss due to sickness or temporary disability.

63

Not more than a third of American working women have such insurance from either private or public sources; only in New Jersey, Rhode Island, and to a limited extent in California and New York are maternity benefits provided by state laws. This is one of the major remaining gaps in the protection of workers against losses of income.

Paid maternity leave or comparable insurance benefits should be provided for women workers; employers, unions, and governments should explore the best means of accomplishing this purpose.

Women Under the Law

Equality of rights under the law for all persons, male or female, is so basic to democracy and its commitment to the ultimate value of the individual that it must be reflected in the fundamental law of the land. The Commission believes that this principle of equality is embodied in the Fifth and Fourteenth Amendments to the Constitution of the United States.

The Fourteenth Amendment prohibits any state from depriving any person of life, liberty, or property without due process of law and from denying to any person the equal protection of the laws. Essentially the same prohibitions apply to the federal government under the due process clause of the Fifth Amendment.

In the face of these amendments, however, there remain, especially in certain state laws and official practices, distinctions based on sex which discriminate against women. Both the states and the federal government may classify persons for the purpose of legislation, but the classification must be based on some reasonable ground. There exist some laws and official practices which treat men and women differently and which do not appear to be reasonable in the light of the multiple activities of women in present-day society.

The Commission considered various proposed methods of achieving greater recognition of the rights of women:

- Test litigation seeking redress from discrimination under constitutional safeguards looking to ultimate review by the United States Supreme Court.

- Amendment to the United States Constitution—the proposed equal-rights amendment provides, in part, that *"Equality of rights under the law shall not be denied or abridged . . . on account of sex."*

- State legislative action to eliminate discriminatory state laws.

Divergent viewpoints on these methods, particularly among national women's organizations and labor-union groups, were made known in documents lodged with the Commission and in oral presentations at two hearings.

CONSTITUTIONAL RECOGNITION

Since the Commission is convinced that the United States Constitution now embodies equality of rights for men and women, we conclude that a constitutional amendment need not now be sought in order to establish this principle. But judicial clarification is imperative in order that remaining ambiguities with respect to the constitutional protection of women's rights be eliminated.

Early and definitive court pronouncement, particularly by the United States Supreme Court, is urgently needed with regard to the validity under the Fifth and Fourteenth Amendments of laws and official practices discriminating against women, to the end that the principle of equality become firmly established in constitutional doctrine.

Accordingly, interested groups should give high priority to bringing under court review cases involving laws and practices which discriminate against women.

At the same time, appropriate federal, state, and local officials in all branches of government should be urged to scrutinize carefully those laws, regulations, and practices which distinguish on the basis of sex to determine whether they are justifiable in the light of contemporary conditions and to the end of removing archaic standards which today operate as discriminatory.

The Commission commends and encourages continued efforts on the part of all interested groups in educating the public and in urging private action, and action within the judicial, executive, and legislative branches of government, to the end that full equality of rights may become a reality.

INTERNATIONAL CONVENTIONS ON HUMAN RIGHTS

The Commission has been sensitive to the importance of equality of rights not alone to women in the United States, but to women around the world, in the new nations and in the older countries. Until December 1962, when the United States signed the United Nations convention on marriage, the only human-rights convention that this country had signed against genocide. Past abstentions have been in response to fea of the treaty power affect practices of the states, but some of th human-rights conventions would require no change in state pr others relate only to federal matters. Many of the minimum rights protected under such conventions are already secured in this country but not in other countries; abroad, the United States policy of abstention has not infrequently been misunderstood as indifference.

The United States should assert leadership, particularly in the United Nations, in securing equality of rights for women as part of the effort to define and assure human rights; should participate actively in the formulation of international declarations, principles, and conventions to improve the status of women throughout the world; and should demonstrate its sincere concern for women's equal rights by becoming a party to appropriate conventions.

JURY SERVICE

The right to trial by a jury that reflects the community is a bulwark of justice. Women became eligible to serve on all federal juries only by virtue of the Civil Rights Act of 1957. The Commission regards further federal legislation as necessary to assure that procedures for selecting the names of qualified persons to be placed in the jury box shall not systematically or deliberately exclude any group from the jury panel on account of race, sex, political or religious affiliation, or economic or social status.

In 3 states, women still may not serve on juries of the state courts, and in 26 others and the District of Columbia, women who are called on for jury service may claim exemptions that are not available to men.

Appropriate action, including enactment of legislation where necessary, should be taken to achieve equal jury service in the states.

It is also desirable for appropriate agencies like the Federal Judicial Conference and the National Conference of State Chief Justices, as well as national and state civic organizations, to give continuing attention to assuring equal jury service without distinction as to sex. Women and men alike should assume their responsibilities for making juries representative of the communities in which they live.

67

STATE LAWS ON JURY SERVICE ARE NOT UNIFORM

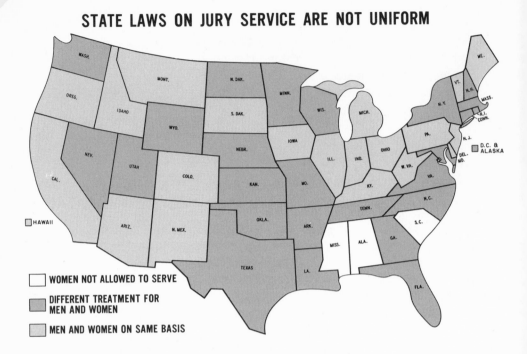

WOMEN NOT ALLOWED TO SERVE

DIFFERENT TREATMENT FOR
MEN AND WOMEN

MEN AND WOMEN ON SAME BASIS

Chart 16.

PERSONAL AND PROPERTY RIGHTS

In many specific areas of state law, the disabilities of married women are considerable. State statutes affecting family law and personal and property rights of women should be modernized.

Single women enjoy equality of legal treatment with men in respect to property and contract law, the only general exception being the lower minimum age at which they may contract to marry. But married women, over much broader legal ranges, are denied such equality.

Limitations on the rights of married women derive from a long history: some go back to concepts of the common law brought to this continent by its English settlers; some, particularly those related to concepts of community property, derive from the law traditional among the settlers from France and Spain. In practically all of these areas of law, remedial action lies under the jurisdiction of the states. Many states have already removed most inequities, but in every state, one kind of disability or another limits the legal rights of married women.

State legislatures and other groups concerned with the improvement of state statutes affecting family law and personal and property rights of married women, including the National Conference of Commissioners on Uniform State Laws, the Council of State Governments, the American Law Institute, and state Commissions on the Status of Women, should move to eliminate laws which impose legal disabilities on women.

Specifically, the Commission directs their attention to these considerations:

- The civil capacity of married women and married men should be equalized through the elimination of legal restrictions on the rights of married women to contract, convey, or own real or personal property, to engage in business, to act as surety or fiduciary, to receive and control their own earnings, and to dispose of their own property by will; the law governing domicile for purposes such as voting, holding public office, jury service, taxation, and probate should be the same for married women as it is for married men.

- Marriage as a partnership in which each spouse makes a different but equally important contribution is increasingly recognized as a reality in this country and is already reflected in the laws of some other countries. During marriage, each spouse should have a legally defined substantial right in the earnings of the other, in the real and personal property acquired through those earnings, and in their management. Such a right should be legally recognized as surviving the marriage in the event of its termination by divorce, annulment, or death. Appropriate legislation should safeguard either spouse and protect the surviving spouse against improper alienation of property by the other. Surviving children as well as the surviving spouse should be protected from disinheritance.

- The prevailing rule in the United States is for guardianship of children during marriage to be vested jointly in both parents; all states should make their statutes conformable to it.

- In line with the partnership view of marriage, while the husband should continue to have primary responsibility for support of his wife and minor children, the wife should be given legal responsibility for sharing in the support of herself and the children to the extent she has means to do so.

Modernization of state law in these respects should be initiated now.

The Commission found that in several areas, legal research and analysis are essential before firm proposals for reform can be recommended. These include:

- The effect of according married women the same right as married men to establish a separate domicile on marital status, rights, and obligations, on alimony and support, on custody and visitation of children.

- Minimum age of marriage for males and females.

- Alimony, support, and property settlements. Such a study should include not only the law and practice pertaining to the rendition of alimony and support decrees, but also methods of locating persons responsible for the support of dependents.

- Differences in substantive law and procedure as between men and women in the field of criminal law and administration, including correction.

The Commission notes the great progress that women have achieved during the last few decades as the result of the efforts of civic and other organizations, including women's groups, to focus public attention on the problem of discrimination based on sex and believes that continuance and increase of these efforts constitute an indispensable condition to the achievement of equal rights for women. Such groups can likewise render service by helping women of all groups and income levels to know their rights; while rights accorded women frequently lag behind those accorded men, many women are inadequately aware of what their current rights actually are.

A know-your-rights pamphlet should be published, under either public or private auspices, to enable more women to become aware of their legal position.

Women as Citizens

For over 40 years, since the Nineteenth Amendment to the United States Constitution gave American women the right to vote in national elections in 1920, political participation by women has grown in many directions. But full participation in all of the functions of a citizen is not yet a fact.

Millions of citizens of both sexes consistently absent themselves from the polls. The generation that struggled to obtain votes for women would have had difficulty believing that use of the right they gained would be as desultory as it is in many communities. Visitors from abroad, alike from countries whose women were active in the early suffrage movements and from countries where newly acquired independence has enfranchised large populations within the past few years, are surprised at the low percentages of the adult American population that appear at the polls.

EXERCISE OF THE FRANCHISE

In the 1960 presidential election, the 68,836,000 ballots cast for president represented 64 per cent of the estimated number of Americans old enough to vote; the 62,015,000 ballots of the 1956 election represented 60 per cent. Presidential elections induce the nation's maximum electoral effort: in off year elections, when, nevertheless, ⅓ of the United States Senators and all Members of the House of Representatives are chosen, the votes cast for candidates for Members of the House of Representatives are materially less. In 1962, they represented 47 per cent of estimated potential voters, and in 1958, 43 per cent. Exercise of the franchise varies by region. It is lowest in the South, where registration of minority groups has been resisted and where poll taxes have discouraged voting by low-income white citizens as well. It is highest on the Pacific Coast.

71

NOT ENOUGH WOMEN EXERCISE THEIR RIGHT TO VOTE
(ADULTS 21 YEARS AND OVER)

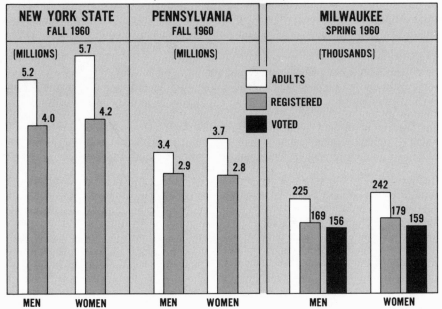

| NEW YORK STATE FALL 1960 | | PENNSYLVANIA FALL 1960 | | MILWAUKEE SPRING 1960 | |

(MILLIONS) — NEW YORK STATE: MEN 5.2, 4.0; WOMEN 5.7, 4.2

(MILLIONS) — PENNSYLVANIA: MEN 3.4, 2.9; WOMEN 3.7, 2.8

(THOUSANDS) — MILWAUKEE: MEN 225, 169, 156; WOMEN 242, 179, 159

Legend: ADULTS, REGISTERED, VOTED

MEN   WOMEN   MEN   WOMEN   MEN   WOMEN

Chart 17.

Women currently outnumber men in the United States population by some 3¾ million, but in terms of registration and election-day turnout, their failure to use their vote converts them into a minority. Statistical records are rarely kept in forms that give breakdowns of voting by sex, but those that exist show women's rates of participation to be lower than men's, alike in the proportions of adults who register and in the proportions of registrants who actually cast votes.

Additional efforts are necessary to interest and educate women on public issues, prepare them for more constructive activity in the national parties, and stimulate them to seek elective and appointive office.

WOMEN IN PUBLIC OFFICE

In the federal Congress, only 2 of 100 Senators and 11 of 435 Representatives are women. Only 2 women have held cabinet rank in the federal government; only 6 have served as ambassadors or ministers. In federal judicial office, no women are on the Supreme Court or the courts of appeals. One woman judge serves on the United States Customs Court and 1 on the Tax Court of the United States. Of 307 federal district judges, only 2 are women.

Among appointive posts in the upper levels of the federal executive branch, a study of occupants of the key offices listed in the *United States Government Organization Manual* shows that under the past 3 administrations women have comprised a constant per cent—2.4—of a rising number: 79 of 3,273 in 1951–52; 84 of 3,491 in 1958–59; 93 of 3,807 in 1961–62.

In the states, as of 1962, of approximately 7,700 seats in state legislatures, 234 were held by women.

Few women have been elected or appointed to state executive offices of cabinet rank; secretary of state, treasurer, and auditor are the posts most commonly held. In some states, appointments of women to public office have clustered in certain fields regarded as "women's areas": those dealing with juveniles, school affairs, health, welfare, libraries. At all levels of government, efforts should be made to widen the range of positions to which women are normally appointed.

The low proportion of women in public office reflects the low proportion of women prominent in the private occupations that normally lead to political activity and advancement. Few women possess the practical experience obtained at middle and upper levels of administrative and executive responsibility, and they therefore lack the public visibility that goes with such posts and in turn becomes a basis for appointment to public office.

Law is commonly the professional background of both state and federal legislators, but only 3.5 per cent of the lawyers of the country are women. In view of this proportion, it is noteworthy that 5.2 per cent of the lawyers in federal agencies as a whole, and 6.9 per cent of the attorneys in the United States Department of Justice, are women.

During their early married lives, women's political participation is limited by the need to work near their homes. Conversely, the very high percentage of political work at the precinct level that is done by women shows the extent of their interest and their skill in activities that can be undertaken close at hand.

As more and more women plan ahead for a career after their children are grown and apply themselves in earlier years to a grassroots apprenticeship, the scale of their political activity is likely to broaden. Even those with active home responsibilities can undertake municipal or county contests for the school board or the town council or accept appointment on local advisory bodies, and more and more of them are doing so. For women whose families are grown, the presence at the state capital required by membership in the state legislature—normally for 2 to 3 months every other year—is not insuperable; it is frequently easier for them to get away than for men other than those who are self-employed.

Women should be encouraged to seek elective and appointive posts at local, state, and national levels and in all three branches of government.

PARTY RECOGNITION

Party recognition of women as practicing politicians is developing. In some areas and at some levels in party hierarchies, it extends to the inner councils where central decisions are made. More often, it is ceremonial Women sit on platforms at campaign rallies and at high tables at party fundraising dinners. National committeemen are matched by national committeewomen, men chairmen by women vice chairmen on committees below the national level and in the national party headquarters.

The fact that many politically minded women active at the precinct level do not expect recognition by a victorious party when plans are made for appointment and advancement following a succesful campaign may be a factor in their being given minor consideration by the party's top power structure. Prejudice against women in politics, though few political inner circles are free of it, diminishes as more women turn in political performances that help the party's record in the eyes of the electorate.

Both major parties carry on a talent search for prospects for top executive appointments, women as well as men. The Commission commends the parties' efforts to maintain up-to-date lists of highly qualified and available women. These should include candidates for posts where special skills—in science, medicine, law, for instance—cause the employment to be excepted from civil-service regulations, and for nonpartisan appointments such as judgeships.

Public office should be held according to ability, experience, and effort, without special preferences or discriminations based on sex. Increasing consideration should continually be given to the appointment of women of demonstrated ability and political sensitivity to policy-making positions.

Continuing Leadership

Throughout this report the Commission has considered women in the context of the total American society, not as a group apart and not as a group whose progress can be secured separately. It is, therefore, recommended that federal action taken as a result of the Commission's proposals become operative through regular and existing federal government structure.

To further the objectives proposed in this report, an Executive order should:

1. Designate a Cabinet officer to be responsible for assuring that the resources and activities of the federal government bearing upon the Commission's recommendations are directed to carrying them out, and for making periodic progress reports to the President.

2. Designate the heads of other agencies involved in those activities to serve, under the chairmanship of the designated Cabinet officer, as an interdepartmental committee to assure proper coordination and action.

3. Establish a citizens committee, advisory to the interdepartmental committee and with its secretariat from the designated Cabinet officer, to meet periodically to evaluate progress made, provide counsel, and serve as a means for suggesting and stimulating action.

We consider the establishment of such a citizens committee to be of real import. Many of our recommendations can be made effective only through

75

private, nongovernmental initiative, or through governmental initiative at other than the federal level.

The Commission has noted with high regard the interest in its work that has already been shown at the state level. By August 1963, a number of states had already authorized or established state Commissions on the Status of Women and action to this end was underway in at least a dozen and a half others.

This report closes, as it begins, with a call to move ahead. Its findings are commended first of all to individual girls and women, with the hope that many will discover in these pages starting points for their own initiative, either to expect more of themselves and prepare for fuller development of all their talents or to be ingenious in locating means of keeping up to date and utilizing skills they have already acquired.

Many of our recommendations concern the improvement of environments, and to this end we invite concerted action, private and public, at community, state, and national levels.

But the best of environments is nothing if not used. The potential of American life depends for realization on the inner fiber of American citizens. For all of the phases of the lives of America's women on which the Commission has concentrated attention, information entirely adequate to a forward step, and in many cases to a breakthrough, is in hand.

This is our call to move ahead.

Robert F Kennedy

Orville L Freeman

Luther H. Hodges

W. Willard Wirtz

Anthony J. Celebrezze

George D Aiken

Maurine Neuberger

Edith Green

John W Macy Jr

Mrs. Macon Boddy

Mary Ingraham Bunting

Esther Peterson

Mary E. Callahan

Henry David

Dorothy Height

Margaret Hickey

Viola Hymes

Margaret Mealey

Norman E. Nicholson

Marguerite Rawalt

Wm. F. Schnitzler

Caroline F. Ware

Cynthia C. Wedel

Richard A. Lester

American Women Today

It is appropriate at this time . . . to set forth . . .
the story of women's progress in a free democratic society.
PRESIDENT JOHN F. KENNEDY, THE WHITE HOUSE, DECEMBER 14, 1961

Today's young girl growing into womanhood finds it easy to believe that life in her time is very different from what it was in her grandmother's day. And in almost any country—certainly in the United States—she is not only right, but right in a variety of particulars.

Important elements in most women's lives are changing rapidly: how long they live, where they reside, when they marry and start homemaking, their age at the time their children are grown, their work outside the home in paid employment and in voluntary activities, their use of their leisure. Recent changes appear still more striking when viewed in perspective; this section presents twentieth-century developments related to women that are pertinent to the recommendations of the Commission.

LIFE AND HEALTH

When a young American now nearing her twenties was born at the end of World War II, she had a life expectancy of 69 years. This was 21 more years than if she had been born in 1900.

In health as well as length of life, gains made in the past 60 years are startling. By and large, the young girls of the 1960's were born in hospitals. Raised by the book on formula and baby food, with regular checkups at well-baby clinics, they were given shots that kept practically all of them

78

from having diphtheria or polio and made scarlet fever a minor illness. There are regional and racial differences, but overall, only 25 babies in 1,000 die before they are a year old today; 145 did so in 1900.

Yet the girls now coming of age and those at the turn of the century have this in common: membership in a rapidly rising population. Then, the increase was due not only to rising birth rates, but also to the fact that immigration was bringing into the country as new citizens large numbers of young adults in the childbearing years. The first decade of the 1900's saw the greatest influx of all.

A downcurve followed. By the early 1920's, World War I and United States legislation had all but halted immigration. In the depression years of the 1930's, the domestic birth rate fell—life expectancy was rising, but economic expectancy was dubious enough to keep families small.

The next great influence on the birth rate was military expectancy. When World War II began, many young couples rushed into marriage, faced with certainty of separation and possibility of death. When it ended, the birth of the daughters now coming of age was part of an upward surge that continued.

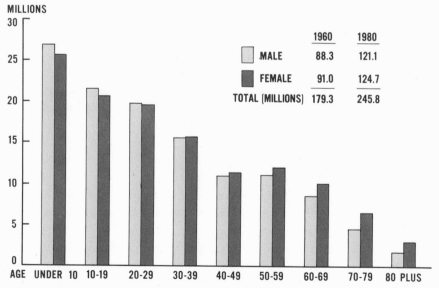

U.S. POPULATION WILL BE MUCH LARGER IN 1980

MILLIONS

	1960	1980
MALE	88.3	121.1
FEMALE	91.0	124.7
TOTAL (MILLIONS)	179.3	245.8

AGE UNDER 10 10-19 20-29 30-39 40-49 50-59 60-69 70-79 80 PLUS

Chart 18.

Young women of the postwar years sought security in the early founding of homes. Between 1890 and 1962, the median age of marriage dropped from 22.0 to 20.3 years for women and from 26.1 to 22.7 years for men. Recently, ¾ million girls have already begun homemaking between the ages of 14 and 19. In 1900, 2 out of 3 women in the total population had been married at some time in their lives; now, this is true of 4 out of 5 women. As of 1960, there were 488 children under 5 years for every 1,000 women of childbearing age; 291 would have been enough to replace the present population.

CONCENTRATION IN BIG CITIES

The homes of today's families are for the most part not where they used to be. At the turn of the century, 2 American families in 5 lived on a farm and many others lived in small towns in rural areas. Mostly, they went to bed by lamplight, drew water from the well in the old oaken bucket. Today, less than 1 family in 10 lives on a farm, and almost all farms have electricity and water systems; many are equipped in the same way as town-dwellers' homes.

From one decade to the next, more and more families live in the metropolitan areas that cover the East Coast from north of Boston to south of Washington, border the Great Lakes from Buffalo to Milwaukee, and center their widening circles on Los Angeles and San Francisco Bay, Pittsburgh and St. Louis, Minneapolis–St. Paul and Houston, Seattle and Dallas, Cincinnati and Kansas City, San Diego, Atlanta, Miami. The countryside is filling up. Within 20 years, 190 million people—as many as the entire population today—are expected to be living in the country's 200 largest cities, though problems of urban and suburban blight, water shortage, air pollution, and traffic congestion are already pressing for solutions there.

In looking at the American woman at home, it is well to remember that there is no such thing as an average American woman or an average American dwelling. The dream house shown in the movies, by the mass media, and on the subdivision circulars is not the only kind of dwelling that shelters American families. The 1960 census registered the increase in new apartments and suburban developments, but it also tabulated the continued existence of substandard dwellings, whether rural shacks devoid even of privies or congested city slums overcrowded with deprived families, especially from minority groups. Shortages of housing for low and lower middle income families continue.

80

THE AMERICAN STANDARD OF LIVING

It is also well to remember that over the years, from the very beginning of this country down to the present, standards of living have had importance to Americans beyond the material goods that they comprise. There is a special reason why this has been so. Successive waves of newcomers—from the Spanish, English, Dutch, and French who thrust the aboriginal Indians westward, to the Irish, the Central and Eastern Europeans, and the others from five continents who came in the nineteenth and the early twentieth century—quit societies where they had been born, looking for greater opportunity and greater freedom in the New World. After emancipation American Negroes sought it, too.

The diversity of backgrounds from which all of these peoples came, and their lack of any common tradition, made it necessary for the nation to find a unifying force that was external, something all could see and look upon as good. In a society where class distinctions were fluid, where there were no privileges based on birth, and where equality of opportunity was a principle that over the years was approached more closely in practice, the attainment of successive standards of material goods was felt to prove something. The desire to have a house, a bathtub, a car was only in part a desire for a material object: its possession was specific and undeniable evidence that the American system had worked.

Consumer goods have always been conspicuous in United States national production, and the American woman has been in large part responsible for their form. But over the last 60 years, her ways of supplying family needs have changed out of all recognition.

TWO IMAGES

At the turn of the century, the popular assumption about the dowry of skills a young woman would bring into marriage anticipated that the young farm wife knew how to cook and bake, keeping the wood or coal stove stoked to the proper temperature; how to can and preserve the annual yield of orchard fruits and garden vegetables to supply a family requirement calculated at 125 quarts per person. She would use a sewing machine to make her long-sleeved blouses, her floor-sweeping dresses, her children's pinafores and her husband's shirts and nightshirts—his Sunday suit might be bought through the catalog of a mail-order house. She expected to nurse the family ailments prevalent at the time—children's diseases, pneumonia, typhoid fever, malaria, tuberculosis. In case there was no school in the back country, she would teach her youngsters herself.

Her home was largely self-sufficient, her outside activities chiefly in her church, its missionary society and its women's circle. Neighboring families, however, could rely on mutual aid at times of crisis—illness, accident, or death; fire; or crop failure.

Today's image of young married women is very different. It shows suburban mothers reading directions on packages or cans as they cook frozen or otherwise preprocessed food by gas or electricity. To buy it, they bundle the children into the car and set forth to market at the local shopping center, where transcontinental trucking systems have assembled in one area most of the consumer goods that suburban families use. They make the rounds from supermarket to five-and-ten, from drugstore to branch department store. Services are there, too: laundromats and dry-cleaning establishments, banks, dentists' and lawyers' offices, and beauty parlors. (In 1960, 267,000 women worked as beauticians; perfumes and cosmetics are a billion-dollar industry.)

The appeal to the modern young housewife of instant coffee and minute rice is a vivid indication that time is always short: perhaps that is why her hair is short; her dresses are short; at home or at play she is likely to wear shorts—and on occasion her temper is short, too. Since ironing is one of the least mechanized and most time consuming of household tasks, she likes drip-dry fabrics and contour sheets.

Except for minor childhood illnesses, suburban wives' nursing is likely to be as aides at the local hospital. But they are expected to be active in sales of TB seals at Christmas and Crippled Children's seals at Easter and to engage in fund drives for research and assistance to sufferers from diseases such as cancer and heart. These have become today's ranking causes of death, particularly afflicting persons in older age groups.

Homemakers' teaching will generally be as organizers of nursery schools or day care centers, as teachers' helpers, or as substitute or full-time teachers in public or private school systems.

The advertisements of a $20-billion business suggest that the family's recreation take the form of outdoor excursions to national parks, beaches, or city recreational areas, sandlot softball, bowling, golf, tennis, fishing or boating, water skiing or skin diving. For most members of a family, football and baseball are spectator sports. So is horse racing. At home, many women are knowledgeable and avid gardeners; many men officiate as the family chef at cookouts.

Their cultural interests may lead them to library or museum, amateur

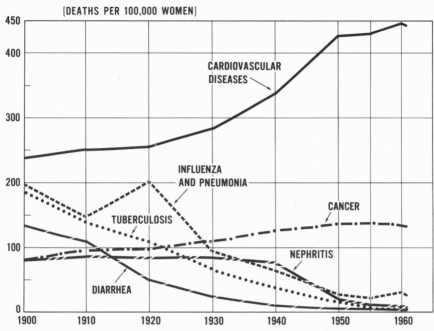

CAUSES OF DEATH HAVE CHANGED SINCE 1900
(DEATHS PER 100,000 WOMEN)

CARDIOVASCULAR
DISEASES

INFLUENZA
AND PNEUMONIA

CANCER

TUBERCULOSIS

NEPHRITIS

DIARRHEA

Chart 19.

theatricals, school band performances, the movies, or, depending on where they live, presentations by stock companies, visiting stars of stage and concert hall, or first-run casts with top billing in major centers. TV sets in the home are omnipresent, with commercially sponsored women's fiction and children's programs of widely varying quality or lack of quality by day, major newscasts and a range of fare from westerns and comics to prestige programs of national corporations by night. Ultrahigh frequency and the educational TV network have their financial problems but are gaining viewers for serious programs.

The suburban norm is for evenings to be highly organized: the young wife and her husband belong to the Parent-Teacher Association, numerous civic bodies, voluntary agencies, and fund drives—United Givers, Red Cross, UNICEF, Girl Scouts, Campfire Girls. Voluntary activities supply many services, from day care for children to projects to prevent juvenile delinquency to pilot programs in arresting urban or suburban blight and developing sound community life. Participation ranges from young girls

83

to mature women to retired professionals, and draws increasingly on widening social groups.

Suburban couples are expected to be active in their church and, to a lesser extent, in their political party, where the wife is called on to do much of the pre-election doorbell ringing.

The suburban wife has constantly impressed upon her the importance of getting along well with people, adjusting easily to new locations. She is likely to move at fairly frequent intervals, and though there is an increasing sameness among American communities, particularly those built since the war, that makes one house or one school or one shopping center very like another, each move means new human relationships.

These images of the modern wife and the old-fashioned girl accurately illustrate some of the twentieth-century changes in the activity of American women in their homes, but there is much that they leave out: the story of Negro progress over the hundred years since emancipation, and the extent to which the opportunities of Negro and other minority groups are still today more limited than those of other Americans, for instance. Neither conveys adequately the range of American women's occupations then or now; neither describes the life of working women or wives of workers in the cities.

WOMEN IN INDUSTRY

Because agriculture was the standard occupation of the American people during the early days of the nation, the idyll of rural life became a national myth. Actually, by 1900, the towns and cities of the United States were well on their way to the predominance they have now attained. Industry, finance, and commerce were booming, and women had begun to work in town outside the home in very substantial numbers. They operated industrial machinery; they tapped the typewriters newly installed beside rolltop desks in urban offices.

The working conditions of the 5 million women who made up 18 per cent of the labor force in 1900 were very different from those of the 24 million women who comprise 1 in 3 of the country's workers today. In 1900, the individual worker had little bargaining power. All wages were low. Arriving immigrants were eager for work on almost any terms. Trade unions existed chiefly in crafts where the workers were men; organization of women was difficult. The historic Triangle fire—in which 146 employees, mostly young women sewing on women's blouses in a New York loft, were burned to death—dramatized the precariousness of much industrial em-

84

ployment. Initial attempts in the states to temper exploitation through protective labor laws setting minimum wages and maximum hours for women were frequently nullified by court decisions declaring such laws unconstitutional. No social security system mitigated disaster for the disabled or those too old to work or those who became unemployed with the downswings of the business cycle. Only workers' solidarity, with the poor aiding the poor, and private charity blunted the cutting edge of prevalent misfortune.

Yet in the first decade of the century, women leaders—many of them developed in the groups associated with the great settlement houses, the House on Henry Street in New York under Lillian Wald and Hull House in Chicago under Jane Addams, and in the National Women's Trade Union League and the Consumers League—began to force increasing public attention on conditions of work, and helped put laws on state statute books requiring inspection and regulation of factory operation and installation of safeguards to reduce industrial hazards. Beginning with a historic court case in 1908, ceilings on hours of women's work began to be sustained by the United States Supreme Court. The first state minimum-wage law was passed in 1912.

These leaders were representative of a determined generation that pioneered to widen opportunities for women as well as to mitigate the economic circumstances in which many of them worked.

THE EARLY FEMINISTS

There had been women's "firsts" all the way back to the second quarter of the nineteenth century, when female academies for the higher education of women began to be founded. A generation later, the first woman was admitted to medical school. Clara Barton, one of the early women government employees, Civil War nurse, international disaster relief worker, and founder of the Red Cross in the United States, was an outstanding example of this group. Spreading from early establishments in New England, public elementary education for girls had become general by the latter part of the century, but only then were such women as M. Carey Thomas of Bryn Mawr literally and figuratively emerging from behind the curtains that initially screened them from the view of men students at the world's great universities.

Agitation to obtain the vote also dated from the mid-nineteenth century; before 1900, 4 western states granted suffrage on the state level. During the first decade of the twentieth century, careful organization led by Carrie

Chapman Catt added 7 more states and 1 territory to the suffrage columns. In 1917, Montana sent to the federal Congress the first woman member of the House of Representatives.

The outbreak of World War I in 1914, and United States entry 3 years later, accelerated a number of trends. With full employment, the end of large-scale immigration, and mounting pressures for production, a climate developed favorable to improvement of working conditions and wages and to trade-union organization. Unionization of the clothing industry was of direct benefit to women workers. Alike in government and industry, women began to be employed on new kinds of jobs. Dr. Alice Hamilton, who had become managing director of the first State Occupational Disease Commission in Illinois in 1910, served through the war as consultant to the federal government on the dangerous trades, and in 1919 was appointed the first woman member of the Harvard medical faculty. In 1920, the wartime Women-in-Industry Service was made permanent as the Women's Bureau of the United States Department of Labor under Mary Anderson. Her first job, as a Swedish immigrant to the United States, had been in domestic service. By this time, the economy included about 8¼ million women workers.

THE NINETEENTH AMENDMENT

Political recognition increased, too. Prior to the presidential election of 1916, the suffrage movement opened a campaign to obtain the vote through a federal constitutional amendment. At the Republican Convention in Chicago, a wind-driven November rain lashed the route of the scheduled suffrage parade, but 10,000 women, umbrellas held high and soggy skirts swabbing the pavement, nevertheless marched. Delegates to the Democratic Party's Convention in St. Louis, on their sun-flooded route to the Convention hall, had to pass between erect and silent lines of women in white with yellow parasols. By 1920, the Nineteenth Amendment had been voted by the Congress and ratified by the states. The League of Women Voters was formed to encourage political participation.

Because of the increase in kinds of work done by women during the war, and resulting performance records, the young women who came of age in the 1920's had before them varied new models representing what women could do. In the course of the decade, a considerable number of women attained standing in the professions.

At the same time, the industrial expansion of the 1920's increased women's earning power and placement opportunities. Low wages continued throughout most of the economic structure, though Henry Ford's daring 1914 decision to pay $5 for an 8-hour day found imitators on the new assembly lines. The then large agricultural sector of the economy was in difficulties, but the standard of living of many families, especially in urban areas and middle-to-upper income groups, rose. Then the stock-market collapse of 1929 triggered the loss of many economic gains, and in the early thirties the Great Depression braked the economy to a near halt. Women and Negroes experienced the truth of the adage that they are last to be hired, first to be fired.

THE ROOSEVELT ERA

The national social legislation passed after inauguration of the Roosevelt administration changed the economic position of women in many ways. For the first time, the Cabinet had a woman member—Frances Perkins, previously Industrial Commissioner of the State of New York, became Secretary of Labor. The right to organize was affirmed in the Wagner Act, and its provisions given effect through the National Labor Relations Board. Industrial unionism, paralleling the craft unionism of the past, brought collective agreements into industries employing many women, such as textiles and telephones.

The social security system instituted in 1935 assured the great majority of both women workers and women dependents of workers that they would have a backlog for their old age and a stopgap for periods of unemployment. Public assistance programs aided the unfortunate. The Fair Labor Standards Act of 1938 placed a floor under wages and established the 40-hour week for the great majority of both men and women whose products moved in interstate commerce.

WOMEN IN WORLD WAR II

The outbreak of World War II in 1939, and United States entry in 1941, brought another period of full employment, and with it new opportunities for women. In 1940, 48 per cent of the country's single women were working; by 1944, 59 per cent. The women's components of the armed services put 266,184 women into uniform. Tillie the Toiler and Rosie the Riveter became classic figures on the American industrial scene; under the Lanham Act, day-care centers took care of the youngsters of many working mothers while they boosted war production.

Both the amount of women's employment and its varieties changed.

Many women, especially in minority groups, who had been in domestic service were able to move into other occupations. The women working as household help had formed 18 per cent of women workers in 1940; the percentage so employed had dropped to 8 by 1950.

After the war, though many women withdrew from the labor force, many others either stayed in or went in. Between 1947 and 1962, the number of women workers increased by 7.6 million.

POSTWAR MARRIAGE AND EDUCATION

The world into which the young women now reaching maturity were born differed from the prewar world in many ways. At the same time that younger marriages increased, general expectations rose as to the number of years of schooling that a young person should complete. In 1950, there were 3,327,000 girls in high school and 727,000 in college and graduate work. Frequently both the man and the woman in a postwar couple were students. To a growing extent, young couples shared the tasks of the home. But, frequently also, the wife halted her own education and worked to support the family while her ex-soldier husband went to college with the aid of the GI Bill of Rights.

Throughout the early postwar period, the economy boomed; worry about a job was not high on the list of a young couple's troubles; to them, the Great Depression was history. Assurance of steady earnings made the use of consumer credit practicable and general; on installment buying, young people were able to start their married years in homes and with equipment for which earlier generations had had to save, obtaining them on a cash basis at a later period in their lives.

NEW INCOME LEVELS

Over the years, the levels of American family incomes materially changed. In 1961, the median family income of America's 46.3 million families was $5,737, up from $3,319 in 1950. With gains in workers' incomes, and with production of consumer goods increasingly aimed at mass markets, the country has become a middle-income country. Whenever one or more workers in the family is regularly attached to the economy, earnings are at levels permitting an increasingly wide range of consumption. Today's poverty, unlike the general poverty due to low wages in the past, centers in the families and individuals who for various reasons cannot attach themselves to the economy or succeed in doing so only irregularly or at the inadequate levels of today's minimum wage. Rising price levels devalue resources available either from welfare or other public programs or from past savings; a new hard core of disadvantaged people, many of them women with children, many of them in upper age groups, is forming in American cities.

Though still far lower than men's, women's earnings bulk increasingly larger. Many single women work throughout their adult lives; the period when the single woman had to rely for support on her father if she did not marry is over. In 1961, the median income of the 19 million women who worked at a full-time job was $2,574. In some 12 million families where the husband was working full time and the wife was in the labor force, the family median was $8,154. Since most of a family's purchases of consumer goods are made by the wife, recent gains have placed on her an increased responsibility to manage money wisely at the same time that they gave her increased options for its expenditure.

LIFE'S SECOND HALF

Earlier marriage, better health and longer life, homes increasingly equipped with laborsaving apparatus, all have greatly altered the second half of the American woman's adult life in the postwar years. Today's married couples have an average of 15 years to share together after their youngest child is grown up and gone. Family responsibilities, lessened from the time the youngest is in school and reduced again when the last child leaves, free many married women in their late thirties and their forties to work or carry on voluntary activities outside the home, part time at first, full time later. These new entrants are in addition to the women who because of economic necessity or other considerations have been in the labor market from early in their lives. In 1940, married women made up less than a third of the female work force; by 1950, their number had reached half, and by 1962, exceeded half of all women workers. The rise has been chiefly due to increased entry by mature women: between 1947 and 1962, the number of women 45 and older who were working doubled. As of 1962, the average age of employed women was 41, as compared with 37 in 1950. In 1900, it was 26. Better health and vigor likewise enable women to work at ages that a few years ago would have been thought advanced. In 1960, 548,000 of the 3.3 million women between 65 and 69 were in paid employment.

89

A woman of 70 has a life expectancy of 12.2 years. The number of women 75 and over rose from 2.1 to 3.1 million between 1950 and 1960; more than half a million are 85 or more.

In spite of the increase in divorce—the number of divorced women in the population rose from 273,000 in 1920 to 1,708,000 in 1960—greater longevity on the part of both men and women results in the maintenance of married life in independent households to older ages than formerly. But as the years go on, both elderly married couples and elderly individuals, mostly widows, find management of a home either too burdensome or too costly. Institutions for their care, with or without medical attendance, and nursing homes for the senile are now being developed on both a commerical and a nonprofit basis. Generally, demand for places in such residences far exceeds currently available supply.

The staffing of facilities of this kind with professional personnel and assistants trained in geriatrics is only one example of the growing requirements for skilled services that are changing the emphasis in all employment.

CHANGING OPPORTUNITIES

A review of the occupations of women in 1960 as compared with 1950 shows very clearly where new opportunities have been opening and where older types of employment are declining or stagnating.

Contraction in agriculture is illustrated by a drop of 46 per cent in the number of women who work on farms. The decline in unskilled work in general appears in a drop of 14 per cent in nonagricultural women laborers.

Recent sluggishness in manufacturing and the extent of automation of existing processes are reflected in a growth of only 8 per cent in the number of women operatives. Trade-union figures underscore the absence of growth in factory employment. In 1960, there were 3.4 million women trade unionists. They constituted 18 per cent of all union members. Their numbers have changed very little in recent years. Women's employment has not been expanding in such long-organized fields as the needle trades and various branches of textiles; the same is true in communications, where automation has kept jobs from increasing with sales. Only 14 per cent of the women who work are in trade unions; the kinds of employment in which most of them work have always been unorganized.

While proportionately fewer of the women in the work force were employed in household employment in 1960 than in 1950, the total number of women so employed rose by 24 per cent. Sales staffs expanded by about the same amount—25 per cent.

90

The really large increases, signaling the areas where economic growth has recently accelerated, were in professional employment, which went up 41 per cent; clerical work, up 46 per cent; and service jobs, up 48 per cent.

ROOM AT THE TOP

These increases showed where jobs were available to be filled and women had filled them. But the numbers of women in top-level executive or administrative positions or in positions demanding the specialized skills of high technology have not risen with the expansion of a segment of the economy that would expand still faster if properly qualified personnel were available in greater numbers. Shortages of highly trained people explain why help-wanted signs are out at a time of relatively high unemployment levels.

An urge toward high professional achievement strongly characterized the generation that came of age in the 1920's. A comparable urge is evident today among women from minority groups to whom opportunities are newly opening. But the desire to excel in intellectual fields has been maintained much less strongly among women from the parts of the American population in which the existence of women's opportunities for high achievement have for several decades been taken as a matter of course.

There are brilliant exceptions. In the postwar period, 2 American women have won Nobel prizes. The National Academy of Sciences has elected 5 women to membership. Newspaper women have won 5 Pulitzer prizes; women authors in the fields of biography, poetry, history, drama, and fiction have won 38 more. In nonfiction and fiction alike, books by women have consistently placed high on bestseller lists. In theater, opera, and ballet, women's performances have received international recognition. There are many women in the country's outstanding orchestras.

Yet the capacities of many other women are clearly not being developed to their full potential. Many able girls graduating from high school do not go on to college, and the fields of specialization of those who do go cluster rather closely in education, social sciences, English, and journalism. It is particularly at the graduate level, however, that women fall behind. The number of women earning B.A.'s was 5,237 in 1900, 76,954 in 1940, and 145,514 in 1961. But since the war, the percentage of M.A.'s to B.A.'s has not risen as it did in the previous period; it has remained static at between 16.3 and 18.8 per cent, standing at 16.8 per cent in 1961. There has been similarly little change in the percentage of Ph.D.'s. In 1961, women earned

24,481 M.A.'s and 1,112 Ph.D.'s; the comparable figures for men afford a sharp contrast—54,459 M.A.'s and 9,463 Ph.D.'s.

Projections of where employment will be located by 1970 dramatize the gap that is developing between women's qualifications and the requirements of the jobs that offer talent greatest scope. The existence of room at the top, and of increasing room as women upgrade their abilities at any level, is easy to demonstrate. Economic rewards are there, too. The median full-time income of women with 5 or more years of college and advanced work was $4,694 in 1961, about $1,500 above the median income of those who are college graduates only, and almost 5 times the $950 median of women who have graduated from elementary school but not completed high school.

CHANGING ATTITUDES

Among the postwar generation of women, the possession of less educational experience than they could have had, and correspondingly less de-

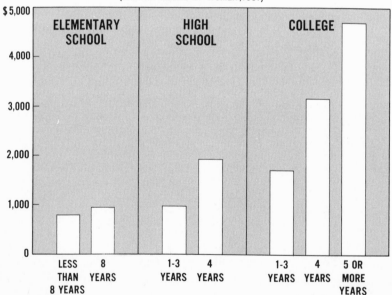

EDUCATION AND EARNING POWER GO TOGETHER

(MEDIAN INCOME OF WOMEN, 1961)

Chart 20.

JOB OPENINGS WILL BE DIFFERENT IN 1970

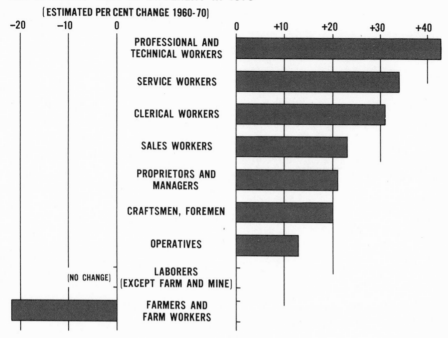

(ESTIMATED PER CENT CHANGE 1960-70)

Chart 21.

veloped skills, was deliberate. For many, the search for security in their homes was a primary objective, and the care of young children became all absorbing during years that in the past have been the conventional time for a young person to carry on full-time advanced study. But now, increasingly flexible and locally available academic institutions are beginning to permit young married women to keep up their interests and skills even while they are busiest at home, and locally organized means of marketing their skills on a part-time basis are developing. A growing feeling on their part that life in a child's world uses only part of their capacities has over the past few years motivated more of them to keep alive their intellectual interests and increased the degree to which American society will have the benefit of all of its human resources.

The young American woman starting out in life today has exceptional need to be self-reliant. Her making of decisions is likely to take place in a community which is new to her, and frequently is itself so new as to be almost without a past. Her husband's work is likely to be far enough away from home for their associates during the working day to overlap only slightly if at all. Her contemporary relatives, and her parents and grand-parents, are likely to be widely scattered over the country. The number of adults other than wives who are related to the heads of families and live in the same household with them has been small for some years; it declined further between 1950 and 1960. Many families, indeed, have members abroad, with civilian organizations from the Peace Corps to the Foreign Service, or with military units, or studying on educational grants, or engaged in business.

In exercising her resourcefulness, however, both in respect to her life as an individual and her life as wife, mother, and homemaker, today's young woman has many special advantages.

TODAY'S HOME MANAGEMENT

Though in too many families the struggle for a bare existence goes on, the majority have enough economic leeway to permit a widening measure of choice. In practically all families, decisions about spending include decisions on how to spend time as well as money. The 8-hour day, the 5-day week, and paid vacations are by no means universal, but they are very common. The new dimensions of life for which the present generation can plan include not only greater length of years but also more free time as they go along. In the 1960's, man's work no longer runs from sun to sun, and woman's work can be finished.

As a result, home management now looks increasingly to the cultural as well as the physical well-being of the family. Homemakers count among their resources the local library and the local museum as well as the local shopping center and the local hispital. Book sales are booming. The paper-back book industry is a new development which puts classic and modern authors within reach of modest incomes. Women in particular are active readers of magazines.

The churches have been important all along; they are now: over 116 million Americans have religious affiliations.

New responsibilities for culture have recently devolved upon the average American family. In the past, philanthropists and connoisseurs have en-dowed universities, libraries, and museums, supported creative artists, col-lected paintings and sculpture, backed theater and ballet. Today, with the changed distribution of incomes, while various foundations have cul-tural interests, the lavish patron has become rare. Funds for the support of the institutions that nourish mind and spirit must now come increasingly from families whose household budgets used to include little for such

94

purposes beyond contributions to their churches and payment of college bills or admission to entertainments. Such families have become a major source of support for universities, orchestras, community theaters, special exhibitions. In some localities, cultural attractions funds are paralleling United Givers organizations, with women active in both.

The attainment of material standards of living reached a stage during the postwar years when 3 of every 4 families had a car, and jokes about fins and status symbols suggested that the urge to keep up with the Joneses was losing momentum. Future American standards are likely to be more inwardly felt than those of the past, to be matters of taste rather than matters of emulation in the possession of material things. The development in recent years, especially among young people, of a knowledgeable interest in music is a case in point. The number of community orchestras in the country went up from 650 to 900 between 1951 and 1961; discriminatingly chosen hi-fi record collections and players personally assembled from selected components are more and more usual in American homes.

Standards in this sense become judgments of excellence. They are of the mind and spirit, and the country is now homogeneous enough to have a common approach to them. Consequently, today's young American woman comes to maturity with a special measure of opportunity—to live in a period when American abundance is coupled with a quest for quality, to show forth excellence in her life as an individual, to transmit a desire for it to her children, and to help make it evident in her community.

SECTION II

REPORTS
OF COMMITTEES

Introduction

by FRANCES BALGLEY KAPLAN

The Report of the President's Commission on the Status of Women synthesizes the Commission's thinking about problems on which it had been expertly briefed by members of its seven working Committees. Each of these Committees prepared a comprehensive report about the area of concern assigned to it, proposing solutions to the problems it found. These reports were an important stimulus to Commission discussions, since the Committees' suggestions formed the basis of most of the Commission's recommendations. In some few instances, the Commission disagreed with its Committees and made different recommendations. In still other cases, the Commission failed to adopt a Committee recommendation without substituting another.

The material presented in this section amplifies and documents the reasoning behind many of the Commission's decisions. It explains the special importance of some recommendations and points out why the Commission disagreed with its Committees about others. Background information has been added to aid the reader's understanding.

In the following chapters, material originally appearing in a Committee report and also included in the Commission Report has not been used. Thus, Section II supplements, but does not repeat the Commission's argument.

Subjects are treated in the same order as in the Commission Report; private and federal employment are again linked in one chapter. "Women in Public Office" is based on ideas discussed by two Committees. "Accomplishments through Continuing Leadership" is a report of progress in all areas considered by the Commission and its Committees. It provides a means of measuring the Commission's influence up to the time of writing.

Of the four consultations with specialists sponsored by the Commission, two dealing with volunteer activity and private employment gave creative advice and insights that were almost completely incorporated in several Committee reports. However, the ideas presented in the consultation report "Portrayal of Women by the Mass Media" were less fully drawn upon. That document is reprinted here along with the report of the consultation that discussed the problems of Negro women. The latter offers a comprehensive review of the special socioeconomic problems encountered by the women members of the largest minority group in the United States.

Twelve tables have been included in this volume; they provide material relevant to an analysis of the status of American women. Three of these, "State Laws with Respect to Jury Service by Women, as of January 1965," "State Laws Governing Domicile of Married Women, as of January 1965," and "Old-Age, Survivors, and Disability Insurance—Range of Benefits Payable in 1964, by Class of Beneficiary" are current versions of those appearing in Committee reports.

The eight tables comprising Appendix IV present a clear and concise comparative picture, state by state, of such subjects as employment, protective labor legislation, unemployment compensation, personal rights, marriage and divorce laws, and jury service. Thus, Section II and Appendixes III and IV help to complete the total picture of American women today, their status, their problems, and, most encouraging their progress.

Education

Today's women, educated as they are to take part in every phase of community life, stand in need of more effective and extensive education than ever before. The object of the Commission's recommendations in the area of education (these were adopted from the suggestions made by the Committee on Education) is to prepare women both to realize their intellectual and vocational potentialities and to fulfill their responsibilities to family, home, and community.

The Commission urged that three considerations be kept in mind when anything is done to improve education for women: the culturally deprived must be motivated; vocational guidance and counseling must be available to girls and women of all ages and circumstances; and part-time study arrangements should be recognized and encouraged.

Though the Committee document concentrated on needs and deficiencies, it did underline, as the Commission Report states, that more women are getting a better education in America today than at any other time or place in history. Having made its recommendations, the Committee was able to cite examples from current educational practice to illustrate the kinds of arrangements it would like to encourage. These may serve as models for other communities or as stimuli to further thinking along related lines. That the Committee found so many examples to cite is proof that educators themselves in various parts of the country have been successfully experimenting and groping toward the kinds of educational opportunities American women need to fulfill their contemporary roles.

The following material, adapted from the Report of the Committee on Education, provides documentation for the Committee's recommendations in addition to that included in the Commission Report, or describes the kinds of programs the Committee deemed particularly useful.

101

IMPROVING EDUCATIONAL OPPORTUNITIES FOR ALL

PRESCHOOL EDUCATION. Interest in learning can be formed during the preschool years, and it is crucial to foster such interest early in a child's life. The primary source of a small child's education is his mother, but many homes cannot or do not offer an environment that encourages intellectual development. The Committee went beyond the Commission in recommending that public and private kindergarten and nursery school facilities be available to all children. This idea was seconded by the Committee on Home and Community, which noted that significant educational contributions could be made by a day-care program for preschool children.

In 1960, only 24 states supported public kindergartens. Some school districts in other states supply funds for public kindergartens, and privately operated classes do exist, of course. However, nursery school facilities as part of the public educational system are almost unheard of, although private and cooperatively run schools for 3- and 4-year-olds are fairly common in some areas of the country. Census Bureau school-enrollment figures published in January 1964 indicate that almost 2½ million children were enrolled in kindergarten in October 1963. However, almost 17 per cent of all 5- and 6-year-olds were not enrolled in school.

GENERAL EDUCATION. Children of low-income families are at a disadvantage in school. Either they must cope with the unfamiliar orientation of a school geared to middle-class standards, or they must make do with the generally poorer quality of the educational program of schools in low-income areas. This is particularly true in large urban centers and the rural South. Often, it is taken for granted that children from culturally impoverished environments will not do well academically under any circumstances. Only recently has there been any sustained attempt to meet these youngsters halfway.

HIGHER EDUCATION. Despite the fact that not all talented students continue their education after high school, President Kennedy referred to a "veritable tidal wave of students" advancing on our institutions of higher education. In his 1963 Message on Education, he reached back to the earliest days of our country in describing the "aristocracy of achievement arising out of a democracy of opportunity."

Though opportunities for higher education are widening each year, they do not keep pace with our growing population. In his book *Excellence,* John Gardner, President of the Carnegie Foundation for the Advancement of

Learning, wrote: "Those who receive the most education are going to move into virtually all the key jobs. Thus the question, 'Who should go to college' translates itself into the more compelling question, 'Who is going to manage society?' "*

More high school graduates want to continue their education than actually do, according to a 1962 article by Wilbur J. Cohen, Assistant Secretary of the Department of Health, Education, and Welfare.† In that year, according to figures published by his Department, 58 per cent of male high school graduates entered college while only 42 per cent of the girl graduates did.

EDUCATION FOR THE MATURE WOMAN

LITERACY. The federal government has cooperated with local educational authorities to offer elementary English instruction to under-educated candidates for job training as provided under the Manpower Training and Development Act.

Volunteer groups have instructed illiterate adults in many communities. The General Federation of Women's Clubs has launched a large-scale effort to combat illiteracy using educational television as well as traditional teaching methods. This promises to be a relatively low-cost way to teach numbers of people, particularly if viewing groups can be organized.

The Laubach Literacy Fund, incorporated in 1955, grew out of the work of Dr. Frank C. Laubach, who for 35 years pioneered in literacy education for adults. The Fund, whose headquarters are in Syracuse, New York, claims that it can prepare a teacher to work with illiterates in 8 to 12 hours of workshop study. It works with groups in 20 states; its materials are used in 40 states and in 10 projects overseas.

Some communities have approached the illiteracy problem informally. In Chicago, for example, the Board of Education runs literacy classes in settlement houses, park field houses, housing projects, churches, Y's, and stores at hours of the day convenient both for workers and for mothers.

GENERAL EDUCATION. The federal government, states, cities, and private groups have all successfully provided education for adults. A study conducted by the National Opinion Research Center indicated that over 17 million adults were enrolled in some sort of adult-education course or

* John W. Gardner, *Excellence* (New York: Harper and Row, 1961), p. 71.

† Wilbur J. Cohen, "College Aspirations and the Future Demand for Higher Education," *Higher Education*, October–November 1962, p. 4.

activity in the year ending June 1, 1962. Participation was lowest among those with only a grade school education. Negroes, it was reported, were under-represented among adult-education participants. Education seems to provide the stimulation and motivation for further education—additional proof of the need for environmental motivation of the less well educated.

Throughout the country every year, some half million adults complete an elementary or high school education in public adult-education classes, the Office of Education reports. Private industry also offers basic education to adults.

COMMUNITY COLLEGES. The low cost and geographic accessibility of community colleges has made higher education possible for many women. These colleges accept older students as well as those of usual college age. Admissions policies are usually nonselective. Schedules tend to be flexible and geared to individual needs. These schools have had a tremendous impact on American education, serving not the educated minority, but the educable majority.

During the school year 1963–64, public or private community colleges or institutions under both auspices were teaching students in every state but Nevada (see Table 1).

Younger students sometimes use these institutions as stepping stones to a 4-year college education. Other students take advantage of their vocational and technical training programs, which are usually planned with local employment needs in view. Courses offered are therefore of great interest to mature women who want to enter or re-enter the labor force.

HIGHER EDUCATION. The exciting success of pilot programs in continuing education for women has been a most important phenomenon. They have illuminated the needs, interests, and potential of mature women.

The Minnesota Plan of that state's university has enrolled about 1,200 women of great diversity of age and academic background in college courses. Counseling is the cornerstone of the program, and academic plans are tailored to the individual. College and graduate work is offered, and the students include some who have never pursued higher education and others who already have completed some graduate work.

The Center for Continuing Education at Sarah Lawrence College acts as a source of educational counsel and referral for women in the New York City area who want to complete interrupted studies or take advanced degrees. In this liaison capacity the Center fills a dual function. It helps women find their places anew in the educational world, and in so doing,

TABLE 1

NUMBER OF JUNIOR OR COMMUNITY COLLEGES
BY STATE AND CONTROL, AS OF 1963–1964

STATE OR OTHER JURISDICTION	PUBLIC	PRIVATE	STATE OR OTHER JURISDICTION	PUBLIC	PRIVATE
Alabama	0	4	Montana	2	0
Alaska	0	1	Nebraska	4	2
Arizona	2	0	Nevada	0	0
Arkansas	0	2	New Hampshire	2	0
California	68	6	New Jersey	1	8
Colorado	7	0	New Mexico	1	0
Connecticut	2	7	New York	27	30
Delaware	0	2	North Carolina	5	17
District of Columbia	0	5	North Dakota	4	1
Florida	28	4	Ohio	0	4
Georgia	8	7	Oklahoma	13	2
Hawaii	0	1	Oregon	5	3
Idaho	2	2	Pennsylvania	1	16
Illinois	17	15	Rhode Island	0	2
Indiana	1	1	South Carolina	0	5
Iowa	16	5	South Dakota	0	3
Kansas	14	4	Tennessee	0	7
Kentucky	1	8	Texas	32	7
Louisiana	0	2	Utah	2	2
Maine	0	4	Vermont	1	3
Maryland	12	4	Virginia	0	13
Massachusetts	9	18	Washington	12	0
Michigan	16	5	West Virginia	1	3
Minnesota	10	2	Wisconsin	23	3
Mississippi	17	11	Wyoming	5	0
Missouri	7	11			
			Total	378	262

encourages other colleges and universities to modify rigid rules and requirements. Sarah Lawrence also offers seminars that help students conquer the problems involved in a return to an intellectual discipline.

The Radcliffe Institute for Independent Study, in Cambridge, Massachusetts, was conceived to help highly motivated women of demonstrated scholarly or creative capacity whose home responsibilities keep them from full-time work and other opportunities. In the fall of 1963, 32 women were Institute scholars receiving stipends designed to give them the freedom they needed for their studies. The Institute also is involved in basic research, and it has set up a guidance laboratory to inquire into women's educational needs and to test methods for meeting them.

Other pilot programs are limited to specific professional or academic fields. The program offered at Rutgers University in New Brunswick, New Jersey, trains women who wish to update or expand their mathematical competence. Edgewood College in Madison, Wisconsin, now offers teacher-training as well as liberal-arts courses in its program for personal development, which has enrolled over 500 mature women in 10 years.

The Harvard Graduate School of Education provides opportunity for part-time study for a small, selected group of mature women seeking to enter the teaching profession. In 1962, the Carnegie Institute of Technology, in cooperation with the Pittsburgh public schools, also instituted a training program for part-time teachers in social studies. For mature women who aspire to college faculty careers, the Educational Foundation's College Faculty Program of the American Association of University Women has provided counseling, referral, and financial support.

MATCHING WOMEN'S APTITUDES WITH SOCIETY'S NEEDS. The Committee specifically called attention to several areas in which the special aptitudes of mature women fit them to meet urgent social needs.

An estimated 200,000 new elementary and secondary school teachers will be required each year during the 1960's. With some retraining, mature women might help alleviate the shortage. Changes in certification rules would probably be necessary; reciprocity of certification and pension plans between states would be helpful.

Those involved in the Radcliffe Institute, the Minnesota Plan, and the Sarah Lawrence Center for Continuing Education have noticed the bent of mature women toward the fields of counseling and mental health.

"Women who manage families and raise children have to be concerned with people, their development, and their problems. Many women emerge

106

from this training ground in interpersonal relations with considerable skill in deciphering unspoken messages, in handling tensions, and in helping people to develop their potentialities. And just as they are becoming experts, the children go away to college and have little, if any, further need of them." So wrote Dr. Margaret J. Rioch, the clinical psychologist who created a program at the National Institute of Mental Health to train housewives as psychotherapists.* Her limited but intensive experiment has shown that mature women with varied earlier experience can become very adequate therapists.

School counseling, vocational-guidance work in or out of school, and related work in community mental-health centers are all jobs that could be filled by educated women of talent and sensitivity who have raised families and who are willing to return to school to train for a second career.

COUNSELING FOR CHOICE

The Committee urged that the help available from sympathetic vocational guidance and counseling be available to all individuals who are contemplating a choice or a change in education or vocation.

Counseling may be obtained in many ways. It may come through reading a book or pamphlet, seeing a film, informal discussions with informed individuals, or through individual or group discussion with professional counselors.

In 1961–62, about 36,000 persons performed some counseling functions in public secondary schools, far too few to meet students' needs. Throughout the country only an estimated 5,000 counselors are working in elementary schools.

In evaluating the training and certification of school counselors, the Committee found that some states require that candidates be licensed teachers before they can win certification as counselors. This prerequisite is unnecessarily burdensome, the Committee believed, and deters many, particularly women, from entering the field.

There is also serious need for simple vocational guidance. A survey in 1962 indicated that of the 3,120 counselors who work in state employment services, only 35 per cent were employed full time.

Not only are there an insufficient number of these advisors, their train-

---

* Margaret J. Rioch, "Training the Mature Woman for a Professional Role," *AAUW* (American Association of University Women) *Journal,* May 1962, pp. 236–239.

ing often does not equip them to advise women realistically. Counselors need education about the differences and similarities between the sexes in such areas as life patterns, role expectations, native abilities, and interests. A growing body of literature about women exists, but is not yet well enough known by those who guide them. Guidance workers also need materials that describe and explore women's status, opportunities for education, vocational training and employment, prospects for part-time work, and so on. This information should present the picture at the local and national level. Guidance workers should be equipped with biographies, films, and taped interviews that will suggest role models to students and enlarge their horizons.

EDUCATION DURING THE YEARS AT HOME

Mothers of young children need help to keep their intellectual interests alive. Both educational and commercial television offer academic courses, but very few of them are shown at hours when housewives are free to watch.

College alumnae groups bring some intellectual nourishment into communities where their alumnae reside, often through the cooperative effort of several institutions and emeritus members of the faculty. The cooperating colleges might give transferable credit for such courses. They might also distribute course reading lists and sponsor two-day alumnae "think" sessions or longer summer institutes for women who are not pursuing degree programs.

If professional organizations treated members who are not in active practice as active reservists rather than as former professionals, young mothers who have been trained in a field might be encouraged to maintain a commitment to their professions.

EDUCATION FOR HOME AND FAMILY LIFE

EDUCATION FOR HOMEMAKING. The content and emphasis of education for homemaking should fit the educational, cultural, and social background of the student. The subject has different relevance at various times in an individual's development.

Under the Smith-Hughes and George-Barden Acts, which have provided federal grants to the states to support vocational and technical training since 1917, the Office of Education helps state departments of education support home-economics programs in the schools. Eight million dollars in federal funds are now being matched almost 8 to 1 by the states. A high proportion of secondary schools offer some home-economics instruction; the foundation in this area given in elementary schools could be strengthened.

Home-economics instruction is increasingly concerned with realistic problems. In early adolescence, education for homemaking begins to have immediate relevance. For many young people, junior high school instruction relates to tasks they have assumed at home. At the senior high school level, students may acquire an informed basis for evaluating early marriage and childbearing.

Colleges are developing new methods to help students prepare for marriage and family life. Courses in family relations and child development, for example, draw on the disciplines of psychology, sociology, and anthropology. In this way they gain enough intellectual vitality and meaning to appeal to college girls studying many different fields.

Extracurricular experiments have also been effective. These include informal discussion groups, cooperative houses, apartment-living arrangements for student groups, and homemaking experience in designated families.

EDUCATION FOR FAMILY RESPONSIBILITY. Both society as a whole and the individuals in it have a vital stake in wise decisions about sexual behavior. It was the Committee's belief than an individual who had an opportunity to acquire a variety of reliable information about the subject and was encouraged to develop moral values would be the most likely to make wise decisions.

The Committee recognized that the subjects of sex education and family planning evoke the inhibitions of many members of our society and that any proposal for large-scale dissemination of this information arouses deep-seated concern among many otherwise education-minded citizens. Parents' apprehension about the teaching of family planning is based in part on the fear of unwise use of the knowledge by young people. However, ignorance of the facts has been the cause of considerable social and personal damage. The problems caused by premarital pregnancies and abortions fall mainly on the shoulders of young women. The effects on their personalities and future lives can well be disastrous, and the neglected children and severe welfare problems that often ensue strain community resources.

Opportunities for women to learn about human reproduction and sexual activity in the context of education for family responsibility are not as

109

available as they should be. Some successful endeavors in this area offer guidelines for expanded programs. For example, courses in many elementary schools deal with human reproduction as part of health education or as part of science courses. The latter include laboratory work with animals.

Junior and senior high schools have developed sex-education courses within the framework of health education, general or biological sciences, or home economics, thus contributing to the student's understanding of the relation between biological drives and personal relations. In a few areas, experiments are underway to make this education practical enough, sometimes through the dissemination of birth-control information, to help lower the illegitimacy rate.

College courses on family life and parental responsibility deal with problems of sex education and principles of family planning. At Howard University in Washington, D.C., freshman girls in a course in family living are taught about birth control by Planned Parenthood Association social workers.

State and community health and welfare departments have begun to see education in family planning as one method of reducing some of their severest problems. Further development of teaching materials in this subject will indicate optimum ways to reach students of different ages and cultural backgrounds. The simplest presentation and the most complicated should stress responsibility—the responsibility of the individual woman to herself, her husband, and her children.

Home and Community

The Committee on Home and Community took its mandate from that portion of the Executive order establishing the Commission that solicited suggestions on "new and expanded services that may be required for women as wives, mothers, and workers, including education, counseling, training, home services, and arrangements for care of children during the working day." The Committee on Education shared responsibility for filling this mandate. The work was divided along obvious lines.

At the outset, the Committee reaffirmed "society's stake in strong family life" and mothers' primary responsibilities in the home. At the same time, it also noted that many women are engaged outside their homes in endeavors related to their families' needs and welfare, and recognized these outside activities as important and legitimate. The Committee recognized that mothers may need help in order to perform all the tasks required of them under such circumstances. The community itself must become the source of help, the Committee believed. Its recommendations suggest the kinds of services communities must make available to mothers in order to help them be the effective homemakers that every family needs.

SERVICES FOR ALL

Though the Committee recognized that the needs of some women and their families are obviously more pressing than the needs of others,* it aimed its recommendations at the needs of all women. In its own words, "It is as important for women in suburbia to have access to needed serv-

* The Committee included in this description women who are heads of families or in low-income groups, women handicapped by minority status or suffering from physical or other disabilities, women who live under migrant conditions, or in congested housing, or who face other special problems.

111

ices as for those in downtown or rural areas, and as important for professional workers to be able to make satisfactory provision for their children's care as for factory or household workers."

The Commission, following the same principle, adopted nearly all the
Committee suggestions. It recommended the establishment of day-care
services and after-school and vacation programs for children of all economic
levels. All segments of the population need the kinds of help that would
be available when such services as the recommended Homemaker Services,
family counseling and community-health programs are in operation. The
suggested reorganization of household employment would lead to an improvement in the status of those engaged in the work and would benefit
employers as well. The satisfactions to be gained from contributing to
the recommended services as a volunteer worker would also be available
to all.

VOLUNTEER ACTIVITIES

Both groups' significant commitment to volunteer activities is worthy
of comment. This focus contrasts with a noticeable tendency in American
life to assign status only to activities on which a money value can be
placed. Both the Committee on Home and Community and the Committee
on Education stressed the variety of nonmonetary rewards that volunteers,
ranging from adolescents through mature men and women, would reap
from their efforts. In its report, the Committee on Education distinguished
between the educational needs of the "career volunteer" and the more
casual worker, and cited instances of successful training programs for
students as well as noteworthy achievements of teen-age volunteers. Both
Committees pointed to potentially greater contributions volunteers may
make by helping to provide the new services recommended. The Committee on Federal Employment commented on the value of "career" voluntary activity as preparation for a role in public life; this is discussed
in the chapter on "Women in Public Office" in this section.

High value was also placed on women's experience as volunteers by
Secretary of Labor W. Willard Wirtz. In discussing his belief that emphasis
in our society is shifting from "rights" to "responsibilities," he said in an
address, "This society is moving very rapidly from an acquisitive society
to a cooperative society. . . . You [women]," he went on, "have a head
start on the attitudes of the cooperative society, . . . we at least have the
disadvantage of having been exposed too much to the characteristics of

112

the acquisitive society and their concentration on self-interest. You are in a better position than we are to move ahead on these fronts which involve the identification of the common interest as distinguished from self-interest."*

RECOMMENDED SERVICES

The services suggested by the Committee, were, with few exceptions, recommended also by the Commission, although in slightly different form. Committee documentation of the need for many of the recommended services, which does not appear in the Commission Report, is presented here.

DAY CARE OF CHILDREN. The Public Welfare Amendments to the Social Security Act, passed by the Congress in 1962 and noted by the Commission, authorized the first appropriation of federal funds specifically for the day care of children in peacetime. (Funds were appropriated under the Lanham Act for child care during World War II to free women needed for the labor force, and such federal grants were discontinued early in 1946. Most of these programs—95 per cent of the projects receiving federal funds— were operated by educational authorities.)

Under current legislation, funds earmarked for day-care services are available to the states under the grant-in-aid program for child welfare administered by the Department of Health, Education, and Welfare. The legislation requires that day-care plans include health and education services as well. The development of satisfactory child-care programs on a scale necessary to meet needs will be costly, but less expensive than the price communities pay because of the neglect and deprivation of children.

CARE AFTER SCHOOL AND DURING VACATION. Care for children after school and during vacation could be handled in existing school and other facilities on a regular schedule. Children then would not be on their own, if their mothers work or for some other reasons cannot supervise them. The program could offer a wide variety of recreational and creative activities. The time could also be used for supervised study, group visits to museums and cultural centers, physical and dental checkups, inoculations, and conferences with vocational counselors. Another possibility is that students might hold part-time jobs under supervision. Such a program could be

* Address to the first Conference of Governors' Commissions on the Status of Women, June 12, 1964.

113

developed by a small, paid professional staff and carefully selected volunteers.

SHORT-TERM OR INTERMITTENT CARE. The Committee recognized a third type of child care: that which is on an intermittent or short-term basis. Women need such service to carry on normal homemaking and community activities, such as visits to the doctor or dentist, shopping, social obligations, and volunteer services. The Committee recommended that such care be available to all mothers at fees adjusted to the individual's ability to pay. The Commission did not adopt or comment on the idea.

HOMEMAKER SERVICE. The term *homemaker service* was used by the Commission in its technical meaning. This service is designed to furnish, for varying periods of time, assistance in the home that will help maintain and preserve family life threatened with disruption by illness, death, ignorance, social maladjustment, or other problems. It is a specialized service, sponsored by a public or voluntary health or welfare agency, and performed by trained workers under professional supervision. While the service was introduced in the United States in the twenties, until recently its growth has been both slow and sporadic.

RESPONSIBILITY FOR PROVIDING SERVICES

The Commission's call for establishment of the services it recommended must be heard and acted upon by all those private and public agencies, professional groups, and individuals that make up the complex structure responsible for them.

The local community, acting through all its institutions, has first responsibility, because the services eventually become available within its boundaries regardless of who administers or finances them.

Voluntary organizations should be involved at all levels of planning. Since public agencies provide income-maintenance programs on a large scale, voluntary agencies have been able to shift their focus to social and health services. They have also explored new methods and sharpened their professional skills.

Professional associations in fields related to education, health, social service, counseling, recreation, and home management should lead in exploring new ways to organize services and use personnel. They should reorganize and subdivide units so that professionals, by relinquishing their

114

subprofessional functions to well-trained and supervised assistants, can extend services while maintaining standards.

The federal role should be one of leadership, stimulation, and selective assistance. The federal government should sponsor or stimulate research, encourage area-wide planning, and concern itself with making available the manpower and facilities that will be required in the long run.

The state government is the most important agency concerned with public-health and welfare services. State agencies need to help new suburban areas and old central city areas adjust to socioeconomic changes. They should also offer technical aid and guidance to local communities.

PRINCIPLES TO BE CONSIDERED IN ESTABLISHING SERVICES

The Commission called for implementation of its recommendations. The Committee demonstrated by its own example that consideration of broad principles as well as minute details must precede action. Before making its own recommendations, the Committee looked at the national picture, bearing a set of principles in mind. It also considered an earlier set of guides to the development of community health, welfare, and related services prepared by the United States Department of Health, Education, and Welfare. Both sets of guiding principles are reprinted here for the benefit of individuals and groups interested in helping to foster needed services. Principles valuable in evaluating the national scene may, with little adaptation, be applied at the state or local level.

Goals for community services (Committee on Home and Community):

"1. Existing services should be examined and strengthened in the light of previous experience and emerging needs; new services should not be developed if others exist which meet the need.

"2. Broad standards and principles should be established that will permit and encourage individual and local initiative, allowing leeway for different approaches in different situations, for example, urban, semi-urban, rural; it is essential to determine which programs and services will need licensing and legal controls.

"3. Services should be provided both free and for a fee paid by recipients; voluntary organizations should be used, especially to initiate projects and programs on a pilot basis.

115

"4. Use should be made of both paid part-time and voluntary services, as these may make programs possible that otherwise could not be handled.

"5. The resources of government, business, educational, or voluntary organizations and foundations should be drawn upon for such help as professional consultant service, research, related information and experience, as well as for funds."

Goals for community services (United States Department of Health, Education, and Welfare):

"1. There should be accessible to the people in the communities where they live a range of community services broad enough to enable individuals and families to cope constructively with their social, physical, emotional, and economic problems. Such services should be planned for in such a way that when they reach the individual they do so as an interrelated whole.

"2. Services should be available without regard to the individual's race, religious affiliation, citizenship, residence, or income. The community should contribute toward the cost of such services. The cost of such services may be borne by the individual to the extent of his ability to pay for them or by the public, depending on the nature of the service and established public policy.

"3. A high priority should be given in over-all planning to the health, social, and related services which will strengthen the ability of families and individuals to manage and plan for themselves, which will enable persons to continue to live in their own homes as long as possible, and which will make it possible for those who have had to be cared for in other ways to return to family living where this is feasible.

"4. Preventive services, those which reduce the incidence of problems requiring community action, should be given a high priority in planning.

"5. Care outside the family setting should be available for persons for whom this is appropriate, such care to be provided in a manner which will safeguard the individual's opportunity for as satisfying and well-rounded life as is possible for him in the light of his particular circumstances.

116

"6. Services should be provided by, or under the direction of, persons fully qualified by professional training to give them.

"7. There should be a continuing program of evaluation and research to determine how well the services provided meet the needs of people, and to add to scientific knowledge about cause and effect, with a plan for utilizing such knowledge as it becomes available in planning programs of community services.

"8. An organized planning and coordinating group is needed in every community with a population of 25,000 or more, and should include broad citizen representation as well as representatives from agencies and organizations, both public and private, providing services."*

RESEARCH IN RELATION TO FUTURE NEEDS

The Committee acknowledged that knowledge of present-day needs is relatively superficial and rests on many untested and traditional assumptions. Little is known, for example, about the meaning and implications of mother substitutes to the mother, the child, and society. Nor is there much information about the ways in which girls and women reconcile within themselves the conflicting self-images, role, and practical realities to which they are under pressure to conform. Nor is there knowledge of the complex motivations that determine their decisions.

It cannot be assumed that trends generated by contemporary pressures will leave women unchanged, nor that traditional wisdom provides sufficient insight into women's changing needs. Only penetrating research, courageous discussion, and imaginative experimentation with new services will help solve the riddle of women's needs for the future.

* *Goals for Community Services,* Planning for Community Needs in Health, Education, and Welfare (Washington, D. C.: United States Department of Health, Education, and Welfare; Office of the Assistant Secretary for Legislation, 1963).

Employment

EQUAL EMPLOYMENT OPPORTUNITY

The Committees on Private Employment and on Federal Employment furnished the Commission with recommendations and documentation that it adopted almost without reservation. Evidence that discrimination in hiring, training, and promotion exists in private industry led the Commission to adopt the Committee's suggestion for an Executive order that would promote the principle of equal employment opportunity. The need to implement this important recommendation was eliminated with the passage of the Civil Rights Act of 1964. Nevertheless, the kinds of proposals the Committee on Private Employment weighed before suggesting the Executive order to the Commission are interesting to compare with the terms of the new legislation.

The Committee members searched their consciences in an effort to determine how much pressure might be exerted on the business community. They were uncertain whether the Executive order should apply to all private employment or only to employment under federal contracts; whether compliance should be voluntary or more strictly enforced by law; if compliance, either voluntary or mandatory, should apply only to employers already holding federal contracts, or whether government procurement officers should consider employers' compliance before allotting contracts.

In the end, the Committee took a rather moderate position. It urged the establishment of a President's Committee on Merit Employment of Women. The Committee's focus would be on federal contracts, and enforcement would be through persuasion and voluntary compliance. Employers having federal contracts would have to demonstrate an effort to comply, and prospective contractors' practices would influence their ability to obtain contracts.

118

The Commission took an even more moderate stand, recommending only that the Executive order should state the principle of equal opportunity and "advance its application to work done under federal contracts."

Among the recommendations made to the Commission by the Committee on Civil and Political Rights was one suggesting study of the need for fair-employment legislation. The Commission did not adopt that recommendation. Both it and the Committee on Private Employment preferred not to link discrimination because of sex with discrimination because of race. Neither group suggested legislative action nor thought it realistic in the case of consideration of sex to press for broad scope of application and enforcement.

At the time the Commission considered its recommendations, only one state, Wisconsin, included "sex" in its fair-employment law. However, at this point, there is no need for implementation of the Commission's recommendation because the Civil Rights Act of 1964 forbids discrimination because of sex in its section dealing with equality of employment opportunity. Details of the Act are discussed in "Accomplishments through Continuing Leadership."

PART-TIME EMPLOYMENT

PRIVATE EMPLOYMENT. Part-time work is particularly important for women; it is sometimes seen as the solution to their problem of balancing home, community, and job responsibilities. Part-time work was discussed not only by the two Committees on Employment, but by the Committee on Home and Community as well. As has been stated, the part-time approach to further schooling was also of paramount interest to the Committee on Education.

Part-time employment of women is increasing. In 1962, 1 out of every 3 employed women worked only part time—less than 35 hours a week. By comparison, only 1 out of 4 women were part-time employees in 1950. Although some women who are part-time workers would undoubtedly prefer full-time jobs if they were available, the large majority of those employed on a part-time basis do not have the time or the desire to work a full week. They are most often women with family responsibilities, students busy with school, or partially disabled or older workers.

The use of employees who do not work a full week also solves specific employer problems. Regular employees sometimes need help in coping with recurring peak loads. Some industries have only limited need for certain specific skills. Other firms employ part-time workers when full-time skilled employees are in short supply.

119

Despite the growing prevalence of part-time workers, the Committee on Private Employment believed that the reservoir of such skilled labor was not yet used as effectively or as extensively as it could be and that industry had not yet found the most efficient ways of using people's talents on this basis. It suggested that studies be undertaken to determine how to improve these aspects of manpower utilization. The Committee on Home and Community also urged employer organizations and trade associations to study employment possibilities for women outside the traditional 9-to-5, 5-day-week, 50-week-year approach. By contrast, the Commission, which was clearly in sympathy with the development of increased opportunities for part-time work in private industry, referred in its Report only to the federal government's deficiency in this respect.

Although more knowledge is needed to insure better use of part-time workers, some information is available about the nature of this aspect of the female labor force. Four out of 5 part-time women workers are employed in 4 broad job categories—professional, technical, and kindred workers; service workers (including those in private households); clerical workers; and sales workers. Over half the women who held part-time jobs during 1960 were between 25 and 54 years of age. Teen-agers accounted for slightly more than a fifth of the total group; women 55 and over made up another fifth; and those past retirement age comprised about 7 per cent. The number of single women workers who held part-time as opposed to full-time jobs was proportionately the same as that of married women living with their husbands.

The care of their children of nursery school age constitutes one of the most serious problems for women holding part-time jobs. Facilities needed for child care are much the same whether a woman is working full or part time, but the relative cost is heavier for the latter workers.

Officials of an employment agency specializing in part-time jobs in commercial occupations contributed several valuable observations. Many employers prefer mature women for this work because of their dependability. Part-time workers generally are paid the same hourly rate as full-time employees, and employers may benefit from use of the former if a shorter work schedule eliminates the need for coffee breaks and paid lunch hours.

FEDERAL EMPLOYMENT. Part-time and intermittent personnel in the executive branch of the federal government as of November 30, 1962, numbered 123,733, concentrated in a few agencies that used them effectively in special situations. (This figure includes individuals employed as experts and consultants.)

Some 15 government agencies in the Washington area supplied information about their use of part-time help. All reported that these workers were at least as productive as those employed on a full-time basis, and that part-time employment was more efficient than full-time in some situations. Most part-time employees hired had qualifications of a kind or at a level that was in scarce supply, and one agency reported that part-time help was usually overqualified for the job to be done.

The use of part-time employees because of a fluctuating work load apparently has not been developed to anywhere near its maximum possibilities. One unusual use of part-time help is detailed here for its value to other employers or workers. The Division of Public Documents of the Government Printing Office (GPO) employs help on Sundays and Mondays from 10 P.M. to 6:30 A.M. to fill orders for publications that have accumulated over the weekend and to get rid of the backlog of orders left from the previous workweek.

The number of employees working at the GPO each weekend varies from 150 to 300, depending on the workload. More than 3 out of every 4 interested in doing this work in 1962 were women. Workers telephone the GPO on Friday of each week to find out if and when they are needed. Without any formal recruiting on the part of the GPO, the number of applicants far exceeds employment needs.

The most important deterrent to the employment of part-time workers in federal agencies is the limit placed on the number of positions most agencies may fill. One part-time worker is regarded as "filling" a full-time position in most cases, rather than allowing the use of 2 or more in the same job. The system obviously discourages management from hiring less than full-time help.

EMPLOYMENT PRACTICES IN
THE FEDERAL GOVERNMENT

Several times in the course of its survey of federal employment practices the Committee on Federal Employment reported instances of discrimination against women. Instant action on the part of government officials was the usual result.

Table 2 reveals the heavy concentration of women in the lower-pay grades in the federal service, and indicates a very slow though fairly consistent increase in the percentage of women in the upper ranks in recent years.

More rapid advancement of women toward the upper grades of the Civil Service has resulted from President Kennedy's directive instructing

121

agencies to appoint, promote, and train employees without regard to sex.

The Civil Service Commission's interpretation of this directive may be of particular interest to workers and employers covered by the Civil Rights Act. The Commission circulated the following policy statement:

"The basic employment concept is that no training or position shall be denied any person on the basis of sex who meets the applicable experience, skills, and physical requirements for the training or duties in question. The Commission has determined that exceptions to this basic concept may be made (1) in law enforcement positions requiring the bearing of firearms, or in some few kinds of institutional or custodial employment, and (2) in certain unusual circumstances where it can be clearly and logically concluded from the facts at hand that a *particular individual* under consideration cannot reasonably be expected to perform effectively the duties of the position.

"Objections of this kind [to a particular individual], if based on *physical requirements* of a particular job, will not be sustained unless it can be shown that the person is not physically able to perform the duties of that particular job. For example, work of an arduous nature will have to be evaluated in the light of the actual physical demands of the job and the physical capabilities of the eligible . . . .

"The following are examples of the kind of employment conditions which, within themselves, will not be considered a basis for sustaining objections because of the sex of any eligible.

"Travel, including extensive travel, travel in remote areas, or travel with a person or persons of the opposite sex.

"Rotating assignments or other shift work.

"Geographical location, neighborhood environment, or outdoor work.

"Contact with public or a particular group or groups.

"Exposure to weather.

"Living or working facilities, except where the sharing of common living quarters with members of the opposite sex would be required.

"Working with teams or units of opposite sex.

"Monotonous, detailed, or repetitious duties.

"Limited advancement opportunities."

122

TABLE 2

DISTRIBUTION OF WHITE-COLLAR WORKERS IN THE CIVIL SERVICE BY GRADE AND SEX *a*

GENERAL SCHEDULE GRADE	ALL EMPLOYEES	MEN	WOMEN	WOMEN AS PER CENT OF ALL EMPLOYEES
Grade 18: b				
1954 *c*	200	199	1	.5
1959 *d*	183	181	2	1.1
1961 *e*	257	254	3	1.2
1962 *f*	337	333	4	1.2
1963 *g*	362	357	5	1.4
Grade 17:				
1954	280	278	2	.7
1959	503	496	7	1.4
1961	569	561	8	1.4
1962	777	768	9	1.2
1963	849	842	7	.8
Grade 16:				
1954	598	591	7	1.2
1959	1,067	1,058	9	.8
1961	1,284	1,271	13	1.0
1962	1,845	1,821	24	1.3
1963	2,376	2,345	31	1.3
Grade 15:				
1954	4,375	4,330	45	1.0
1959	8,506	8,416	90	1.1
1961	11,321	11,159	162	1.4
1962	13,409	13,170	239	1.8
1963	14,054	13,806	248	1.8

a Based on surveys by the Civil Service Commission.
b Grade 18 is the highest grade.
c All statistics for 1954 are as of August 31 of that year; all statistics for other years are as of the dates given in the following footnotes.
d As of October 31, 1959.

e As of October 31, 1961.
f As of October 31, 1962.
g As of December 31, 1963. This survey covered only grades 12 and above. The 1954 and 1963 data are for the continental United States; other years include American citizens employed in foreign countries.

TABLE 2

DISTRIBUTION OF WHITE-COLLAR WORKERS IN THE CIVIL SERVICE BY GRADE AND SEX

GENERAL SCHEDULE GRADE	ALL EMPLOYEES	MEN	WOMEN	WOMEN AS PER CENT OF ALL EMPLOYEES
Grade 14:				
1954	9,210	9,054	156	1.7
1959	17,914	17,563	351	2.0
1961	22,778	22,283	495	2.2
1962	26,173	25,529	644	2.5
1963	29,118	28,362	756	2.6
Grade 13:				
1954	22,248	21,756	492	2.2
1959	39,343	38,185	1,158	2.9
1961	49,159	47,628	1,531	3.1
1962	55,070	53,241	1,829	3.3
1963	59,459	57,435	2,024	3.4
Grade 12:				
1954	35,984	34,655	1,329	3.7
1959	60,228	57,594	2,634	4.4
1961	71,442	67,998	3,444	4.8
1962	78,147	74,211	3,936	5.0
1963	84,517	80,167	4,350	5.1
Grade 11:				
1954	51,986	49,045	2,941	5.7
1959	81,934	75,960	5,974	7.3
1961	96,205	88,657	7,548	7.8
1962	101,419	93,034	8,385	8.3
Grade 10:				
1954	12,871	12,110	761	5.9
1959	14,065	12,571	1,494	10.6
1961	14,900	12,916	1,984	13.3
1962	15,207	12,996	2,211	14.5
Grade 9:				
1954	76,848	69,103	7,745	10.1
1959	100,767	86,942	13,825	13.7
1961	109,915	93,615	16,300	14.8
1962	118,507	100,459	18,048	15.2
Grade 8:				
1954	21,041	18,377	2,664	12.7
1959	25,609	20,113	5,496	21.5

TABLE 2

DISTRIBUTION OF WHITE-COLLAR WORKERS IN THE CIVIL SERVICE BY GRADE AND SEX

GENERAL SCHEDULE GRADE	ALL EMPLOYEES	MEN	WOMEN	WOMEN AS PER CENT OF ALL EMPLOYEES
Grade 8:				
1961	22,510	16,136	6,374	28.3
1962	23,381	16,039	7,342	31.4
Grade 7:				
1954	85,900	68,504	17,396	20.3
1959	92,446	62,425	30,021	32.5
1961	93,407	63,003	30,404	32.6
1962	97,038	64,355	32,683	33.7
Grade 6:				
1954	39,126	24,383	14,743	37.7
1959	48,383	23,135	25,248	52.2
1961	53,604	22,286	31,318	58.4
1962	56,355	22,196	34,159	60.6
Grade 5:				
1954	94,232	45,231	49,001	52.0
1959	111,283	43,084	68,199	61.3
1961	125,594	45,968	79,626	63.4
1962	131,324	46,314	85,010	64.7
Grade 4:				
1954	138,854	46,647	92,207	66.4
1959	160,091	45,170	114,921	71.8
1961	169,419	46,234	123,185	72.7
1962	173,655	46,979	126,676	72.9
Grade 3:				
1954	182,766	45,455	137,311	75.1
1959	165,804	46,528	119,276	71.9
1961	153,585	44,584	109,001	71.0
1962	150,318	43,655	106,663	71.0
Grade 2:				
1954	102,136	39,840	62,296	61.0
1959	41,709	18,057	23,652	56.7
1961	34,077	15,805	18,272	53.6
1962	31,858	14,675	17,183	53.9
Grade 1:				
1954	11,396	7,930	3,466	30.4
1959	3,571	2,625	946	26.5

TABLE 2

DISTRIBUTION OF WHITE-COLLAR WORKERS IN THE
CIVIL SERVICE BY GRADE AND SEX

GENERAL SCHEDULE GRADE	ALL EMPLOYEES	MEN	WOMEN	WOMEN AS PER CENT OF ALL EMPLOYEES
Grade 1:				
1961	2,581	1,749	832	32.2
1962	1,985	1,443	542	27.3
Grade Not Specified: h				
1954	420,185	372,466	47,719	11.3
1959	485,820	422,675	63,145	13.0
1961	520,454	452,188	68,266	13.1
1962	557,338	485,156	72,182	13.0
Totals:				
1954	1,310,236	869,954	440,282	33.6
1959	1,459,226	982,778	476,448	32.7
1961	1,553,061	1,054,295	498,766	32.1
1962	1,634,143	1,116,374	517,769	31.7

h Includes positions under the Postal Pay Act and DMS schedules of the Veterans Administration, as well as all other positions which were not comparable to the positions in GS grades.

FURTHER STUDY NEEDED

Few hard facts are available to buttress the reasons commonly advanced to explain women's relatively subordinate position in the labor market. In addition to the subjects on which the Commission requested further study, the Committee on Private Employment listed three matters needing illumination: (1) the factors that influence women in the selection of their careers; (2) the reasons why labor shortages in certain occupations traditionally considered women's work cannot be overcome; and (3) alleged increases in production costs when women are employed in certain occupations and industries.

126

RETRAINING OF DISPLACED EMPLOYEES

The federal government, like industry, often displaces employees because of technological advances. Such changes promise to increase at an accelerated pace. Many workers thus displaced are unskilled or semiskilled; some lack the basic education required for retraining in skills useful in the new technology. Frequently, a high proportion are women.

The federal service, as a model for other employers, should be sure that human suffering is not the price of greater efficiency. The Committee on Federal Employment recommended that agencies make long-range plans for fitting changes, including employee education and placement. Stimulated by the interest of Congressional investigating committees, federal agencies do seem to be paying close attention to human considerations. The Internal Revenue Service (IRS) is now in the midst of one of the largest technological conversions yet made in the federal service. About half of approximately 12,000 permanent field positions will be abolished on a gradual basis, the over-all conversion being scheduled for completion in 1967. The Bureau of Labor Statistics, believing that this experience of the IRS will be of value to others, has published a study of the reorganization in a Bulletin titled *Impact of Office Automation in the Internal Revenue Service.*

Protective Labor Legislation

Laws to regulate the conditions under which men and women labor were called for as early as the 1830's. But a real drive for their passage, fueled by public dismay over deplorable working conditions, starvation wages, and inhumanly long hours, was not begun until the turn of the century. Since then, primarily through state and federal legislation, most workers have been protected in regard to maximum hours of work, minimum wages, health and safety hazards, and other aspects of employment. Labor legislation was first enacted to protect both men and women workers. However the United States Supreme Court upheld the constitutionality of such laws only insofar as they applied to women, whose dual role as workers and as mothers stirred humanitarian concern. The Supreme Court decisions cite "women's health and welfare" with stress on their childbearing functions.

In recent years, however, men as well as women have been included in minimum-wage and certain other types of labor legislation. Until then, as the Commission Report noted, men made progress through union membership and collective bargaining, while not many women could achieve such protection because so few work in occupations that are organized.

Both federal and state labor legislation are needed to protect workers because different groups are affected by each set of laws. In general, federal statutes apply only to those engaged in work concerned with interstate or foreign commerce or to workers employed by firms operating under government contract. State laws, in general, apply primarily to trade, service, and production industries within the state. In some cases, state laws deal with aspects of work not covered by the federal ones, or they may cover the same occupations but apply to workers in establishments that do not come under federal jurisdiction; or federal and state statutes may overlap. It should be stressed that the standards set by this large body of state and federal laws differ. There is little or no uniformity in the provisions included, the wages required, the limits imposed, or the means of procuring compliance. This mass of legislation is seriously in need of standardization, the Committee on Protective Labor Legislation found.

The various kinds of protection offered by labor laws may be organized under several general categories. Minimum-wage legislation may stipulate the minimum wage to be paid for an hour's work; or it may set up wage boards that determine and "order" into effect appropriate minimum wages for individual industries; or it may combine both types of procedure. Frequently, the number of hours to be included in a basic workweek is spelled out, and if an employee works longer hours, he must be paid at a higher rate for the overtime. The Federal Fair Labor Standards Act is an example of this kind of law. It has been amended several times since its passage and provides for a minimum wage of $1.25 an hour for all covered workers as of September 1965, with overtime pay of time and a half for work in excess of 40 hours. The Act also stipulates that men and women doing equal work must be paid equal wages.

A second category limits the number of hours women may work during any one day or week. Women are sometimes forbidden to work at night, or their night work may be regulated in some way.

A third kind of law sets standards for such matters as weight lifting, seating, and physical facilities in the place of employment.

Other labor legislation covers subjects such as industrial homework, maternity benefits, occupational safety and health, protection against income loss, and medical care and rehabilitation of workers injured on the job. Tables 5 and 7 of Appendix IV give details of some of this legislation state by state. Legislation dealing with protection against loss of income caused by unemployment, retirement, and death was reviewed by the Committee on Social Insurance and Taxes and will be discussed in that chapter.

Laws in all these categories were appraised by the Committee on Protective Legislation to determine how they affected women's employment opportunities and general status.

In the broad view, the Committee found the general record of improvement during the past 50 years impressive. The general development of the

American economy was responsible for some advances in labor standards, but labor legislation accounted for many improvements. Since the turn of the century, industrial homework and the sweatshop have virtually disappeared. Children under 14 no longer work in industrial factories. An average workweek of 40 hours replaces the 50–60-hour week of times gone by. Women's opportunities for employment have greatly expanded. Their average weekly wages have risen—the average wages of most full-time women workers are 2½ times as high as they were 50 years ago. Women's wages have indeed increased faster than men's. In the period between 1900 and 1919 a woman made about ½ as much as a man did, on the average. In 1961 and 1962 the median earnings of full-time women workers were almost ⅗ as high as men's.

Now, problems of protective legislation for women stem from the fact that many women are still underprotected and some feel overprotected. As Commission and Committee noted, millions of low-paid women workers who most need protection are not covered by either federal or state wage-and-hour laws. By contrast, however, other women workers feel that regulations that strictly limit the number of hours they may work or specify other working conditions for them discriminate against them. They feel hampered in their efforts to compete freely and equally with men on a job and to earn overtime pay on the same basis that men do.

MINIMUM WAGE

Minimum-wage legislation has made a significant contribution to the economic position of American families. It has lifted their living standards and narrowed the gap between the wages paid women and men in the same or similar occupations. It has helped to remove excessively low wages, which impose hardship not only on the employee but also upon society in general.

Fears of dire consequences to business and industry, and to employment, as a result of the enactment of minimum-wage legislation have proved groundless. To the contrary, by enlarging purchasing power, minimum-wage legislation has contributed to the general expansion of the economy; it has also helped remove the unfair practices that might otherwise have been engaged in by unscrupulous employers.

Of some 68 million workers in the employed civilian labor force, about 28 million are covered by the FLSA. Approximately 24 million are not covered because they are specifically exempted or because they are self-employed, government employed, or in professional or executive occupations, which generally are excluded from minimum-wage statutes. Most of the specifically exempted workers, with the exception of those employed in agriculture and nonprofit organizations, would routinely come under the coverage of a federal law.

Outside the present scope of federal minimum-wage protection, about 16 million nonsupervisory workers in private employment are subject to coverage by state action. The most recent estimate made by the Women's Bureau of the United States Department of Labor indicates, however, that state statutes give protection to only about 4 million of these 16 million workers. About half of the remaining 12 million are women, or nearly 1 in 4 of all women in the work force. Generally excluded from state as well as federal labor laws are employees of nonprofit organizations, and those in agriculture and private household work. Minimum wages stipulated by state laws range upward from the $1.25 a *day* provided by Arkansas's statute.

Many state boards that recommend minimum wages have reached the conclusion that at least $55 to $60 a week is required to maintain a standard of health and decency. A United States Bureau of the Census Report dated 1961 indicates that the median amount earned by women employed on a full-time year-round basis as service workers, except private household workers, was $2,357 or about $45 a week. Private household workers earned a median of $1,045 or about $20 a week, and sales workers, a median of $2,409 or $46 a week. These studies published by the United States Department of Labor in 1962 revealed shockingly low wages prevalent in certain occupations not covered by the FLSA. The extreme lows found were an average of $0.46 an hour for chambermaids in one city and $0.48 an hour for dishwashers in another. In general, the lowest wages were paid in Southern cities, but the pattern in those in the North also left much room for improvement.

In addition to recommendations urging the extension of the federal Fair Labor Standards Act and the passage, extension, and improvement of state minimum-wage laws that were adopted by the Commission, the Committee suggested that the minimum wage now fixed by federal law at $1.25 per hour be raised as rapidly as practicable. The Commission made no mention of this.

EQUAL PAY

Even in states that have equal-pay laws, not all women workers are guaranteed equal wages. Some legislation exempts certain groups of workers or limits coverage to specific industries. Moreover, the passage of an equal-pay statue does not necessarily insure equal pay in practice. Authorities in one large state frankly admit that salary differentials based on sex continue to be in effect though state law is violated.

Need for additional legislation to insure equal pay for equal work may be further highlighted by these facts. In an unpublished study conducted in 1960, Professors Lola B. Dawkins of Arizona State University and E. Lanham of the University of Texas conducted a mail survey of 120 firms in 20 states. Employers were asked whether they always paid women the same salary as men if they held the same position. Of the companies who responded, 83 per cent indicated that they always paid the same salary and 17 per cent said they "sometimes" did. A Women's Bureau representative who visited public employment offices in 5 cities in 1961 found about 120 examples of job orders containing wage differentials based on sex.

HOURS OF WORK

The Commission and the Committee were not in complete agreement when they considered those aspects of labor legislation that are occasionally thought to discriminate against some women. The recommendations made by the Commission and the Committee in respect to maximum hours of work are not exactly the same.

Such differences as there are may be traced to two contrasting points of view about protective laws for women. On the one hand, there are those who link the improvement in women's working conditions very closely with the labor legislation that has protected them. The Committee tended toward this view. On the other hand, there are those who feel that at this stage of our economic development, all workers, men and women alike, should have equal protection against long hours, unhealthful conditions, substandard wages, and undesirable conditions of labor. The Commission favored this approach. Many women who hold this view point out that rigid maximum-hours laws deter some employers from hiring women. They note that present statutes may prevent women from earning overtime pay on the same basis as men; this often creates hardship in families for which a woman is the main or sole breadwinner. And a woman's advancement toward executive rank is made more difficult or impossible if overtime work is prohibited. Both the Committee and the Commission agreed that women employed in executive, administrative, and professional capacities should be exempt from hours laws.

Neither side would repeal laws limiting hours or setting conditions for night work and the like. Both recognize that there are many women who

132

are completely unprotected in relation to the number of hours they may be forced to work. There is no federal law covering the question of maximum hours. Even in the 43 states with such laws, many women work in occupations not covered by them; for example, farm workers and private household workers are generally exempted from these regulations. Their pay is notoriously low and their hours often unhealthfully long.

The difference between the Committee and the Commission emerged in their approach to the problem of extending regulations concerned with maximum hours women may work. The Commission termed broad and effective minimum-wage coverage based on an 8-hour day, 40-hour week, and overtime pay "the best way to discourage excessive hours for all workers." The Commission encouraged the passage and strengthening of maximum-hours laws for women only until minimum-wage laws exist throughout the nation. It based its point of view on the success of the FLSA in cutting down excessive hours of work.

The Committee saw maximum-hours legislation for women as their main bulwark against excessive hours of work. It recommended that statutes be passed in all states establishing for women a maximum workweek of 48 hours or less and a maximum 8-hour workday. It recommended also that these maximum-hours laws be extended to cover more workers. Recognizing that premium-pay legislation acts as a deterrent to excessive hours of work, the Committee also suggested the insertion of premium-pay requirements for work beyond 40 hours a week in state laws governing hours of work and minimum wages for men as well as women. However, it regarded this legislation as a complement rather than an alternative to maximum-hours limitations. The Committee held that legislation governing and limiting working hours does not present a significant barrier to employment opportunities or promotion of women. Its Report said: "The standards established under this type of legislation have created a climate within which American women can function effectively and productively as workers and, at the same time can participate in community and citizenship responsibilities."

NIGHT WORK

The Committee noted that there are problems to be considered when women work at night other than the mere regulation of hours. One suggestion was for the provision of safe and suitable transportation.

A significant relationship between night work and eligibility for benefits under unemployment-insurance laws sometimes creates hardship for women. In some states where the law permits women to work at night, a woman accustomed to the day shift may be disqualified and refused unemployment-insurance benefits if she declines to accept work on the second or third shift. Conversely, women who have customarily worked on a night shift and cannot, because of family responsibilities, reasonably accept employment during the day, are sometimes similarly penalized. This practice, the Committee believed, may have undesirable social results, particularly for women who must care for family and home needs. It should be eliminated.

RIGHT TO ORGANIZE

Women, like men, can achieve through union membership certain protections that are not otherwise usually available even through legislation; namely, opportunity to improve their employment conditions, grievance machinery to defend them from arbitrary individual discrimination and abuses, and means to secure enforcement of protective labor legislation. It is generally true that in those states having legislation restricting the right of workers to organize and bargain collectively, protective labor legislation is weaker than in the others, and in some instances it is almost nonexistent. The Committee-sponsored recommendation, adopted by the Commission, regarding legislative protection of workers' rights to organize grew out of the realization that a relatively few women workers are union members and that many work in industries where employers are under no obligation to refrain from anti-union practices.

OTHER COMMITTEE ACTION

Several subjects were bypassed by the Commission because it considered them of equal importance to both men and women workers. The Committee had discussed these areas. Its significant recommendations follow.

OCCUPATIONAL HEALTH AND SAFETY. Occupational health and safety statistics for 1962 revealed 13,700 deaths, 83,300 injuries involving some permanent physical damage, and close to 2 million injuries of a temporary nature. Extension of occupational health and safety programs, to keep pace with new industrial developments, such as the use of atomic substances, is necessary, the Committee said.

WORKMEN'S COMPENSATION. With the exception of programs administered for federal employees and longshoremen and harbor workers, workmen's-compensation programs are state operated, and are financed entirely by

134

taxes on employers who are subject to state law. In all states, the District of Columbia, and Puerto Rico, a worker injured on the job has recourse to the benefits of workmen's-compensation laws. These provide cash payments to the disabled or to survivors in case of death, and medical care and rehabilitation services to the injured. Many of these laws are deficient in several ways. Only 28 of them are compulsory. They leave uncovered many occupations in which the majority of employees are women, for example, domestic service and jobs with charitable and religious groups. Half the laws exempt employees in small establishments, though occupational hazards are just as severe as in large firms. The statutes of only 30 states, the District of Columbia, and Puerto Rico cover all occupational diseases as well as accidents. Moreover, the fixed cash benefits stipulated in many of the laws have become inadequate in the face of heightened living costs and increased wages. The benefits now paid are often out of keeping with the original intent of the legislation, which aimed to provide the injured worker with between $\frac{3}{5}$ and $\frac{2}{3}$ of the wages he lost because of his temporary disability (See Table 5 in Appendix IV). The Committee recommended that the states remedy these deficiencies and make the laws compulsory. It also asked the Congress to explore a way to insure minimum standards for workmen's compensation laws in all the states.

GOVERNMENTAL ADMINISTRATIVE ACTION. The Committee underscored the need for efficient and well-administered departments of labor at the state and federal levels. To that end it asked that such departments be given enough funds to function adequately in fields of enforcement, administration, education, and research. The governors of all states were requested to direct state labor departments, with the assistance of statewide public committees, to review unmet needs as well as existing legislation and its administration, and where necessary to recommend improvements. It urged the strengthening of the Women's Bureau of the United States Department of Labor, and asked the Secretary of Labor to appoint a broadly representative committee to advise the Women's Bureau about further improvement in the field of protective labor legislation.

Noting the wide disparity in regulations, standards, coverage, and exemptions and the lack of uniformity in policy and enforcement, the Committee urged the strengthening of the Bureau of Labor Standards and asked the federal government to explore means by which uniform minimum standards for protective labor legislation in the states might be promoted.

Social Insurance
and Taxes

The Committee on Social Insurance and Taxes devoted the largest portion of its study of social insurance to the two main income-maintenance programs provided under public auspices—Old-Age, Survivors, and Disability Insurance (OASDI), commonly known as social security, and unemployment compensation. The Committee also dealt with deficiencies and inequities in the federal income-tax program and considered several proposals for changes in tax laws that were suggested to it.

Most of the Committee's recommendations about social insurance were adopted by the Commission. The pattern of the Commission's acceptance or rejection of recommendations indicates that it held to a fairly strict interpretation of the "social" nature of government income-maintenance programs, avoiding suggestions that would favor any one group.

Both the Committee and Commission noted that these otherwise fairly comprehensive programs of income maintenance failed to provide benefits for working women at the time of childbirth and urged that such a program of income maintenance be established.*

Because it is necessary to recall some of the important features of income-maintenance programs in the United States to understand the significance

* The Committee on Protective Labor Legislation was more specific than either the Committee on Social Insurance and Taxes or the Commission, and recommended the passage of legislation to provide for maternity benefits under state temporary disability laws. It called for reasonable maternity leave without loss of re-employment and seniority rights, and urged labor and management to promote these benefits through collective bargaining.

of specific suggestions, a brief review precedes the discussion of recommendations.

OLD-AGE, SURVIVORS, AND DISABILITY INSURANCE

The social-security program is administered by the federal government uniformly in every state.* The program protects workers and their families against three major contingencies: permanent and total disability, retirement in old age, and death.

As originally passed in 1935, the Social Security Act authorized the payment of monthly benefits to an insured worker upon his retirement from active employment at 65. The benefit, which was closely related to the worker's contributions, was intended to help replace the income he lost when he could no longer work, and thus to ensure his security in his old age. Before any monthly benefits became payable, however, it was apparent that the program, as originally authorized, would not provide effective family protection.

In 1939, the Congress, acting upon recommendations of the Social Security Board and the Advisory Council on Social Security, amended the Act to provide payment of benefits to certain members of the worker's family who were dependent on him when he retired or when he died.

Since the husband traditionally was the wage earner in the family and the wife the homemaker, benefits were provided for wives, widows, and children on the basis of presumed dependency upon the husband. Proof of financial support by the husband was not required. Benefits were also provided for the worker's parents if they could show they were receiving more than half their support from him. Since 1939, other categories of dependents whose eligibility for benefits is based on proof of support have been added to the law, and some of the eligibility requirements have been liberalized. At the present time, the husband or widower, and a worker's divorced wife (if she has in her care a child of the deceased worker entitled to a child's benefit) are also eligible for benefits on the earnings record of the worker if the worker provided one half of their support.

Under OASDI, the worker builds up his future security as he earns his living, paying toward the cost of his protection out of his earnings. When he suffers a loss of work income, benefits are paid to him and to his family

---

* Special groups of workers benefit from other programs. Among them are railroad workers, federal civilian employees, the uniformed services of the United States government, employees of the Tennessee Valley Authority, Foreign Service Officers, and the Board of Governors of the Federal Reserve System.

as a matter of right. There is no need to prove he needs the money. It is this aspect of the program—that an individual's security and that of his family grows out of his own work—that makes the program an effective mechanism for preventing economic dependency.

When a worker, man or woman, becomes disabled or retires, he is paid a benefit based on his monthly earnings averaged over his working lifetime.

A worker may elect to retire at any age after 62. If he retires at 65 or later he receives his full monthly benefit. If he retires between the ages of 62 and 65, his monthly benefit is actuarially reduced.

Benefits payable to dependents or survivors are related directly to the worker's benefit but generally are not as high, and the total payable on any earnings record is limited to an amount specified in the law for each benefit level. Table 3 lists benefits payable in 1964.

Eighteen million people were getting benefits in 1962, with more than 9 out of 10 mothers and their children protected against loss of income resulting from the death of the family breadwinner. Eighty-seven per cent of the people who became 65 in 1962 were eligible for retirement benefits.

At present, most of the beneficiaries of the program are women. About 8 million women were receiving payments at the end of 1961 as workers or as dependents of workers. Because most of these women depend on social-security money as their major source of income, the level of benefits under the program is very important to their economic status. Until 1950, the Congress had not attempted to keep the level of benefits in line with the increase in wages and prices. In that year, though, benefit amounts were roughly doubled, and since then the Congress has enacted several general increases in recognition of the rise in wages and prices. As a result of these increases, the benefits have more than kept up with prices but have consistently, although only slightly, lagged behind increases in wages.

Two of the four recommendations the Committee made about widows and divorced wives of workers (that a widow's benefits should equal what her husband would have received and that under certain circumstances divorced wives should be entitled to a wife's or widow's benefits) were adopted by the Commission; one that broadened the definition of dependents of single persons was also adopted; and another, on the question of "dual entitlement" of working wives to benefits, was rejected.

DUAL ENTITLEMENT. Married working women often complain that they receive little or no return on their own contributions to the social-security system. If they did not work and made no contribution to the system at all, they would still be entitled to benefits as the wives of retired workers or as

TABLE 3

OLD-AGE, SURVIVORS, AND DISABILITY INSURANCE—
RANGE OF BENEFITS PAYABLE IN 1964,
BY CLASS OF BENEFICIARY

CLASS OF BENEFICIARY	MONTHLY BENEFIT AMOUNT	
	MINIMUM	MAXIMUM
RETIREMENT BENEFITS:		
Retired worker, aged 65 or over *a*	$ 40.00	$127.00
Wife, aged 65 or over *a*, or under age 65 with a child beneficiary in her care	20.00	63.50
Dependent husband, aged 65 or over *a*	20.00	63.50
Child under age 18, or over that age if disabled before age 18	20.00	63.50
SURVIVOR BENEFITS:		
Widow, dependent widower, or parent aged 62 or over	40.00	104.80
Widow, generally under age 62, and dependent former wife divorced, with child beneficiary in her care	30.00	95.30
Child under age 18, or over that age if disabled before age 18 *b*	30.00	95.30
Lump-sum death payment	120.00	255.00
DISABILITY BENEFITS:		
Disabled worker under age 65	40.00	127.00
Wife, aged 65 or over *a*, or under age 65 with a child beneficiary in her care	20.00	63.50
Dependent husband, aged 65 or over *a*	20.00	63.50
Child under age 18, or over that age if disabled before age 18	20.00	63.50

a. If the beneficiary elects to begin receiving benefits at ages 62–64, the amount shown would be actuarially reduced.
b The minimum amount shown is the minimum benefit payable if there are two survivor beneficiaries getting benefits on the worker's earnings record. If there is only one survivor beneficiary, the minimum benefit payable is $40.00.

the widows of former jobholders. As the number of married women in the labor force has increased, this question of "dual entitlement" has become more important.

In 1939, when dependents of workers became beneficiaries, the Congress recognized that among the groups normally considered dependent, there would be individuals who worked and earned their own benefit rights. It reasoned that since a woman could not be completely dependent on her husband's earnings and at the same time be dependent on her own earnings, she should not receive the benefit based on her own income as well as the full benefit based on her husband's earnings. The law, therefore, provides that a working woman always receives the full benefit she earns for herself; if her own benefit is less than that due her as a wife or widow, the difference between the two amounts is added to her benefit as a worker. If the sum due her as a worker is larger than what she would receive as a wife, she receives only the former. Thus the wife who works and qualifies for benefits gets her *full* benefit, but she does not get both this and her full benefit as a dependent wife or widow.

Although a married woman who qualifies for benefits on the basis of her own earnings may not get a larger total amount than she would receive as a dependent, she ordinarily has additional protection. She is covered by the disability-insurance provisions of the program and would receive disability benefits if she were disabled before she reached retirement age. On her death, a lump-sum death payment, and possibly monthly benefits as well, would be paid to survivors. If her husband died and she remarried, the benefits from her own account would still be payable; a widow's benefit would generally terminate on her remarriage.

The Committee saw some justice in a married woman worker's complaints, not only because both she and her husband contribute to the program, but also because the family unit suffers greater loss of income when two wage earners retire than when only one does. It recommended therefore, that a working wife receive both a primary benefit as a worker and a secondary benefit as a dependent wife, but that her benefit as a wife be reduced on a sliding scale in proportion to the primary sum. Under the Committee's plan, a working wife would receive more than she does now unless she were entitled to maximum benefits as a worker.

The Commission did not adopt the Committee's view on the issue, believing it was too narrow a conception of the social-security program. The Commission stressed that it is principally a social program, and therefore individual equity must be given secondary consideration. Groups other than married women can point to inequitable benefits in relation to their contributions. For example, some workers contribute for many more years than others before claiming benefits. The Commission took the view that such inequities are inevitable and must be overlooked in order to preserve the social nature of the program.

REMARRIED WIDOWS. The Committee considered the treatment accorded the remarried widow of an insured worker. The law now provides that such a widow permanently loses her entitlement to benefits based on her first husband's earnings. Should her second marriage end in divorce, she does not regain her rights to the widow's benefit based on her first marriage, regardless of how short a time her most recent marriage has lasted. This provision seemed unnecessarily harsh to the Committee, since many older persons who remarry find it difficult to adjust to new mates and therefore separate from them. The Committee recommended that a woman in such circumstances become re-eligible for a benefit as a widow when her divorce becomes final, providing she brings action for divorce within a year after her remarriage. The Commission did not comment on this.

READJUSTMENT ALLOWANCE. The Commission did not adopt the Committee's recommendation to pay a readjustment allowance to a widow, ineligible for other benefits, for a year after her husband's death. Such an allowance would alleviate the problem faced by a woman widowed in middle age who must make the transition from supported wife to self-supporting widow. The Social Security Board recognized this problem in 1939 and indicated then that a temporary monthly benefit might facilitate readjustment. The Commission also recognized the problem, but believed it should be solved in a different way.

POSSIBLE SOLUTION FOR THE FUTURE. In the course of Committee discussion, a novel conception was advanced that might open a new approach toward solution of some of these problems. It was suggested that earnings be imputed to a woman's work as a homemaker so that she would accumulate "credits" toward benefits on the basis of her own work, whether she worked at home, in industry, or elsewhere. This plan would perhaps raise the status of women's work in the home, in that a woman who devoted her life to homemaking would become eligible for benefits through her own efforts rather than through her dependence on her husband. The basic principle of a woman "earning" her own benefits by her own efforts might also be considered in other types of labor and social legislation. The Committee saw so many practical difficulties in applying this principle to the social-security program that it did not recommend it, but believed it worthy of further study.

141

UNEMPLOYMENT INSURANCE

Unemployment insurance, in the main a federal-state program, provides a partial replacement of wages to unemployed persons who are able and available for work. Separate federal programs cover railroad workers, federal civilian workers, and members of the Armed Forces. The Railroad Retirement Board administers the program for railroad workers; the other two programs usually pay benefits in accordance with the law of the state in which the claim is filed, and benefits are paid by the state agency as agent for the federal government. While these programs are designed primarily to assist workers during relatively short periods of unemployment, they also have been of great assistance to workers experiencing longer spans of unemployment during recessions or during periods of technological displacement.

Contributions and benefits under unemployment insurance are based on wages received. Taxes to finance the program are paid by employers on the basis of wages paid to the employee; benefits are based on the former wages of the unemployed individual, and are paid to him without investigation of his need.

The federal-state program is financed by a federal tax on the payrolls of all covered employers. Employers may receive partial credit for the federal tax if they have contributed taxes to a state unemployment system that meets certain federal requirements. The federal government pays the administrative expenses of state unemployment insurance and employment service programs, and makes loans to states whose reserves are near depletion.

An average of 46.2 million workers per month were covered by unemployment-insurance laws in 1961; of these, 40.4 million were covered by state laws; 2.6 million were in the Armed Forces; 2.4 million were federal workers; and 800,000 were railroad workers. In April 1963, 4.1 million workers were unemployed and 2.1 million were getting unemployment benefits. The federal tax is imposed on employers with 4 or more workers but, as the Commission Report noted, exempts certain categories of workers. Some state laws are more comprehensive than the federal one in that some states cover employers with fewer than 4 employees and some cover workers in categories exempted from the federal law.

Unemployment compensation usually is paid at the rate of approximately 50 per cent of former earnings, but this is subject to maximum and minimum amounts that vary from state to state. Twelve states also pay allowances for certain classes of dependents, mainly children and their mothers. Table 6 in Appendix IV gives general information about unemployment-insurance programs in the states.

SPECIFIC DISQUALIFICATIONS. A most significant recommendation made by both Committee and Commission attempted to counteract a growing tendency to undermine the eligibility of certain women workers for unemployment compensation. From 1962 until January 1965, the number of states refusing to pay unemployment compensation to pregnant women workers, regardless of their availability for work, rose from 35 (and the District of Columbia) to 38 (and the District of Columbia). At the same time, the number that refuse compensation to women who are available for work but unable to find it, on the grounds that they quit their last job because of marital obligation, rose from 22 to 25 (see Table 6 of Appendix IV).

EXTENSION OF COVERAGE. Although over ¾ of all salaried workers are covered by unemployment insurance, approximately 14.3 million workers still were excluded from coverage in 1961. In recommending coverage for many of these men and women, the Committee noted that some of the workers had originally been excluded from protection because of the administrative difficulties their coverage would have entailed. Some 23 states have solved the problems connected with the protection of employees in establishments having fewer than 4 workers, and several states have overcome the difficulties involved in bringing household workers into the program. Extension of coverage under the federal law would lead more states to protect larger numbers of these workers.

In 1961, approximately 1.5 million persons were employed in nonprofit organizations—religious, charitable, educational, and other institutions—that were exempt from income taxation. In 1957, over 700,000 were employed in exempted hospitals, where women workers predominate. Several factors have hindered the coverage of employees of nonprofit organizations (except in Alaska, Colorado, and Hawaii), one of them being the traditional exemption of these organizations from taxation. In the OASDI program, this difficulty was overcome by providing for voluntary election of coverage. Although most states permit voluntary election of coverage under unemployment insurance, few nonprofit organizations ask to be covered. They contend that they do not have any real unemployment problem and that even if they did, they could not afford to pay the unemployment tax. Such coverage as there is has resulted primarily from union pressure.

143

EXTENSION OF COMPENSATION. The Committee urged that the federal government provide additional benefits for members of the labor force who exhaust their state benefits in periods of high unemployment. The Commission refrained from approving this recommendation not because it disagreed with the principle, but because it felt that it would affect men as much as women.

Most states now provide 26 or more weeks of benefits to some claimants, but 2 states and Puerto Rico still provide less than 26 weeks. In all but 8 states and Puerto Rico, the duration of benefits varies with the length of previous employment or the amount of wages. As a result of both these limitations, a high proportion of workers exhaust their benefits before they are called back to work or find new employment. This is particularly true in periods of recession. During 1961, the proportion exhausting their regular state benefits ran over 48 per cent in 1 state and exceeded 25 per cent in all but 5. As a result, almost 2½ million workers exhausted their regular state benefits during that year. A little over half of these men and women had received the maximum duration provided under their state law, while ⅓ had received fewer than 20 weeks of benefits.

During each of the last two recessions, Congress enacted legislation to provide extended benefits to workers who exhausted their regular unemployment compensation. In 1958, the Temporary Unemployment Compensation Act gave financial advances to the states, enabling them to extend payments to workers who had exhausted their regular benefits by an additional 50 per cent. The Temporary Extended Unemployment Compensation Act of 1961 provided workers additional benefits equal to 50 per cent of what they had received under state legislation, up to a maximum of 39 weeks of combined regular and extended benefits.

FEDERAL TAXES

The Committee considered a number of recommendations in regard to inequities in federal taxes relating to women, adopting some and rejecting others.

DEDUCTIONS FOR CHILD CARE. The Commission adopted the recommendation of the Committee regarding liberalizing the federal income-tax law in regard to deductions for care of children or disabled dependents, and discussed it in the context of "Home and Community" without going into specific detail. The Committee on Social Insurance and Taxes had been quite specific in its suggestions and recommended more liberal terms than were adopted in the Revenue Act of 1964, which is discussed in the chapter "Accomplishments through Continuing Leadership." The Committee recommended that the maximum income a couple may earn while still claiming child-care deductions be raised to $7,500; that a deduction of $600 for the first child, $300 for the second, and $100 for each additional child be allowed without imposing a dollar limit on the total deduction; and that the age limit for children for whom the child-care deduction may be made be raised above 11 years. (The Committee had considered various ages ranging up to high school age as the cutoff, but had reached no agreement.)

SUPPORT TEST FOR DEDUCTION FOR DEPENDENTS. Some low-income widows whose children are partially supported through tax-exempt public benefits, such as those provided under the Social Security Act, are unable to demonstrate that they contribute half their children's support and therefore cannot claim a deduction for their children as dependents. Higher-income widows can more easily demonstrate that they have made this contribution to their children's support even when public benefits received are taken into account. As a result, some lower-income widows pay relatively more in income taxes than widows whose income is higher.

The Committee recommended that tax-supported, but nontaxable benefits received by a child be disregarded in determining who supports him. The Commission made no recommendation on the subject.

EXTENSION OF THE HEAD-OF-HOUSEHOLD SCHEDULE. It had been suggested to the Committee that it recommend that all widows and widowers who have not remarried, all individuals who have attained 35 without marrying, and all who have been separated or divorced for 3 years or more, be eligible to use the head-of-household tax schedule.

This schedule was created after single persons complained about the more favorable one available to married couples who file joint returns. Congress went halfway by allowing widows, widowers, or single persons who maintain a household and support dependents to pay a tax midway between that paid by single persons and that paid by those who are married and file joint returns.

The Committee pointed out that some individuals in these groups may claim the head-of-household schedule even though the dependents they support live in separate homes. The main effect of the proposal therefore would be to extend the head-of-household schedule to individuals over 35 with no dependents. The Committee did not think that the fact a person had attained this age created a presumption that he or she was maintaining a

145

household. It also believed that the whole question of the relative equities of the three schedules for joint husband-wife, head-of-household, and single-person returns raised issues beyond its purview. The Committee made no recommendation.

EXTRA EXPENSES OF MAINTAINING A HOUSEHOLD. The Committee had been asked to recommend that working wives be allowed a tax credit for the additional expenses they incur in the maintenance of their households.

There is no doubt that wives incur additional expenses when they work outside the home; many of these expenses are common to men and women. However, a wife maintaining a household usually has—in addition to any costs for the care of her children—extra expenses for household help, laundry done outside the home, prepared foods, and so on. The Committee recognized that such costs are also incurred by women who are strictly home-makers, and that it would, therefore, be very difficult to establish whether the additional household expenses were caused by the fact that a woman was working. The Committee made no recommendation on this matter.

EXCISE TAXES ON ARTICLES NEEDED BY WOMEN. At present, a number of articles that women usually use and consider necessary are subject to excise tax. The most common articles in this category are handbags and cosmetics. The Committee considered whether to recommend removal of all such articles from the excise-tax list or to suggest that only those above a moderate price, that is, luxury articles, be taxed. The Committee recognized, however, that there are excise taxes on many other articles that could be classed as common necessities, such as electric light bulbs and refrigerators. It therefore made no recommendation.

Civil and Political Rights

Although women in the United States are more equitably treated now than they have ever been, discriminations against them based on sex still remain in both law and practice. Reports of the Commission and its Committees document a wide variety of examples of inequitable treatment. Indeed, there would hardly have been need for a Commission on the Status of Women had the belief prevailed that women's rights were fully recognized. Those concerned with the status of women have long held that it would be easier to identify and eradicate many kinds of discrimination if broad recognition of the principle of women's equality were embodied in the law. While this objective is widely accepted, disagreement has existed on the best means to attain it, with the greatest controversy centering around the pros and cons of an equal-rights amendment to the United States Constitution.

CONSTITUTIONAL RECOGNITION OF THE EQUALITY OF WOMEN

THE EQUAL-RIGHTS AMENDMENT. The proposed equal-rights amendment to the United States Constitution provides in part: "Equality of rights under the law shall not be denied or abridged by the United States or by any State on account of sex."

This or a similar proposal has been introduced in each Congress since 1923 and has repeatedly been reported on favorably by the Senate Judiciary Committee. The Senate approved the proposed amendment in 1950 and in 1953, but added the "Hayden rider" to it on the floor. The rider provides that the amendment "shall not be construed to impair any rights, benefits, or exemptions now or hereafter conferred by law upon persons of the female

147

sex." Supporters of the equal-rights amendment generally oppose the "Hayden rider" because they believe that it is under the guise of special "rights," "benefits," and exemptions that women have been denied opportunities that are available to men and that such exceptions contradict or nullify the principle of legal equality. Most supporters of the amendment think its passage is necessary because they believe that the Fifth and Fourteenth Amendments, as interpreted by the courts, do not afford women protection against discriminatory legal treatment.* Those who oppose the amendment are fearful that it would threaten protective benefits that women have acquired over the years. They further believe that such a broad constitutional declaration is not a satisfactory way of dealing with a host of complex and varied provisions ranging from laws governing family relations to those relating to women in industry.

The equal-rights amendment apparently is not intended to require identical legal treatment of the sexes. The Report of the Senate Judiciary Committee in 1962† indicated that the amendment probably would render unconstitutional laws restricting the legal capacity of married women, those dealing with jury service that treat women differently than men, and restrictive work laws applying only to women. The Senate Report stated further that the amendment would not affect laws granting maternity benefits or criminal laws governing sexual offenses, nor would it require equal treatment of men and women for purposes of military service any more than all men are treated equally for purposes of military duty, but women apparently would be equally subject to military conscription. With respect to alimony and support, the Report indicated that under the amendment alimony laws probably could not favor women solely because of their sex, but a divorce decree could award support to a mother if she was granted custody of the children.

It would, of course, ultimately be a matter for the courts to determine when equality of rights under the laws has been denied or abridged on account of sex, just as it is for the courts now to determine when due process of the law or equal protection under the laws is denied women under the Fifth or Fourteenth Amendments.

---

* "A Brief in Favor of an Equal Rights Amendment," prepared for the Committee on Civil and Political Rights by Judge Libby Sacher and Joyce Capps, on behalf of the National Federation of Business and Professional Women's Clubs (1963), is available for study in the offices of the Women's Bureau.

† Senate Report 2192, 87th Congress, 2nd Session.

LITIGATION UNDER THE FOURTEENTH AMENDMENT. The Commission and the Committee studied these arguments, and others,* and concluded that the Fifth and Fourteenth Amendments *do* embody the principle of equality for women, but that clarification by judicial interpretation is urgently needed.

The opinion of members of the Committee and the Commission were strongly influenced by a document prepared at the request of the Committee by one of its members, Miss Pauli Murray.†

Miss Murray's comprehensive legal memorandum analyzed court opinions and separate opinions expressing concurrence and dissent, in cases involving sex distinctions based on the Fourteenth Amendment. She noted that great changes have occurred in women's activities and interests and in society's attitude toward them since these decisions were handed down. She concluded that the Supreme Court, if presented with an appropriate test case, would today interpret the Fourteenth Amendment as prohibiting unreasonable discrimination based on sex.

In the past, the courts have consistently upheld laws providing different treatment for women than for men, usually on the basis of the state's special interest in protecting the health and welfare of women. In its opinions on cases alleging discrimination on account of sex brought under the Fourteenth Amendment, the Supreme Court has never held that a law classifying persons on the basis of sex is unreasonable and therefore unconstitutional.

The Fourteenth Amendment to the United States Constitution provides in part: "No State shall make or enforce any law which shall abridge the privileges or immunities of citizens of the United States; nor shall any State deprive any person of life, liberty, or property, without due process of law; nor deny to any person within its jurisdiction the equal protection of the laws."

* In addition to the brief prepared by the National Federation of Business and Professional Women's Clubs already noted, the Committee received the varying views of other organizations on this question. Opinions were presented by the American Association of University Women, American Civil Liberties Union, American Federation of Labor and Congress of Industrial Organizations, American Medical Women's Association, American Nurses' Association, League of Women Voters of the United States, National Association of Women Lawyers, National Council of Catholic Women, National Council of Jewish Women, and National Woman's Party.

† "A Proposal to Reexamine the Applicability of the Fourteenth Amendment to State Laws and Practices Which Discriminate on the Basis of Sex Per Se," (1962) by Pauli Murray, Senior Fellow, Law School, Yale University is available for study in the offices of the Women's Bureau.

In the nineteenth century, the Supreme Court held that the Fourteenth Amendment did not confer upon women the right to vote or the right to practice law within a state. As has been noted, in a series of cases decided between 1908 and 1937, the Court upheld various state labor laws that were applicable to women but not to men. In 1948 it held that a state law forbidding the licensing of females (with certain exceptions) as bartenders did not violate the Fourteenth Amendment. And as recently as 1961, it upheld a Florida law providing that no female be taken for jury service unless she registers with the clerk of the court her desire to serve.

The language of the Fourteenth Amendment appears sufficiently broad to reach all arbitrary class discriminations and would therefore seem to cover discrimination based on sex.

In one case, the Supreme Court stated:

"Throughout our history differences in race and color have defined easily identifiable groups which have at times required the aid of the courts in securing equal treatment under the laws. But community prejudices are not static, and from time to time other differences from the community norm may define other groups which need the same protection. Whether such a group exists within a community is a question of fact. Where the existence of a distinct class is demonstrated, and it is further shown that the laws, as written or as applied, single out that class for different treatment not based on some reasonable classification, the guarantees of the Constitution have been violated. The Fourteenth Amendment is not directed solely against discrimination due to a 'two-class theory'—that is, based upon differences between 'white' and Negro."*

In very recent decisions on cases concerning school desegregation (1954, 1955),† the extension of the concept of state action (1961, 1963),‡ reapportionment of state legislatures (1962),§ and the right of persons under arrest to have counsel (1963)‖ the Supreme Court has enunciated principles illustrating the capacity of the Constitution to reflect modern concepts of the importance of human values and individual rights.

"The genius of the American Constitution is its capacity through judicial

---

* Hernandez v. Texas, 347, U.S. 475, 478 (1954).

† Brown v. Board of Education, 347 U.S. 483 (1954), 349 U.S. 294 (1955).

‡ Burton v. Wilmington Parking Authority, 365 U.S. 715 (1961); Peterson v. City of Greenville, 373 U.S. 244 (1963); Lombard v. State of Louisiana, 373 U.S. 267 (1963).

§ Baker v. Carr, 369 U.S. 186 (1962).

‖ Gideon v. Wainwright, 372 U.S. 335 (1963).

interpretation for growth and adaptation to changing conditions and human values," Miss Murray wrote. " . . . It must be recalled that the earlier decisions on women's rights reflected the prevailing attitudes of a parochial society in which human rights had neither gained recognition as a universal concept nor received the comprehensive analysis which they are being given today. Archaic notions expressed in some of those cases would hardly be countenanced by an enlightened court of the nineteen-sixties. The more important precedents were established nearly fifty years ago before the worldwide technological, social, and political revolution which has followed two World Wars had made its impact upon American society and institutions."

The Supreme Court has not reviewed the constitutionality of some of the discriminatory legal provisions noted in the Commission Report. Examples of state laws that the Committee thought should be subjected to judicial scrutiny include provisions totally excluding women from jury service, domiciliary rules that operate to restrict a married woman's right to vote, and provisions restricting married women but not married men in the right to contract. In addition, there are undoubtedly instances of official practices that discriminate against women, as, for example, discrimination in public employment. It should be noted that the equal-employment opportunity provisions of the Civil Rights Act of 1964 will not apply to public employment.

Members of the Committee and Commission were unanimous in their hope that, in a properly presented case, the Supreme Court would give full effect to the principle of equality of rights for men and women, thereby clarifying and establishing this principle in federal constitutional doctrine.

JURY SERVICE

Women are still ineligible to serve on state juries in Alabama, Mississippi, and South Carolina. Twenty-six states and the District of Columbia permit women to claim exemptions not available to men (see Table 8 in Appendix IV). The Commission's desire to equalize jury service for men and women would, if implemented, require changes in all states except the 21 that permit women to serve on juries on the same basis as men. The removal of sex distinctions in state laws in regard to jury service would not mean that women having the care of small children would be forced out of the home; it would mean only that eligibility for an exemption and excuse from jury service would be the same for either sex. Indeed, some states now permit members of both sexes to claim exemption for child care.

PERSONAL AND PROPERTY RIGHTS

The Committee's survey of married women's personal and property rights disclosed many instances in which the law sanctions their inequitable treatment. In suggesting remedies, the Commission balanced a desire to find and eliminate discrimination with an equivalent interest in encouraging women to assume appropriate responsibility. Both the Commission and the Committee were influenced by recent developments in matrimonial property systems around the world reported in the 1958 United Nations Report on the Legal Status of Married Women.* These systems reflect widespread recognition of married women as independent persons before the law, and recognize the economic partnership involved in marriage and the financial contribution of the wife who works only in the home.

The material that follows documents the Commission's recommendations in this area and is adapted from the Report of the Committee on Civil and Political Rights.

OWNERSHIP AND CONTROL OF PROPERTY. In 42 states and the District of Columbia, earnings and property acquired during marriage are owned separately by the spouses; in 8 states, all in the West or Southwest, earnings and most property acquired by either spouse during marriage are owned in common. Thus there are two basic types of matrimonial property systems in the United States.

The systems of the separate-property states derive from the English common law. The common law concepts of matrimonial property evolved from the needs of an agricultural, feudal society in which the husband was regarded as the head of the family and the guardian of his wife. A woman was considered as having lost her personal entity upon marriage, a fiction that furnished the basis for close to total legal disability of a married woman.

Common-law rules have been modified by statute in most states, so that today a wife generally has full capacity to own and control her separate property. Traces of the old common-law system may be seen in 3 States— Alabama, Florida, and Indiana—which still require the joinder† of the husband in the conveyance of the wife's real property, irrespective of his release of any inheritance right in the wife's property.

The 8 community-property states—Arizona, California, Idaho, Louisiana, New Mexico, Nevada, Texas, and Washington—adopted the French or

* "Legal Status of Married Women," United Nations Publication ST/SOA/35.

† The joining of two or more causes of action in the same declaration.

152

Spanish civil-law concept of community property. In general, under this system, whatever is acquired by the efforts of the husband or the wife during marriage constitutes part of a common fund. Management and control, however, generally vests in the husband. Either the husband or wife, or both, may also have "separate property," such as that belonging to either at the time of marriage or that acquired through gift, inheritance, or in exchange for other separate property. Most of these states subsequently adopted the common law as the law of decision where the statutes failed to cover a particular situation.

In all states, a wife is able to control her separate personal property independently of her husband. The last exception, the Texas law requiring a husband to join in the transfer of his wife's stocks and bonds, was repealed during the 1963 state legislative session.

All states, in varying degrees, have modified by statute some of the outmoded disabilities of married women, but some inequities remain even in the operation of state matrimonial-property systems. For example, in the separate-property states, a wife has no legal rights to any part of her husband's earnings or property during the existence of the marriage, aside from a right to be properly supported. Hence, if she does not have earnings or property of her own, she is completely dependent upon his largesse for anything above and beyond the money she needs for support. On the other hand, under community-property systems, a wife has an interest in the commonly owned property, but a husband generally has exclusive authority to manage and control that property.

CIVIL CAPACITY. Under the common law brought to the United States from England, a married woman was virtually a legal nonentity. In addition to the prohibitions on owning or controlling property, she could not enter into contracts, sue or be sued in her own name, engage in business in her own name, act as surety* or fiduciary (trustee), receive her own earnings, or dispose of her property by will.

Beginning in the middle of the nineteenth century, various states adopted the married women's property acts, which were designed to remove the legal disabilities imposed on women upon marriage. The provisions of these statutes, and also the judicial interpretation of these laws, vary considerably from state to state.

Although today all of the states have removed most of the common-law

---

* A person who has made himself responsible for another and who remains primarily liable for such things as the payment of a debt, settlement of a claim; one who makes himself responsible for the appearance of another in court on a specified date.

153

disabilities of married women, some remnants of past centuries still remain. In some states, a married woman does not have legal capacity to become a surety or guarantor.* A number of states limit her right to sue or be sued in her own name. Earnings under the community-property system belong to the common fund. While some of the community-property states permit a wife to receive and control her own earnings within the communal-property concept they generally qualify her right to do so. For example, in California she has control of her earnings only until such time as they are commingled with the community property. In Nevada and Idaho she has absolute control only if she is living separate and apart from her husband. In Texas, as part of the community property, a wife's earnings are subject to the control of her husband.

A few states still restrict the right of a wife to engage in a separate business. These states have enacted "free dealer" or "sole trader" statutes that require some type of formal procedure before a wife may engage in an independent business. For example, 4 states—California, Florida, Nevada, and Pennsylvania—require court approval, and in Massachusetts a married woman and her husband must file a certificate with the city or town clerk in order to prevent the personal property of her business from being liable for her husband's debts.

INHERITANCE RIGHTS. Under the influence of feudalism, the English common law developed rules by which land descended to the lineal offspring, males being preferred to females. Neither spouse was the heir to the other spouse's lands. The estates of dower† and courtesy‡ provided a wife and husband respectively with an interest in the other's real property. Thus, dower became the chief support of a widow.

Today in nearly all states a widow has a statutory share in her husband's property, both real and personal, of which he cannot deprive her by will. In some states the statutory share is in addition to dower, in some it is in lieu of dower, and in some she can elect which to take. State laws generally provide a husband with a similar share in his wife's property.

The disposition of community property follows a different pattern. In Arizona, California, Idaho, Louisiana, Nevada, and Washington, the surviv-

---

* One who contracts to be answerable for the performance of another's obligations or promises.

† "Dower" represented that portion of a deceased husband's real estate, usually a third, in which a widow had a legal lifetime interest.

‡ "Courtesy" represented the life interest or tenure a man had in the landed estate of his deceased wife in case she had borne him children capable of inheriting.

ing spouse takes ½ of the community property while the other half is subject to the testamentary disposition of the decedent. In the absence of a will, the second half may go to the surviving spouse as well, or to the children or to both. In Texas, the surviving spouse takes title to the entire community property if there are no surviving children and to ½ if the deceased spouse is survived by any children or their descendants. In New Mexico, upon the wife's death, the entire community property may vest in the husband, whereas upon the husband's death, the wife's right to obtain the entire property is subject to the husband's right to dispose by will of his half of it.

The statutory shares as provided by state law generally apply only to property owned at the time of death. Although the estate of dower prevents a husband from disposing of real property without his wife's consent during their marriage, there is usually no like safeguard against improper alienation of personal property. State inheritance laws give some protection against improper alienation of property to a surviving spouse, but generally do not provide similar safeguards to protect the surviving minor children.

DOMICILE. A person's domicile or legal residence is important because it may determine many personal rights and obligations. For example, the place of domicile determines in which state the right to vote may be exercised, where an individual may run for public office, where one may be called for jury service, where a divorce may be filed, where personal property and income taxes may be levied, where the assets of a decedent will be administered, where one may receive welfare benefits, and where one may be eligible for admission to state hospitals and other state institutions.

A person's domicile generally is the place which he intends to be his permanent home. However, this rule does not normally apply to married women; the common-law rule with respect to the domicile of a married woman is that her domicile, by automatic operation of law, is her husband's, without regard to her intent or actual residence. This rule, if not modified, can restrict the basic rights of a married woman, particularly if she is not living in the same state as her husband. A married woman in such circumstance may be barred from voting, running for public office, and sitting on a jury, because she lacks the required domicile. Further, because state tax laws vary, a wife's personal property located with her in one jurisdiction may be taxed by a state with a higher rate if such a state happens to be her husband's domicile.

In a special study of state law on domicile, the Women's Bureau of the United States Department of Labor found that most of the law on the subject has been established by court decision. Since case law is subject to some interpretation, classification is difficult. However, on the basis of this study, it appears that today there are only 4 states—Arkansas, Delaware, Hawaii, and New Hampshire—recognizing a married woman's right to acquire her own domicile, independently of her husband, for all purposes, without limitation. Forty-two states and the District of Columbia permit a married woman to acquire an independent domicile for all purposes if she is living apart from her husband for cause; of these, only 18 permit a married woman to acquire an independent domicile if she is separated from her husband by mutual agreement or if her husband acquiesces to the separation. All states permit a married woman to establish a separate domicile for purposes of instituting divorce proceedings. However, in addition to Arkansas, Delaware, Hawaii, and New Hampshire, only 15 states permit, without limitation, a married woman to acquire her own domicile for the purpose of voting: 6 for the purpose of election to public office, 5 for the purpose of jury service, 7 for the purpose of taxation, and 5 for the purpose of probate. (See Table 9 in Appendix IV.)

RESPONSIBILITY FOR FAMILY SUPPORT. In dealing with problems of family law occurring during or at the dissolution of a marriage, the Commission and the Committee emphasized women's responsibilities as well as rights in the partnership.

The husband generally has primary legal responsibility for family support. However, in most states, a wife has secondary liability, and in more than half the states, the wife is liable for the support of her husband if he is in need and unable to support himself.

Whether or not a wife works outside the home is a matter to be decided within each family. When it is decided that a wife should take outside employment, it is reasonable that her income as well as her husband's be used to help support the children. On the other hand, when a family decides that it is necessary or desirable for the wife to work only in the home and the wife has no independent income, the husband must necessarily bear the full responsibility for family support.

As a practical matter, a dispute as to which party should pay how much of the family expenses does not arise in a normal family situation. It is only when agreement cannot be reached or when the marriage is disrupted that problems regarding family support obligations arise. It is for those situations that the law must provide standards and means for enforcing those standards.

156

Neither the Commission nor the Committee intended the recommendation regarding women's responsibility to support herself and her children to be used to pressure women to leave their homemaking functions for paid employment. Neither group expressed any opinion on whether a wife should be responsible for the support of her husband when he is capable of supporting himself.

GUARDIANSHIP OF CHILDREN. Under the old common law, the father was considered the natural guardian of his minor child and, as such, had the care, custody, and control, and the responsibility of the education of the child. Today, this rule has been abrogated by statute and court decision in the majority of states, which provide that natural guardianship of a minor child is vested jointly in both parents.

However, 6 states—Alaska, Georgia, Louisiana, North Carolina, Oklahoma, and Texas—still provide by statute that the father is the preferred natural guardian of a minor child.

HOMESTEAD LAWS. Most states have enacted some type of homestead law to prevent the family home from being sold to satisfy debts. Such statutes usually specify the size of the homestead and include a monetary limitation; in some states, the monetary value of the homestead exemption is unrealistically low. In North Carolina and Ohio, for example, the homestead exemption is limited to $1,000, and in Michigan, to $2,500. In addition, some state laws appear to be too restrictive concerning the persons who may claim the homestead exemption. For example, in West Virginia, where only a husband or parent residing in the state or the infant children of deceased or insane parents may claim the homestead exemption, the law offers no protection to a childless widow.

This Committee recommendation on the Homestead Laws and another, which proposed study of the need for fair-employment legislation (which is discussed in the chapter on employment), were the Committee's only suggestions that the Commision did not endorse. The Commission believed that the problem involved in the Homestead Laws affected too few women to warrant a formal recommendation.

157

Women in Public Office

The well-organized drive that characterized women's pursuit of the franchise has never been transformed into a purposeful march toward public office. In truth, though the Nineteenth Amendment to the Constitution opened the door to public elective and appointive posts to women, relatively few have been invited or have attempted to walk through.

The Commission recognized that home responsibilities and limited experience in fields from which public figures are usually drawn often prevent women from gaining responsible public office. It realized also that political parties often give little more than lip service to women's claims. Two Committees looked for further reasons for this seeming lag in the acceptance of women as public representatives and for women's apparent lack of interest in the pursuit of prominence.

That few women have high positions is not because of legal bars against them, the Committee on Civil and Political Rights acknowledged. However, some provisions of state laws do impose legal disabilities on married women that indirectly hinder their participation in public life. Women do not try to attain high office, either because they are unaware of possibilities open to them, or because they are reluctant to strain traditional social patterns and attitudes. Men's failure to appreciate women's leadership abilities is also a factor. But an element of prejudice undoubtedly plays a role when appointments are made, and it excludes women from public opportunities for which they may be fitted.

The Committee on Federal Employment suggested one interesting explanation for the fact that so few women are prominent in the competitive fields from which public figures generally emerge. Women, often free from any pressure to achieve monetary success or fame, tend to seek work that expresses their concern for others and offers them an opportunity to make

158

a personal contribution to human welfare. Such activities generally do not make women "visible" in a way that suggests to the general public their qualification for public office. Nevertheless, leadership in volunteer activities, in which many women engage, may well develop the same kinds of abilities that public leaders need. A woman who has held a responsible position in one of the many large volunteer organizations will have directed many unpaid workers in their jobs. In so doing, she will have had to exert her power in a democratic fashion. She will have had to harmonize conflicting personalities and compromise diverse views without sacrificing principles. Since these skills are also of primary importance to political executives, it might be well to re-evaluate the ways in which needed political and administrative skill is thought to be developed.

One of the Commission's recommendations asked for "increased consideration to the appointment of women of demonstrated ability" and the elimination of discrimination in regard to the holding of public office. The Committee on Civil and Political Rights had gone further in its suggestions to the Commission and in effect asked for temporary discrimination in favor of women. The Committee wrote: "Attainment of a more reasonable division between men and women of the powers and responsibilities of public office —appointive and elective—is desirable as a matter of national policy. Ultimately, the desired objective is, of course, distribution of public office among our citizens—men and women—according to ability, experience and effort. But interim measures which, for a time, may artificially favor women should be considered as a means of hastening the realization of this objective and achieving more effective and representative government. Early increase in the numbers of women serving government will help men and women to develop more rapidly the sound attitudes toward women in public office which are essential."

Obviously the Commission did not go along with the Committee in asking for privileges for women. Nevertheless, the previously discussed Civil Service Commission study of employment profiles, which indicated that experience working with women supervisors improves men's attitudes toward them, would seem to confirm the view expressed in the last sentence of the Committee's statement.

CAPT. CECIL STOUGHTON—OFFICIAL WHITE HOUSE PHOTO

She [my daughter] will need to know not only how to be a good homemaker, but perhaps at some time how to be a good breadwinner and at all times to be a participating member of society throughout her life.

Children do grow up. Children do leave home as inevitably as summer follows the spring and fall follows the summer. Therefore, it would be important to my daughter and to all of our daughters that she have an opportunity to make use of whatever skills she has learned, and it is equally important to our society that it have the opportunity to make use of her skills.

Somehow, some way, we must find a method by which this talent may not be lost or grow stale. If we have enough brains to send a sophisticated communications system hurtling within ten thousand miles of Venus, surely we have the brains to organize a society in such a way that this talent will not be wasted.

LYNDON B. JOHNSON
Washington, D.C.
September 24, 1962

My whole aim in promoting women and picking out more women to serve in this administration is to underline our profound belief that we can waste no talent, we can frustrate no creative power, we can neglect no skill in our search for an open and just and challenging society. There is no place for discrimination of any kind in American life.

LYNDON B. JOHNSON
Washington, D.C.
April 13, 1964

Accomplishments
Through
Continuing Leadership

THE COMMISSION CASTS A SHADOW

"No year since passage of the Nineteenth Amendment in 1920 can be compared to the period October 1963 to October 1964, in terms of new opportunities offered to women."* This quotation measures both tangible and intangible advances made since the Commission presented its report to President Kennedy on October 11, 1963.

The most potent, although the most intangible of these advances is the new "climate of awareness." Most communities, and the channels of communication that serve them, seem more aware of women, their problems, their aspirations, and their potential. The position of American women is even being discussed across the oceans, as people in Italy, Japan, Sweden, and Western Germany read the Commission's Report in their native tongues. Denmark has gone a step further by establishing a Commission of its own.

Tangible improvements can also be tabulated. The list of accomplishments was begun in Washington while the Commission was still in office.

* *Progress Report on the Status of Women*, First annual report of the Interdepartmental Committee and the Citizens' Advisory Council on the Status of Women. Single copies available from the Women's Bureau, United States Department of Labor, Washington, D.C.

It has since grown considerably, and the rate of advance may be expected to increase geometrically as centers of action, which now include state capitals as well as Washington, move further out to county seats, cities, and towns.

Major accomplishments affecting the status of women and revealing the impact of the Commission are given in this chapter.

ACCOMPLISHMENTS THROUGH NATIONAL ACTION

Even though the Commission could confidently have expected strong support for its recommendations from the executive branch of the federal government, the changes produced within the government have been impressive.

The work that President Kennedy began was taken up with obvious enthusiasm by President Johnson, whose speeches and appointments have been important factors in creating the climate of awareness noted above.

CONTINUING LEADERSHIP. The Commission had the foresight to urge the appointment of an official body to continue its work. It knew well that all traces of discrimination against women could not be eradicated from the American scene within its lifetime and that the momentum it had generated would dissipate or die without stimulation.

President Kennedy's Executive Order 11126, issued on November 1, 1963, establishing an Interdepartmental Committee and a Citizens' Advisory Council on the Status of Women, was a direct result of a Commission recommendation.

The Interdepartmental Committee, chaired by the Secretary of Labor, includes also the Attorney General, the Secretaries of State, Defense, Agriculture, Commerce, and Health, Education, and Welfare, and the Chairman of the Civil Service Commission, all ex officio. The Director of the Women's Bureau of the Department of Labor is also an ex-officio member and serves as Executive Vice-Chairman of the Committee. Members of this Interdepartmental Committee are the same officers of the executive branch of the government who served on the original Commission with the addition of the Secretaries of State and Defense.

The Citizens' Advisory Council on the Status of Women consists of 17 members and meets at least twice a year. Members of the current Council are for the most part the same individuals who served on the original Commission. Miss Margaret Hickey, who was chairman of the editorial committee of the Commission during the preparation of its report was designated Chairman of the Council.

Both groups were instructed to stimulate, review, evaluate, and report progress in the advancement of the status of women. The first annual report was issued in October 1964.

EDUCATION AND COUNSELING. Several new developments in federal aid to education will expand educational opportunities for women. These laws were enacted between July 1963 and December 1964.

- Public Law 88–210 modernized the legislative base of federal aid to vocational education. The program was made permanent, and $806 million in matching grants to states for expanded programs was authorized for the first 5 years. About 4.3 million students were enrolled in federally aided programs in the year ending June 1963. One hundred fifty million dollars was authorized for work-study programs in experimental residential schools.

- The Higher Education Facilities Act of 1964 authorized $1.2 billion aid for construction in fiscal years 1964, 1965, and 1966.

- The Health Professions Educational Assistance Act of 1963 authorized $175 million for construction of medical education facilities over a 3-year period, plus $61 million for loans to students entering medical schools during fiscal years 1964, 1965, and 1966.

- The Library Services and Construction Act of 1964 expanded federal aid to help raise the level of public library services in urban as well as rural areas. For fiscal year 1965, $55 million was appropriated.

- The Nurse Training Act of 1964 authorized a $90 million, 4-year construction program for nursing schools; a $58 million, 5-year program to improve and expand training programs; and an $85 million, 5-year student-loan program.

- The Mental Retardations Facilities and Community Mental Health Centers Construction Act of 1963 authorized a total of $329 million over a 5-year period to provide grants for construction of research and treatment centers for the mentally retarded and mentally ill, and for the training of teachers of handicapped children.

Increase in the number of accredited junior colleges continues. It is estimated that between 15 and 20 new community colleges were established in the fall of 1964, bringing the total close to 670.

163

In the area of counseling and guidance several significant developments have occurred:

- The 1963 and 1964 amendments to the National Defense Education Act have extended guidance services until June 30, 1968 and strengthened them. Coverage now includes junior high and elementary schools, public junior colleges, and public technical institutes. The authorized appropriation of $24 million for fiscal year 1965 represents an increase of $9 million over fiscal year 1963. The number of fellowships authorized under the Act will increase each year, from 1,500 in fiscal 1964, to 3,000 in 1965, to 6,000 in 1966, and 7,500 in 1967 and 1968.

- In 1963–64 some 1,740 trainees, including 804 women, satisfactorily completed training as counselor aides and youth advisors for employment by state agencies and other youth guidance services. Training was provided by the Bureau of Employment Security of the Department of Labor through 27 colleges and universities. The Women's Bureau furnished guidance publications.

The Women's Bureau of the Department of Labor has been active in stimulating the development of effective guidance and counseling:

- In cooperation with the Office of Education it met with 6 state directors of guidance to discuss special aspects of vocational counseling for girls and to plan for regional and State conferences.

- It added 3 bulletins to its series of publications on occupations.

In the meantime, more women have been taking advantage of education available; barriers have been falling.

- Part-time students, carrying at least half of a normal full-time schedule have become eligible for loans granted under the National Defense Education Act as a result of 1964 amendments to that law. In fiscal year 1963, when only full-time students were eligible for assistance, 91,000 women received loans or fellowships, representing 42 per cent of all student borrowers.

- The Economic Opportunity Act of 1964 included women in the Job Corps as well as in other programs of that Act.

The wife of an unemployed man may now be paid a training allowance while she is training under the Manpower Development and Training Act. Prior to the enactment of Public Law 88–214 on December 19, 1963, only heads of families and youths were eligible for allowances.

HOME AND COMMUNITY. Interest in day-care services has been stimulated by the grants to the states authorized by the 1962 amendments to the Social Security Act.

The Congress appropriated $4 million for use in fiscal year 1964 (July 1, 1963–July 1, 1964) and the same sum for fiscal year 1965. During fiscal year 1964, 44 states, the District of Columbia, and Puerto Rico used these funds; Idaho, Montana, Nevada, New Hampshire, Vermont, and Wyoming did not. Among projects being financed are day-care centers for babies of very young parents who are receiving training under the Manpower Development and Training Act, day-care centers for mentally retarded children, and a center where mothers attend with their children to learn better methods of child care and homemaking skills.

A pamphlet, *Determining Fees for Day Care Services,* was prepared by the Welfare Administration, and single copies may be obtained from the Children's Bureau, Department of Health, Education, and Welfare.

Tax deductions for child care were liberalized by the Revenue Act of 1964, Public Law 88–272. The joint income level above which deductions are not allowable was raised from $4,500 to $6,000. The new law permits deduction of up to $600 for 1 dependent and up to $900 for 2 or more dependents; $600 was the maximum deductible under previous law, without regard to the number of dependents. Definition of a dependent child was changed from a child under 11 to a child under 13. The law also allows a husband to make a deduction for his wife if she is incapacitated.

The following facts evidence progress in homemaker services:

In October 1961, some homemaker service was available in 40 states, the District of Columbia and Puerto Rico. In the whole country, 208 agencies employed 2,664 homemakers (⅔ of them full time), who served a total of 5,454 families in 1 month. Nearly 70 per cent (142) of these agencies were voluntary and the remainder (66) public.

Between 1961 and 1963, services increased though they are still extremely limited. As of October 1963, six states—Idaho, North Dakota, South Carolina, Utah, Vermont, and Wyoming—still had no programs at all, and none had complete statewide coverage. In the whole country, 303 programs were in operation—close to 40 per cent of them under public auspices (118) and the rest under voluntary agencies (185). A total of 2,539 full-time and 1,369 part-time homemakers were employed. And a total of 9,547 families were helped during the month of October.

If the need for homemaker services is to be met, public agencies must share much more extensively in the development of programs. Financial and technical assistance are currently available to the states through five units of the Department of Health, Education, and Welfare—the Office of Education, Public Health Service, Vocational Rehabilitation Administration, Social Security Administration, and Welfare Administration.

National awareness of the need for these units has been further stimulated by a National Conference on Homemaker Services, called by the National Committee on Homemaker Services in April 1964. The Welfare Administration of the Department of Health, Education, and Welfare provided staff services; 800 persons attended.

HOME MANAGEMENT ADVISORY SERVICES. These services are now being used more frequently in pilot studies.

The Cooperative Extension Service of the Department of Agriculture, whose programs the Commission cited, is now concentrating its efforts on "hard-to-reach" families in both rural and urban areas. Pilot projects with low-income families have been begun in Hartford, Connecticut; Providence, Rhode Island; Boston, Massachusetts; Kanawha County, West Virginia; Lee County, South Carolina; Lane County, Oregon; and 4 counties in Alabama. Major emphasis is placed on helping families raise their aspirations, restore their self-respect, and improve their level of living by learning skills in money management, housekeeping, and child care and in clothing, home, and food management. The Chicago, Illinois, and St. Louis and Kansas City, Missouri, programs have been expanded. These projects are supported by the land-grant colleges and are substantially financed by funds from county and city governments.

A "concerted services" approach to welfare needs, which brings together welfare services and education in home and money management and housekeeping skills, has also been initiated in selected low-income public-housing projects by a task force of specialists from the Department of Health, Education, and Welfare and the Home Finance Agency.

Health programs have been strengthened by the Maternal and Child Health and Mental Retardation Planning Amendments of 1963 (Public Law 88–156), which provided for expansion and strengthening of maternal and child-health and crippled-children services, including a 5-year project grant program for comprehensive maternity care to high-risk, low-income mothers and a 5-year grant program for research relating to maternal and child health.

PRIVATE EMPLOYMENT. As has been noted, at the time of the publication of the Report of the President's Commission on the Status of Women, only one state, Wisconsin, included "sex" in its fair-employment law. Since then, Hawaii has passed a fair-employment statute that makes it unlawful to discriminate against persons on the basis of sex. New York recently amended its law to recognize and declare as a civil right the opportunity to obtain employment without discrimination because of sex. Colorado amended its FEPC law in 1963 to prohibit discrimination, including such action on the grounds of sex, in apprenticeship and on-the-job training programs and in vocational schools. In the same year, the Governor of Washington, Albert D. Rossellini, issued an Executive order barring discrimination, including sex in its definition, in public employment. In 1964, the Governor's Commission on the Status of Women in the same state recommended that the word *sex* be added to age, race, creed, color, or national origin in state laws prohibiting unfair employment practices.

On a national scale, the Civil Rights Act of 1964 represents a much stronger approach and takes a firmer stand than the Commission's statement in its Report. The Act provides legal means for redress of women's grievances about discrimination in private employment. Several developments can be cited that helped change the climate of opinion and made it possible to include women in legislation concerned with discrimination. The Report of the Commission, which presented evidence of discrimination against women in employment, was widely distributed and discussed. President Johnson's speeches and his appointment of women to high executive posts in the government strongly influenced officialdom in Washington. Moreover, the strength of the civil rights movement on behalf of Negroes doubtlessly helped carry women's cause as well.

In any event, by July 1964, it was possible to obtain passage of legislation that includes "sex" along with the more usual "race, color, religion, and national origin" in its definition of grounds on which discrimination in employment is prohibited. Title VII of the Civil Rights Act deals with equal employment opportunity and sets up a 5-member Equal Employment Opportunity Commission (EEOC) to enforce it. According to the legislation, enforcement was scheduled to begin on July 2, 1965, when employers and unions with 100 or more workers must comply. Coverage was to be extended each year to employers and unions with fewer workers until 1968, when establishments with as few as 25 workers would be covered.

Under Title VII, employers, labor unions, and employment agencies are required to treat all persons without regard to their race, color, religion, sex, or national origin. Such treatment must exist in all phases of employment, including hiring, promotion, firing, apprenticeship, and other training programs and job assignments in industries affecting interstate or foreign commerce.

When a woman believes she has been discriminated against, she may bring her complaint to the EEOC or to the Attorney General. After giving priority to state fair-employment agencies where they exist, the EEOC is authorized to settle valid complaints by conciliation and persuasion. If the EEOC fails, the aggrieved individual may take his case to a federal court. The court, on finding discrimination, will order the offending employer, employment agency, or union to take corrective action, which may include hiring or reinstating employees with or without back pay.

Although employment in the federal service is not subject to the provisions of the Act, Congress expressed its desire that the principles be applied to government employment.

On June 11, 1964, the date on which the Equal Pay Act of 1963 became generally effective, an Equal Pay Conference was sponsored by the National Committee for Equal Pay and the Labor Department. During 1963, the Wage and Hour and Public Contracts Divisions of the Department of Labor held training sessions throughout the country to ensure that enforcement personnel were fully informed of the provisions of the new Act.

Selection of apprentices in federal apprenticeship and training programs must be made on the basis of qualifications alone, without regard to non-objective factors, including sex; Rules and Regulations on this subject were issued by the Secretary of Labor effective January 17, 1964.

In March 1963, the United States Employment Service of the Bureau of Employment Security, United States Department of Labor, issued a policy statement to promote equal employment opportunities for applicants of both sexes, based on their skills, abilities, and qualifications for the job.

FEDERAL EMPLOYMENT. In July 1962, while the Commission was still functioning, President Kennedy issued a directive to heads of agencies revising the right of the Civil Service Commission to allow appointing officers to specify sex in hiring, promotion, and in other personnel action.

A high-ranking official of the Civil Service Commission has been designated to discuss the President's program to fill positions without regard to sex with organizations of federal officials and community leaders in 12 large centers of federal employment outside Washington.

During the first 9 months of 1964, the executive agencies appointed 311 women and promoted 1,231 others to positions at salary levels of $10,000 and above. (These figures include some, but not all of the 68 women appointed by President Johnson.)

On January 26, 1963, standards for state merit systems concerned with grant-in-aid programs of the Departments of Health, Education, and Welfare, Labor, and Defense were revised to prohibit discrimination in such areas as hiring and promotion for reasons not concerned with merit.

The percentage of women in the entering class for Foreign Service Officers advanced from 9 to 12 per cent from 1963 to 1964.

Correction of specific injustices in the federal service has been accomplished in these instances:

- The Federal Employees Health Benefits Act was amended so that married women now pay the same premium as married men for health insurance for themselves and their families (Public Law 88–284).

- More married women employed overseas are eligible for quarters allowances and travel allowances for their husbands and dependents under revised regulations of the Departments of State and Defense.

- By administrative action, the Department of Defense is applying the minimum-wage provisions of the Fair Labor Standards Act to certain nonappropriated fund activities, such as post exchanges, commissaries, officers' clubs, and laundries where large numbers of women are employed.

- Legislation authorizing payment for representational travel of Foreign Service Wives has been enacted (Public Law 88–205).

- The Department of Defense has amended its regulations so that married women receive the same consideration for appointment overseas as married men.

CIVIL AND POLITICAL RIGHTS. In July 1963, President Kennedy sent three human rights conventions to the Senate for ratification. Two, both United Nations Conventions, are of special concern to women. One, on Political Rights of Women, provides that women shall be entitled to vote, to be eligible for election to national offices, and to hold public offices established by national laws. The other is a Supplementary Convention on the Abolition of Slavery and deals with the removal of practices akin to slavery such as debt bondage, serfdom, involuntary marriage or transfer of women for consideration in money or in kind, transfer of widows as inherited property, and the exploitation of children. The third convention sent to the Senate for ratification is the International Labor Organization Convention on the Abolition of Forced Labor. As of this writing hearings had not been held on it.

A pamphlet titled *Know Your Rights*, which the Commission had suggested was needed, is now in preparation in the Women's Bureau of the United States Department of Labor.

WOMEN IN PUBLIC OFFICE. Both women and government officials have paid heed to the Commission's recommendations in this area.

In 1964, for the first time in United States history, a woman, Senator Margaret Chase Smith (Republican), of Maine, announced her candidacy for her party's nomination for president, and campaigned actively in state primaries.

President Johnson led the nation to fuller recognition of women's ability to fill responsible positions by announcing 68 new appointments of women to important government posts between January 1 and October 2, 1964. One woman was named Assistant to the President. Two were appointed to serve abroad as Ambassadors, bringing to 8 the number of women ever to hold the rank of Ambassador or Minister. Four became Assistant or Deputy Assistant Secretaries, in the Departments of Agriculture, Defense, and State. Four were named to Federal Commissions—Atomic Energy, Civil Rights, Federal Trade, and Interstate Commerce—and one to the Board of Directors of the Export-Import Bank.

ACCOMPLISHMENTS IN INDIVIDUAL STATES

PROTECTIVE LABOR LEGISLATION. Several states took action with respect to minimum-wage and equal-pay legislation:

- Michigan enacted a minimum-wage law. The Michigan law, in effect on January 1, 1965, sets a statutory rate of $1.00 an hour applicable to men and women and provides for 2 step increases to $1.25 an hour by 1967.

- Massachusetts and South Dakota increased the statutory rate of their minimum-wage laws.

- More than 30 minimum-wage orders were revised upward in 8 jurisdictions, including 13 orders in California establishing a rate of $1.30 an hour.

CIVIL AND POLITICAL RIGHTS. In accordance with the Commission's belief that legal research and analysis are essential before firm proposals for reform

170

can be recommended on some problems, several research projects have been initiated:

- The Judicial Committee of the Massachusetts Legislature is investigating the effects of permitting husbands and wives to sue each other. The Committee has also authorized a study of certain matters relating to parents and guardians.

- The Virginia Legislature has requested the Virginia State Bar and the Virginia State Bar Association to study questions relating to the removal of minority disabilities of married minors between the ages of 18 and 21.

- The Wisconsin Legislature has created a State Family Council for Home and Family, one of whose functions is to study marriage and divorce laws, family support, and family disintegration.

GOVERNORS' COMMISSIONS. In response to the urging of many women's organizations, 36 state governors have appointed Commissions on the Status of Women. The efforts of these Commissions have brought results quickly. The governor of at least one state has established a policy of nondiscrimination in state employment at the suggestion of his Commission. A Working Code for Household Employment, developed by another Commission, is already in use. Another Commission effectively helped secure enactment of a long-sought minimum-wage bill.

Table 4 (page 172) lists existing Governors' Commissions and includes selected information about them. The suggestions of many of these Commissions will provide the country with a detailed picture of the needs and aspirations of women in relation to conditions in various areas of the country. These Commissions and the countless numbers of organizations and individuals working with them will doubtless take advantage of the more friendly climate in which women now live and bring improvement in the daily weather.

TABLE 4 · GOVERNORS' COMMISSIONS ON THE STATUS OF WOMEN,

STATE, GOVERNOR *a*, AND COMMISSION CHAIRMAN	NO. OF MEMBERS (No. of Men in Parentheses)		COMMITTEES	FILING DATE FOR REPORT
Alabama: Hon. George C. Wallace Dr. Minnie C. Miles	26	(11)	Education Home and Community Private Employment Public Employment Social and Labor Legislation Political and Legal Rights and Responsibilities	Final Report March 1965
Arkansas: Hon. Orval E. Faubus Mrs. Charlotte Gardner	22	(6)	Education New and Expanded Services Protective Labor Legislation Social Insurance and Taxes	
Colorado: Hon. John A. Love Mrs. Virginia Neal Blue	32	(2)	Women in Employment Labor Standards Women Under the Law Women as Citizens Home and Community	Final Report Due December 1965
Delaware: Hon. Elbert N. Carvel Mrs. Rosella T. Humes	21	(5)	Education Home and Community Private Employment and Labor Standards Public Employment Civil and Political Rights Tax Structure Health and Recreation	Interim Report Filed July 1964
Florida: Hon. Farris Bryant Mrs. Aleene Kidd	27		Education Women as Volunteer Workers New and Expanded Services Public and Private Employ- ment Labor Standards Civil and Political Rights Social Insurance and Taxes Legislative Program	Final Report May 1965
Georgia: Hon. Carl E. Sanders Mrs. Mamie K. Taylor	116		Education and Counseling Home and Community Women in Employment Women Under the Law	Final Report Filed October 1964
Hawaii: Hon. John A. Burns Mrs. Mary Ellen Swanton	30	(5)	Education and Counseling Home and Community (*continued on next page*)	Final Report February 1966

a Governor in office at the time Commission was established.

STATE, GOVERNOR, AND COMMISSION CHAIRMAN	NO. OF MEMBERS (No. of Men in Parentheses)		COMMITTEES	FILING DATE FOR REPORT
Hawaii, continued:			Employment Policies and Practices under State Contracts Labor Standards Legal Rights Insurance and Tax Laws	
Illinois: Hon. Otto Kerner Rep. Esther S. Saperstein	18	(6)	Education Home and Community Public and Private Employment Protective Legislation Legal Rights	
Indiana: Hon. Matthew E. Welsh Dr. Eunice C. Roberts	33	(4)	Education Home and Community Labor Legislation Civil and Political Rights	
Iowa: Hon. Harold E. Hughes Dr. Marguerite Scruggs	25	(3)	Educational Needs of Women New and Expanded Services Employment Practices State Labor Laws Legal Treatment	Interim Report Filed November 1964
Kansas: Hon. John Anderson, Jr. Mrs. Mary Barnett	19		Education Home and Community Private and State Employment Political Rights	
Kentucky: Hon. Edward T. Breathitt, Jr. Miss Chloe Gifford	26		Education Employment Culture Citizenship Legal Status Volunteer Services Home and Community	
Maine: Hon. John H. Reed Dr. Madelyn Dyer	25		Education Home and Community Public Employment Private Employment Labor and Social Legislation Political and Legal Rights	
Massachusetts: Hon. Endicott Peabody To be announced	25	(4)	Not established yet	

TABLE 4 · GOVERNORS' COMMISSIONS ON THE STATUS OF WOMEN,

STATE, GOVERNOR, AND COMMISSION CHAIRMAN	NO. OF MEMBERS (No. of Men in Parentheses)		COMMITTEES	FILING DATE FOR REPORT
Michigan: Hon. George W. Romney Mrs. Paul G. Goebel	25		Education Home and Community Public Employment Private Employment Social and Labor Legislation Civil and Political Rights	
Minnesota: Hon. Karl F. Rolvaag Mrs. Charles Hymes	46	(9)	Education Home and Community Employment Opportunities Civil and Political Rights	Interim Report Filed November 1964. Final Report July 1965
Mississippi: Hon. Paul B. Johnson Judge Mildred W. Norris	16	(4)	Not determined	
Missouri: Hon. John M. Dalton Dr. Blanche Dow	27		Women and Education Women in the Home and Community Women at Work Women as Citizens	Interim Report Filed January 1965
Nebraska: Hon. Frank B. Morrison Miss Sarah J. Cunningham	36	(5)	Education and Counseling Home and Community Women in Employment Labor Standards Women Under the Law Security of Basic Income Women as Citizens	
Nevada: Hon. Grant Sawyer Mrs. Hope Roberts	8	(4)	Education Expanded Services Employment Policies and Practices Protective Legislation Civil and Political Rights Social Insurance and Taxes Public Information	Preliminary Report Filed December 1964
New Hampshire: Hon. John W. King Miss Margaret E. Normandin	18		Education Employment Practices Social and Political Rights	

AS OF JANUARY 1965, SELECTED INFORMATION

STATE, GOVERNOR, AND COMMISSION CHAIRMAN	NO. OF MEMBERS (No. of Men in Parentheses)	COMMITTEES	FILING DATE FOR REPORT
New Jersey: Hon. Richard J. Hughes Miss Doris Hubatka	19 (4)	Education and Counseling Home and Community Women in Employment	
New York: (Committee on Education & Employ- ment of Women) Hon. Nelson A. Rockefeller Mrs. Oswald B. Lord	14 (5)	Education Employment Policies Register of Women Law on Civil Service	Final Report Filed December 1964
North Carolina: Hon. Terry Sanford Dr. Ann Scott	17 (5)	Education and Training Volunteer Organizations and Expanded Services Family and Welfare Services Employment Policies Protective Labor Legislation Civil and Political Rights Citizen Participation Social Insurance and Taxes	Final Report Filed November 1964
North Dakota: Hon. William L. Guy Miss Dagny Olsa (Act.)	13 (4)	Education Home and Community Federal and State Employ- ment Private Employment Civil and Political Rights Protective Labor Legislation Social Insurance and Taxes	Interim Report Filed December 1964
Oklahoma: Hon. Henry Bellmon Mrs. Ettamae Reed	25	Education Home and Community Rights Private Employment Protective Labor Legislation Civil and Political Rights Social Insurance and Taxes	
Oregon: Hon. Mark O. Hatfield Mrs. Gertrude Hauk Farris (Act.)	19 (4)	Education Home and Community Employment Protective Labor Legislation Civil and Political Rights Social Insurance and Taxes	

TABLE 4 · GOVERNORS' COMMISSIONS ON THE STATUS OF WOMEN,

STATE GOVERNOR AND COMMISSION CHAIRMAN	NO. OF MEMBERS (No. of Men in Parentheses)		COMMITTEES	FILING DATE FOR REPORT
Pennsylvania: Hon. William W. Scranton Mrs. Betsy P. Meyers	20	(7)	Education Employment Legal and Political Status	Final Report July 1965
Rhode Island: Hon. John H. Chafee Mrs. Dorothy Burkholder	11	(4)	Employment Policies and Practices State Labor Laws Legal Rights of Women in Rhode Island Education	Final Report Due November 1965
South Dakota: Hon. Archie Gubbrud Mrs. Winifred Echelberger	13		Education New and Expanded Services Employment Policies and Practices (State, County, and Private) Political and Civil Rights	Interim Report Filed December 1964
Tennessee: Hon. Frank G. Clement Miss Flora Rawls	15		Education Employment Practices under Government Contracts and State Labor Laws Legal Treatment State Social Insurance and Tax Laws	Final Report Filed November 1964.
Utah: (Committee on the Status of Women) Hon. George D. Clyde Mrs. Edith S. Shaw	25	(1)	Employment Community Services Family Services Political and Civil Respon- sibilities Legal and Tax Status	Progress Report Filed December 1964
Vermont: Hon. Philip H. Hoff Mrs. Raymond Stark	Not appointed		Not determined	

176

STATE, GOVERNOR, AND COMMISSION CHAIRMAN	NO. OF MEMBERS (No. of Men in Parentheses)		COMMITTEES	FILING DATE FOR REPORT
Washington: (Continuing Commission for followthrough) Hon. Albert D. Rosellini Mrs. Mildred Dunn	41	(8)	Education Legal Rights Employment Policies and Practices Community Volunteer Citizens Employed Woman and Her Family Women in Government Legislative Action Public Relations Research Coordinating	
Washington: (Original study Commission) Hon. Albert D. Rosellini Mrs. Mildred Dunn	29	(8)	Education Legal Rights Employment Policies Family and Employed Women Expanded Services Women as Citizens—Volunteers	Final Report Filed December 1963
West Virginia Hon. William W. Barron Mrs. John Scott	27	(7)	Education Women as Volunteers Expanded Programs to Help Women as Wives, Mothers, and Workers Family and Employed Women Employment Policies and Practices Labor Laws Legal Rights	
Wisconsin: Hon. John W. Reynolds Mrs. Kathryn F. Clarenbach	34	(8)	Education and Counseling Family and Community Life Employment: Public and Private Legal Rights and Protection Citizen Participation	Progress Report Filed October 1964. Final Report March 1965

EPILOGUE

Epilogue

by MARGARET MEAD

The work of the President's Commission on the Status of Women can be used as a guide to the future of American women, and so to the prospect for all Americans. Like a solid, protective wall, the Commission's Report divides the past, with its limitations and difficulties, from a future in which it may be expected that these hindrances will be overcome. Nothing in this report is farfetched, unworkable, or utopian. It contains no recommendation that has not been tested somewhere, in one or another state or in another modern country.

PROGRESS TOWARD EQUALITY

The Report is, first of all, a review of the progress that has been made in giving American women practical equality with men educationally, economically, and politically. Social and religious issues are not discussed. The basic standards by which the status of women is assessed are those used in the modern world to judge the progress of disadvantaged groups in general—those who are disadvantaged because of sex, race, color, class, education, minority group membership, previous complexity of culture, or level of regional or national economy.

From a contemporary point of view, conditions of inequality should be examined so that they may be abolished, and where disadvantage is extreme, special measures should be taken to overcome the handicap. At the international level, there is a widespread and increasingly compelling demand to eliminate, or at least compensate for, the differences between the

181

peoples of the world who are relatively well off and those who, for whatever reason, are disadvantaged.

In all cases, the standards are fundamentally the same. Against the opportunities of the disadvantaged group are weighed those that men of the most privileged race, with the best available education, living under the most favorable economic circumstances *have now*. This is so whether the subject of discussion is the level of opportunity of the people of Algeria, Ghana, or Thailand, or whether, in the United States, it is the disabilities that arise from darker skin, lack of literacy, or membership in the female sex. Carried a little further, these standards also apply to the physically and the mentally handicapped, all of whom should be educated at whatever necessary extra expense and effort so that their level of functioning will be as close as possible to that of the well-equipped and the well-endowed.

Stated very simply, it is at present assumed that any barrier whatsoever to full participation on the level of the privileged white, adult, American male—wherever it exists in the world and whoever is affected by it—should be treated as a handicap so that it can be overcome. All should have an equal chance to win the prizes offered in life's race. Inequalities must be compensated for in the same spirit of fair play in which, historically, the idea of handicap developed, as a device for equalizing the chances of all competitors. In its broadest sense, the desire to compensate and atone for injury, or loss, or lack is an idea that has its origins in the very best tenets of Judaic justice, Christian compassion, and the English sense of fair play.

Within the context of the assumption that everyone should participate in all the rights and opportunities and hopes of privileged males in American society, the Commission and the Committees worked with responsibility and clarity. If some treatment of women that differentiated them from men was considered necessary, compensation for this was very carefully suggested. For example, the Committee on Education pointed out that if the demands of early marriage mean an earlier removal of women from school, this must be compensated for by better educational opportunities for them at a later age. If women with young children can only work part time, then industry and government should provide for more part-time jobs. If women are withdrawn from the labor market while their children are young, then full retraining opportunities should be available when they are ready to return as full-time workers. And it was pointed out that homemaker services, nursery schools, and day-care centers are needed to provide protective care for children so that homemaking duties will not interfere with a woman's work outside the home, whether the job is undertaken from choice or out of necessity.

In such a framework, women's capacities as childbearers and as mothers are to be treated as handicaps to be overcome. This is precisely like considering blindness and deafness as handicaps that should not, in a fair and equitable society, interfere with the opportunity to hold well-paid jobs with equal pay for equal work. So defined, everything connected with a woman's childbearing and child-rearing functions is open to sharp scrutiny. Aspects of these functions that interfere with the rest of a woman's life should be removed or, if they are not removable, compensated for.

BASIC ASSUMPTIONS UNDERLYING RECOMMENDATIONS

The first assumption underlying—though not explicit in—the Commission's recommendations is that in the modern world anything peculiarly feminine is a handicap.

The second assumption is that both males and females attain full biological humanity only through marriage and the presence of children in the home, whether these are born to a couple or are adopted by them. More and more women are marrying earlier and oftener and, if the trend continues, most women and men will marry. The unmarried in the population will then consist of the very young, the divorced, widowers, and, especially, widows. The present longer life span of women means that many outlive their husbands and so are robbed of being married all their adult lives.

The Commission did not concern itself with matters of sexual behavior as such. In our religiously diversified society, such an inquiry would raise questions that could not have been dealt with felicitously in the Report, for its responsibility was to work toward establishing a commonality of law, practice, and usage. But back of the trend toward growing numbers of marriages lies the American idea that a life that includes a legal and continuous sex relationship is the only good life.

The Report overwhelmingly deals with the typical woman, who will marry early, have several children, and live many years after her children are grown. Here it makes the following assumptions: all women want to marry; marriage involves having (or at least rearing) children; children are born (or adopted) early in a marriage; the home consists of the nuclear family only; and special attention must be given to women not in the state assumed to be normal—the single, the divorced, and the widowed.

Historically, it was regarded as a victory when women obtained freedom and some form of public equality with men. Today, on the contrary, the emphasis is on the individual right of women, no less than men, to marriage and parenthood (that is, to the attainment of biological maturity). But the enjoyment of this right should not interfere with women's right to a working life on the same terms as men.

This second set of assumptions has had profound repercussions in American life. It has particularly affected attitudes toward marriage in adolescence, on the one hand, and toward careers for women that require complete dedication on the other.

The third assumption underlying the Commission's Report is that the right to work at a paid job is an intrinsic condition of human dignity. Yet, just as any obstacle to a woman's right to work outside the home should be done away with, so her right to full economic opportunity should not adversely affect her life at home. A report to the Committee on Social Insurance and Taxes makes the complementary suggestion (not recommended by the Committee) that homemaking can be dignified by making it equivalent to a paid job. The housewife, taking care of her home, would build up an equity in social-security benefits. Yet girls as well as boys should be educated to want and to hold paid jobs. Discriminatory practice or law should not interefere with this right. Protective labor legislation often prevents women from doing night work. Yet night work may be more convenient for a working mother, because her husband (who has worked all day) can take over the task of caring for the children while she (who has spent the day tending these small children) works for money at night.

In summary, these are three of the basic assumptions underlying the Commission's Report: (1) all roles and statuses should be equalized toward those of the American, white, Protestant, well-educated, adult male; (2) sex, marriage, and parenthood are fundamental human rights and no sacrifice should be made of them, nor should sacrifice be made to them; and (3) a sense of full humanity involves working for money or at least having a monetary value placed on the work one does.

TWO FURTHER ASSUMPTIONS

It is easy to see how these three assumptions are interwoven with the ethos and ethics of the post–World War II world. Contemporary thinking about these matters has been affected by the dicta of the Commission on Human Rights of the United Nations, the world-wide efforts to give technical assistance and bring about technological change, the active concern within the United States over economic and social deprivation because of race or color and poor education, and the cult of sexuality and a child-centered life that has developed in the United States during the last 50 years.

The Commission, which represented the spectrum of responsible American thinking, also had to take into account certain other conflicting values. For example, the emphasis placed on choice and on individual human dignity can be measured in other ways than by the monetary value placed on one's work by an employer in private business, by a public agency, by the Social Security Board, by a trade union seniority committee, or by others. Thus, two further assumptions were expressed in the Report.

First, the individual should be able to make choices. A woman with young children should not be forced to work, nor, on the contrary, should she have to stay home. A highly educated woman should not be forced to market her trained abilities; alternatively, she should be able to undertake responsible volunteer work as a way of expressing her sense of being a full, responsible, and participating member of the larger society. In the work of the Committees a great deal of attention was given to working conditions and to the educational and community conditions necessary for fitting together a job and homemaking responsibilities. However, very little consideration, by comparison, was given to those conditions in our society that force poorly educated women with young children to seek employment and, simultaneously, prevent women with gifts and education from working.

Implicit in this discussion is the second additional assumption, one that is made explicit in certain other current discussions of the status of women. It is the equation of the *job* (something one does for sufficient pay to meet one's obligations as a person enjoying the benefits of our modern civilization) and the *career*. (Yet, by another definition, a career is pursued with commitment, for its own sake; for the privilege of following it, one would be willing to pay rather than be paid. It is something for which one is willing to put in years of education and hard work and to forego the pleasures that others enjoy.) The failure to distinguish between job and career in the case of women is merely a special case of the more general failure to do so in our entire society. Men increasingly are evaluating their work as it relates to their private lives, and both men and women are re-evaluating occupations that once demanded dedication and commitment—teaching, medicine, law, nursing, social work, and high-level achievement as a scientist, an engineer, a career government employee, or a businessman—in terms of money and the demanding hours spent at work as compared with those given to leisure.

185

Related to this assumption is the question of whether college education should be paid employment. It arises in part because of the disappearance of jobs for adolescents and the difficulty of finding paid summer work for high school and college students. Moreover, complications arise from the current willingness to let college students assume the burdens of marriage and children. They must then work for money in addition to pursuing their studies. A more reasonable course would be to provide college students with a salary on the grounds that they are learning to be the kind of persons needed by their society. Instead, we insist that wherever possible someone—their parents, their wives, or they themselves—should work for wages to support them while they go to college.

The very serious problems arising from retirement may be considered in the same context. This is especially so of the forced early retirement accompanying the obsolescence of certain occupations, such as mining, and the displacement of clerical workers and middle management as a result of automation. In all cases, a very heavy emphasis is placed on finding other kinds of *paid* employment as a way of helping retired persons to uphold their dignity and feel needed and wanted.

HOMEMAKING AND VOLUNTEER SERVICE AS PAID WORK

Increasingly, our society is losing the ability to make people feel needed and wanted in ways other than by paying them money for their services. This American insistence that one's value as a person can be measured by money (or some measurable equivalent of money, such as grades in school, number of persons supervised on a job, articles published annually, awards won, or the size of one's name in neon lights) is rapidly changing attitudes toward volunteer work and the volunteer worker. Area after area in which women and older men have worked tirelessly as volunteers is becoming fully professionalized. The volunteer is being demoted to the performance of tasks for which no one will pay: driving children to the dentist, addressing envelopes until money is raised to buy an addressograph, or painting furniture that is past repair.

The Report recognizes that women should be free to choose how they will use their talents and energy. However, given the belief that the value of an activity must be expressible in quantifiable terms, what women will choose to do will be valued only to the extent that they engage in activities that can be so measured. On this basis, homemaking and volunteer work as we now conceive of them are not highly valued activities, and they can

186

do little to give women a sense of dignity and choice. Only paid jobs can do this.

The idea of treating homemaking as having a real monetary value, and so a kind of dignity, has important repercussions for women's choice of where and how they will work, for it could do much to change the present status of the woman domestic worker. Neither the Committees nor the Commission recommended very great changes in present homemaking patterns. Such alterations would be involved, for example, in more communal types of living, with homes closer to places of work, creches for babies, family restaurant eating, and full summer care for all school-age children. Yet it is expensive and time consuming to maintain our present style of small-unit family living. In fact, a woman (or a man) must always be free to remain in the home all the time. Placed against our actual style of living, the notion that the mother of school-age children is free during school hours is an illusory one. The present homemaking style can be attained and maintained only when another woman, or a man, replaces the homemaker who leaves her home to work. Wherever this is impossible, everyone suffers: the husband's job capacity is threatened; the children's health and psychological needs are less well met; and the woman working away from home is under the pressure of continual worry about what may be happening in the home she left that morning.

Sufficient day, night, and weekend nurseries, nursery schools, after-school groups, summer camps, and so on, could mean that healthy children would be cared for by trained, well-paid, proud personnel, who were committed to the task of watching over other people's children. Even this would not be enough to solve the conflicts between the requirements of a job or a career and the task of the homemaker, in the home. There she must deal with a burst pipe, a defective refrigerator, the telephone call about a dying relative. Someone must prepare meals, accept the delivery of food, or fuel, or a registered letter. And there are unexpected contingencies, such as the emergency care of a sick child, taking the place of the sitter who does not show up, or the long-term care of a convalescent or an aged adult. As the Committee on Home and Community recommended, it is only by redignifying domestic service of all kinds that a real working life for homemaking women who choose to work away from home can be made possible.

Essentially, then, the means must be found to reverse the downward trend in the number of women in domestic service, and this must be done in ways that are consonant with the present standards of dignity. Possibly it will be necessary to set a positive monetary value (instead of merely

187

allowing a tax deduction for a wife) on the job of homemaker. This might dignify domestic work sufficiently so that far more women would do it for money. Furthermore, because she has fixed hours and an impersonal employer, the woman who clerks in a five-and-ten-cent store or who sews on buttons in a shirt factory somehow feels like more of a person than the woman who does housework. It may be necessary to set up new styles of domestic work complete with impersonal employment, special uniforms, and workers' responsibility to the service instead of to the housewife for whom cleaning, cooking, or child care is done by the hour or by the week.

However, inevitably, as the areas in which money is received impersonally for services rendered impersonally are enlarged, another, and conflicting American value is encroached upon—the importance of volunteer activity. On this has been built the American community, the church separated from the state, the school that is the center of the town's life, the community plan that grows out of and is realized through the shared interests of a special group. Underlying the concept that voluntary work is somehow good is the assumption that work done for love, whether it is love of an individual human being, community, country, or God, is of a different quality from work that is done primarily for pay.

This is tied in with the traditional idea that money itself is somehow "filthy" and that those who handle it are themselves somehow demeaned. It was once expressed in taboos against discussing money, in the social distinction made between wholesale and retail trade, and in the idea that the superiority of the professions lies in the fact that, in a profession, love of work and professional ideals can supersede pecuniary considerations. Today, many of these traditional attitudes are becoming obsolete.

Now that the taboos against handling and discussing money have been eliminated, a high premium is set on all paid work. But the question must be raised: Have we not lost something? If it is recognized that the essential conflict is still unresolved, especially for women, other questions cannot be avoided: Would a woman rather care for her own children in her own home for love, or for other people's children, homes, clothes, and meals for money? Is the dignity accorded the working woman when she is paid for her work so rewarding that she will choose to work outside her own home in the absence of some other compulsion (the need for enough money to live on, the need to escape from uncongenial home conditions to more congenial working conditions, or the need to exercise her trained and special skills in a real career)? Would it make a difference

188

if a married woman were entitled legally to some share of her husband's wages?

As men's choices have become more restricted and the opportunity to start one's own business has decreased, American women have become the heritors of the American dream of "being one's own boss," once the prized possession of men. Within a well-equipped, independent house, in the management of which only her husband and children can help, advise, or interfere, the married homemaker is indeed her own boss. She determines the time and the order in which she will do her work and how well she will do it. The work itself has the diversity and the interest that are associated with running one's own business. Her husband may come home at the end of a day's work frustrated by red tape, capricious supervision, and inefficiencies that he is powerless to alter, and feel himself to be a mere cog in a machine. Meanwhile, she has been hardworking but free ranging, and she can offer him, evenings and weekends, participation in the family's freedom to go where its members choose, sleep where and when they like, eat when and what they like, and choose what television show or movie they will watch. The home, as it is constituted for the millions of women who can afford to stay in it while their children are young, has areas of freedom that are almost wholly lacking in much American employment. Yet the Commission, valuing choice, concentrated on the extent to which modern conveniences make it possible for women to escape from the home into well-paid work.

THE GROWING IMPORTANCE OF PAID WORK

If work done at home, for love, is devalued, all volunteer work is devalued also, whether it is connected with politics or is done for the church or for some other community organization. Subtly, the theme, "everything that is worth-while should be worth money," pervades both losses of value. When a community can choose between two talks given by the same lecturer—one of which is free and one for which admission is charged—the auditorium for the paid talk will be filled to overflowing, but not the other. Apparently, it is assumed that a lecturer will give more to a paying audience. Turning every kind of work into paid work could well mean the end of aspects of society that in the past depended very heavily on the millions of hours of volunteer time given by women during the day and by men in the evenings and during weekends.

The underwriting of paid work as valuable for everyone is the key to the solutions reached on questions of structural unemployment and the increasing rate of productivity per man hour in agriculture, government, and private industry. According to one school of thought, the resulting problems will be solved by the creation of new jobs to meet the new needs of an affluent society and to gratify the society's expanding leisure-time demands. It is argued that as the need for workers in industry and agriculture shrinks, the service and the governmental occupations will absorb those who are freed. Thus there will be full employment potential for youths, married women, and the elderly who do not wish to retire. To ensure this, the number of jobs should be consciously increased. Far from disapproving of moonlighting for men and "sunlighting" for women, we should welcome a consumption system and a kind of individual demand that create the shortages to which these men and women respond. For adherents of this theory, the only trouble with our economy at present is maldistribution of worker capacity. The pattern of education should be changed so that the lack of need for unskilled labor and the high demand for dignity for every worker are recognized. This will result in a functioning economic system in which things are just as they are now, or more so. The job, the life lived for pay, will be basic to every adult—male and female, young and old—and leisure, which will be basic to so many jobs, will still be hard won and yet less valued than work.

According to a different school of thought, American workers will be increasingly divided into two groups. First, there will be those who are working very hard at what they want to do, with the assistance of poor help in the home, in the office, and in the laboratory. On the other hand, there will be those who are working as little and as badly as possible at jobs they have not chosen, feeding back into the economy their increasingly high wages and the demands for more jobs arising from their increased leisure time. As a distinction is made between those who are putting everything they have into careers they want and those who are putting as little as possible into jobs they are forced to do, the view of the homemaker's role changes with extraordinary rapidity.

In the 1930's and early 1940's, the fulltime homemaker was inclined to apologize and to describe her busy and exacting life as "doing nothing." In the next decade, with the glamorizing of "togetherness," early marriage, and the large family in the suburban home, the homemaker contended that hers was a wholly fulfilling life; in fact, she claimed to belong in the high-prestige category because she was doing what she chose and loved to do. Only a few years ago, a leading women's magazine published a symposium on women and marriage in which happy, frenetic young mothers reported on the crowding of their days with household tasks and told how they loved every overoccupied minute. But in 1964, when a compensating shift in the other direction was under way, the same magazine published a special issue reporting on women's enjoyment of their freedom to get away from home into paid jobs and their willingness to pay for their gain by doing household chores far into the night.

In 1964, women were promised the same rewards for working that previously had been offered them for staying home. They would be more attractive to men, more vital and interesting to their husbands, better mothers to their children, and they would stay young longer. More dreary and less filled with happy promises are the articles in the Spring 1964 special issue on women published by *Daedalus* (the journal of the American Academy of Arts and Sciences). They indicate that women are settling down, adjusting themselves to compromise jobs and compromise home lives, without the dash and daring of an earlier age. No one today, one article suggests, speaks for the American woman of this generation as Jane Addams did for an earlier one.

Both the popular and the scholarly approaches emphasize the value of employment, with the implication that achievement through education and work is the only way anyone over 14 and under 90 can feel valued, needed, and fulfilled. It might be argued that the Commission's focus on work is a natural consequence of the fact that the Women's Bureau—under which the Commission functioned, the only agency of the federal government with a specific responsibility for women—is in the Department of Labor. However, even a cursory examination of other publications and discussions indicates the prevalence of the idea. Furthermore, current studies of the status of women resonate to the sound of other battles—against race discrimination, unemployed youth, premature retirement, and the growing number of unemployables in our rapidly changing society.

THE POSSIBILITY OF GUARANTEED INCOME

A third view of our changing economy suggests that the decrease in paid jobs and the increase in choice of work should be welcomed. Paid work should not be equated with contribution to society. According to this view, every adult should be guaranteed a modest, but adequate basic income. This money, spent for the satisfaction of basic needs (food, clothing, shelter, recreation, and so on), would keep the economy rolling. Beyond this, the management of complex and special aspects of society, such as computers, hospitals, schools and universities, laboratories, mass-communication industries, and space research would be maintained by an elite group who wanted more than a basic income and who chose to do a particular kind of work. Every individual—whether he or she was a poet, painter, fisherman, fashion designer, teacher, or someone without employable skills because of illiteracy or some physical handicap, such as deafness—would have the choice of living on the guaranteed basic income or doing what was necessary to obtain and hold a job.

The inclusion of all adult women as well as all adult men in this plan would remove marriage and homemaking from the category of unpaid work. But the question would still arise as to whether homemaking should be one of the paid occupations that would qualify a woman for membership in the elite group.

The provision of a subsistence income would guarantee security to those individuals on whose occupations a low monetary value is set although they are honored (the poet, musician, priest, and minister, for example). In these circumstances, it is possible—but very unlikely—that voluntary homemaking might be included as one of the chosen occupations that was honored but not specially paid. That we do recognize the importance of an individual's contribution to society is reflected in the obituary pages of a newspaper like *The New York Times*. There, those who have served their community well and those who have made great contributions in the arts and sciences are honored above those who have merely earned high salaries or made great fortunes. Nevertheless, if monetary rewards were to go to an elite group that chose to work hard, it would be desirable to set a high monetary value on such occupations as homemaking, the ministry, and creative work in general. For in circumstances where the elite of the world were highly paid and given other emoluments and privileges, it seems most unlikely that any labor of love, conducted on a subsistence income, would be specially valued by anyone.

Yet the most cursory examination of our economic prospects should make it clear that in the near future not larger, but smaller numbers of workers will be needed. Most necessary for our general well-being will be more income spent on consumption of goods, more people in school for longer periods of time, and far more people engaged in activities that require either outstanding talent, skill, and training or else dedicated enthusiasm for the task of caring for people or other living things, or for the production of ideas or of objects. It would not make sense to construct a society in which all married women were more highly rewarded for leaving their homes than for staying in them. The desirability of a social system in which those women can work who need or want to, is obvious. But the deliberate construction of a social system that compels or even encourages all women to work outside the home no longer makes sense in the United States (as it still does in Soviet Russia and mainland China). That this is the case becomes apparent even if all consideration of the kind of personal life for children and adults that is most in accord with our other values is laid aside and the problem is considered only in terms of a viable economy.

WHO SHOULD WORK OUTSIDE THE HOME?

The next step is to differentiate among women—women with a grade school education, high school graduates, college graduates, those with specialized professional skills, women who are unambitious and those who have high ambitions, the shy and the outgoing, the poorly endowed and the richly gifted. It is clear that economic necessity, opportunity, and the way women live their lives mesh together very differently indeed. The poorly educated girl who lacks experience and background and has children to care for is a less useful employee than her equally poorly educated husband who is struggling with the responsibility of supporting his wife and children in a shrinking labor market. Again, for the poorly educated widow or divorcee with small children, an adequate social security allowance may be a better economic arrangement than one that forces her into the labor market while someone even less skilled and ambitious cares for her home and children. In contrast, the well-trained teacher, nurse, chemist, or computer programmer, the first-class secretary, administrative assistant, librarian, or laboratory technician may be so desperately needed that it would pay the community in which she lives to set up the services making it possible for her to work away from home. In these circumstances, it would also pay the nation to make suitable income-tax provisions. A married couple with children should be permitted to subtract from their income the actual cost of replacing an educated wife and mother in the home with help that would allow her to concentrate on work just as her husband does. The present system of income-tax allowances takes into account only the very low-income family where the services of the wife are partly replaced by still lower income domestic help. Society can reap the full benefit of work done by a really competent married woman only by taking cognizance of the need for trained housekeeper-nurses as knowledgable and trustworthy, if not as devastatingly efficient, as the better-educated professional women they would replace. And those who replace working women in their homes must be assured a reasonable income.

193

A wide area of choice for individual women and for married couples and, where it is appropriate, the option to engage in paid work—these are possibilities that can be realized only if the opportunity to work is open to *all* women. This the Commission rightly insists on. But once the right of all women, including those who are married, to work for equal pay and with equal protection has been given full legal and economic support, it is still necessary to consider the intangible climate of opinion within which choices are made.

After World War II, no one forced American women back into their homes. It is true that many mature women lost the jobs they had obtained by default during the war, in the years when men in civilian life were scarce and prejudices against women were temporarily in abeyance. But in the postwar years, young girls just finishing high school or in the first years of college chose marriage and, in great numbers, a suburban life. Yet the professions and industry were formally open to them, and they were offered more interesting work at better pay than ever before. Despite this, young women chose against real careers and well-paying jobs. Instead, they accepted temporary employment, often far below the level of their capabilities and education, shied away from the exercise of their talents, and dropped out of school or college in favor of marriage or to support their young husbands' years in college or graduate school.

These young homemakers went gladly, in droves, into the kitchens where, in other countries, only political dictatorship or the pressure of old tradition could still force young women to remain. They accepted with enthusiasm a life of rapid childbearing from which other generations of women had cried for deliverance. In the small American household, the wife-mother has to take full responsibility. She is her own cook, nurse-maid, laundress, cleaning woman, and chauffeur. Too often, she is also, with the possible cooperation of her husband, her own painter, upholsterer, electrician, and gardener.

Within the last five years there has been some rebellion, chiefly engi-neered by women who are no longer fully engrossed with the care of young children. But that this tremendous swing back into the home is still in force cannot be ignored. In the case of the well-educated woman, it took place in the very face of freedom, in a period in which—because of the war—women had been doing many new kinds of things. This sug-gests that other very important factors affect the position of women and the choices they make, factors that will not be altered by the removal of legal, educational, and economic handicaps alone.

Nowhere is this more clearly illustrated than in the poor showing made by American women in political life. It cannot be claimed that the reason women do not play an important role in American politics is related to inequality of pay or legal disability. Yet in comparison with women in many other countries, American women make little use of their potential political strength and freedom to participate. And if the talent search that followed on President Johnson's expression of interest in the appointment of women to high-level executive positions had laid a greater emphasis on younger candidates, it would have been even more difficult to find women of stature to fill such positions.

At the bottom of the economic ladder, married women work because they must or because their home conditions are unbearable. The victims of poor pay and poor working conditions, they are exploited in the same fashion as any other helpless minority group. In fact, women in the United States are not a minority, and it is doubtfully of use to assimilate their status to that of a minority group that must be freed and given the opportunities open to the majority. Further, the interpretation of wifehood and motherhood as defects and handicaps to be compensated for by a fair and gallant society does not answer the question of why American women, who are permitted to work at high-level careers, have on the whole chosen not to do so.

WOMEN AND THE HUMANE VALUES

Here it is necessary to return to the assumption that there are values besides those defined essentially by money payment and to clarify the conflict between this assumption and the others on which the Commission's Report is based. Perhaps it is inaccurate to call these the "gentler" values, for the gentleness of the embattled mother has been grossly exaggerated. It is, however, accurate to call them the humane values, for they affect what happens to the individual self and to others. These are the values that inform a mother's preference to care for her own child. They draw the teacher into teaching in spite of the low salary. Men and women having these standards feel a call to the unpaid service of God or of mankind or feel it right and important to compose music or write poetry for which there is no immediate market; they seek out, instead of fleeing from, time to read and ponder, feel and think. They are values women have cultivated in the home while men have worked hard and for long hours on the farms, in the factories, and in the business world.

For a long period in American history there was a tendency to make a division between the kinds of values appropriate to men and those appropriate to women. It was considered appropriate for women to be concerned with the community, with schools and libraries and playgrounds, with the "finer" things in life, churchgoing, the care of those in trouble, and upholding the moral taboos against drinking, gambling, and fighting. This division weakened our culture. It made caring for many important things seem effeminate, unworthy of the attention of real men. Counterpointed to the values upheld mainly by women, those of the masculine worlds of business and politics appeared to be lower, more ruthless, and (in the case of politics) "dirty."

Given this frame of reference, there is always the danger that the incipient male poet or painter may throttle his talent and that the choice of becoming an intellectual may be based on protest against a "masculine" world. Or men who abhor business and public life as they exist may use whatever power they gain to build a world on the campus or in the laboratory that is more ruthless or "dirty" than the world they believe they have rejected.

None of these confusions should obscure the fact that Americans have made it the province of women to think about and conserve individual human beings, while men have taken over the world of things and the organization of people in groups. The distinction is sometimes blurred by men's tendency to enter and eventually monopolize any occupation that becomes financially rewarding. This has been the case, for example, in the medical field of pediatrics, which would have been an appropriate specialty for women. Similarly, in teaching, men have until recently all but monopolized the areas with better pay and more prestige, to the disadvantage of well-trained, promising women. Again, certain special roles in the care of individuals have been traditionally assigned to men, for example, the priest-confessor and the physician.

In her role as caretaker of the individual, woman's tending of young children historically has been the prototype of cherishing, listening, and care. As long as infants were breast fed, mothers had to stay close to home or carry their infants with them, and the woman at home became the anchor of family life. (It is not yet known whether there is also some other deeply biological basis for woman's homemaking role.) In any culture it has been enough for women whose lives have been centered on a few persons to rear little girls to follow in their own footsteps to establish, generation after generation, woman's role as intensively related to a few individuals, whose physical and emotional well-being are her chief concern. To the hearth the hunter brought his game for food, the wounded warrior returned to recuperate, and the bruised child came for help and comfort.

THE PRESENT ROLE OF HOMEMAKING

Today the same kind of home is not necessary. Meat comes from the supermarket and the deep freeze; the fresh berries have been gathered far away. The infant can be bottle fed as well by the father as by the mother, and so even the most necessitous tie is broken. The mother can take the children with her in the car, miles and miles from home. There are hospitals now for childbirth and for treating illness, mental institutions for the mentally ill, nursery schools and kindergartens for small children, old-age homes for the senile, and funeral parlors for laying out the dead. Even the tasks of housework have been eased or eliminated; there are laundries to wash clothes, disposable table linen and dishes, bread that comes fully baked or partially prepared and ready for the oven, stoves for which no one need gather fuel, and restaurants, hotels, country clubs, and professional caterers who can supply meals.

It is very easy to make a case for the idea that a changing world has changed the home. But the alterations that have taken place are no more radical than those that occurred when agriculture and pastoral activities replaced hunting and people assumed a sedentary life, or when, in some island society, all the men took to the sea. The stress on the new technology of the home obscures other functions that the home performs, now as in the past.

Children still are cared for in the home. Here married couples have privacy for their love, and children sleep safely in the knowledge that the others are nearby. Here boys dream of their future, and men bring their disappointments and their triumphs. Here prized possessions are safe however far and long a journey away from home may be. The bride still goes forth from the home.

In the home each individual can be a whole human being with the full right to be a person without bargaining or reservation. Essentially, nothing has changed for children in their closest relationships. As far as material things go, the modern world has made it easier for adults to live a single life comfortably, but the family home is the one place where companionship comes without planning and where affection and care are given and accepted as a matter of course.

In the family, children learn to be people. The boy learns from his

197

father how to be a man and from his mother how to care for women. The girl learns from her mother how to be a woman and a mother and from her father what men are like. No known society has found a permanent substitute for the family as a way of shaping whole human beings. Many societies have tried other systems of child care. In our time, the Soviet Union and Israel are notable examples. In both of these countries, however, a slow drift is taking place toward closer relationships between parents and children, more time together, and more individualization and intimacy.

A narrow emphasis on the idea that women, like men, should be free to work outside the home and on the extent to which modern conveniences and new institutions have freed women to do other work, in effect ignores very important aspects of home life. For the home to fulfill its functions, at least one person must be endlessly alert to the needs of all the others. Sometimes this person is a grandmother, sometimes it is a housekeeper. It can be the father, if his work allows him to stay at home, but usually it is the mother.

At present, homemaking is treated as an episode in a woman's life filling only a limited number of years, and the traditional role of women is de-emphasized. It is assumed that girls and boys should be educated exactly alike; if there are any family-life education courses, boys should take them too. Young women's first positions should not be dead-end jobs but ones that will prepare them for their life after child rearing. Then they will be legally supported in competing with men in every kind of occupation. Since no occupation should be closed to women, very little support is given to emphasizing those occupations that extend the home-making role—nursing, teaching, social work, and so forth—as women's special fields.

A girl now is formally educated to use her mind in the same way a boy uses his. She is encouraged to specialize, concentrate her interests, and do first-class work. Then, alienated from her mother by the style of her education and by the size and shape of the modern small family, which cannot tolerate the prolonged presence in it of the late adolescent, the girl marries and suddenly must assume the role of wife and mother in her own home. Here she is expected to become a full-time generalizer, something for which she has not been trained. Along with a great variety of activities she is expected to carry a heavy load of manual work and to be willing to subordinate her own wishes and desires to the needs and desires of infants, small children, and a husband whose image of his role is as unformed as hers is unpracticed. It is not surprising that this kind of marriage so often works badly. The real wonder is that it so often works well, that the young mother can enjoy her husband and baby, that the young father can take pride and joy in his wife and child.

In our own historical past, women who did not wish to play the role of homemaker, spending all day and every day on small repetitive chores and endless responsiveness to others, could make other choices. They could remain as unmarried daughters and sisters in homes where the pattern of life was already formed and their own task was to continue it. Alternatively, they could select one part of woman's traditional role —the care of children or of the sick—and, bypassing marriage, they could become teachers or nurses, devoting their lives to many individuals instead of a few. Young couples could live with parents, and the domestic tasks, instead of falling on the shoulders of one young woman alone, could be shared. Among the educated and the privileged, maintaining a home did not mean polishing floors and washing dishes. Raising her children, sustaining her husband, and the care of the old could be animated and activated by a woman who, because she had domestic help, still had time to read, garden, and play a role in the community or in society.

THE AMERICAN STYLE OF LIVING

Our dilemma, which will not be resolved by equal pay for equal work or by more schooling for women in their middle years, is primarily the outcome of the American style of living, which today is prescribed for every woman and man. It involves an early marriage, an isolated house, and children born close together. Moreover there is a desperate rush to accomplish all this before one is thirty. No domestic help is available except that contributed by the husband, and no allowances are made for individual differences in career desires, temperament, or personality.

The sudden realization by educated women of the emptiness of their lives once their children are grown is only in part a belated recognition of more life to live. For a generation that deeply feared there would be no future and grasped at all of life at once, this emptiness is also a feeling of anticlimax. With everything over at thirty, their hands lie lax on empty laps. Now the sense of being trapped in an endless and meaningless round develops. This is not true for all women, probably not even for the majority. Yet it does hold for many—outstandingly for two groups of women: those who do not enjoy devoting themselves to the needs of individuals, who are unwilling to pay the price our present style of living demands, and those who prefer concentrated, specialized tasks to the

199

generalized, endless, mixed routine of homemaking. Among these people are the woman who goes to work and makes enough money so that she and her husband can eat in restaurants, the woman who heaves a sigh of relief just at getting out of the house, and the woman who welcomes a job that permits her to concentrate on one thing. They have all detested the price exacted of them for marriage, and they escape from the round of household work as quickly as possible.

A SOCIETY IN TRANSITION

The Commission's Report assumes that, in the future, our style of early marriage and family life will continue more or less unchanged. The outside job, as it is practiced now and as it is anticipated—part time and then, perhaps, full time—will compensate women for the exacting years during which they must center their interests on love and companionship within a nuclear family. But other solutions may be more consonant with changes that can already be foreseen. First, there is the enormous transition from a society in which there is enough to eat only if everyone works to one in which a small portion of the population, using complex machinery, can provide for the needs of all. There are also the problems of a world in which the greatest need no longer is to increase population but, on the contrary, to balance it. If these problems can be met, two of the heaviest weights on humanity will be removed—the burdens of unrelenting work and of unwilling childbearing. But throughout the ages, those societies whose members worked hardest and had the most children flourished, and a society withdrew large porportions of its men and women from work or reproduction at its peril. It is hard, then, to assess the repercussions these changes will have on our lives.

In the years since World War II, the United States has had its last fling at high reproductivity and high employment (which has also meant high unemployment). For Americans the large family became a central aim of life and the nuclear family, consisting of parents and immature children, was the ideal living unit. We idealized a way of life that isolated every family and required for its maintenance the expenditure of immense amounts of time, energy, and money. The home life of the postwar years reflected the mood of a society that was weary of the idealism, only partly subscribed to, demanded by the war and that was shocked into fear by the bomb. But the dream bubble finally burst in the terrible realization of what a "togetherness" that excluded all others would mean in the isolated family bomb shelter.

EPILOGUE

The old era is over. But many of the problems it produced remain unsolved. World stability is far from being accomplished; the population explosion, like the danger of nuclear war, still threatens the welfare of the human race. Now, perhaps, some of these issues will be faced as our society begins to turn away from its concentration on one style of family living, exclusively devoted to mating and breeding, that was fostered by a generation who were careless of the rest of the world and expected no future.)

Americans have become newly alert to the existing inequalities and deprivations, more conscious of our great resources, and are giving a new kind of recognition to the contributions that can be made by capable, well-educated men and women. And Americans are becoming more fully aware of how urgent it is to eliminate the unbearable burdens of underachievement, cultural deprivation, regional imbalance, and the cankerous dissatisfactions of a society whose ideals are not in accord with its realities.

It is in this developing climate of opinion that the Report of the President's Commission on the Status of Women appeared. It has been accompanied by a spate of articles, books, and broadcasts on the dissatisfied housewife and the middle-aged woman going back to school. Educated, articulate women, who are demanding freedom and are jubilant about its delights, are providing the necessary push to alter the kind of life that has been urged on young women since World War II. It is important to recognize what is happening and to take what we can from the turmoil and shouting, but we should not be misled.

The early feminists fought for the right to be equal with men. Then women found themselves with the freedom to study and think, but it was too often at the price of sacrificing a personal life. So they went back into the home. In the present generation, women who have devoted themselves to homemaking have rediscovered its hardships and limitations and are demanding the right to leave the home. But this time they do not want to give up anything homemaking entails. They would have the period of child rearing considered a special episode. In their view, the woman with a job is to be more admired as a mother and is more stimulating as a wife. It would be well to ask: is this an expression of anything more than another swing of the pendulum?

The problems facing articulate, educated women remain as vivid today as they have been throughout European history. The continuous care given to small children, a husband, and a household usually is incompatible with the single-minded pursuit of a career. The life style of the good wife and mother contrasts sharply with that of the good scientist, artist, or executive.

SHOULD ALL WOMEN MARRY?

It was the assumption of the Commission—an assumption increasingly made throughout the country—that women who are not fitted for or who do not like marriage and motherhood will continue to marry and to try to be wives and mothers. But they will try to get through this phase quickly in order to go on to a work life in which no ties to individuals will be strong enough to absorb their interests.

Yet other solutions are made possible by changing attitudes toward sex and parenthood. Our conscience has been reawakened to the contribution individuals can make not merely by being good parents but also by using their individual gifts. A woman's life as a homemaker need not be opposed to her individual self-realization, with the one treated as a noble duty and the other as selfish and self-seeking. Instead, personal life can be separated from parenthood as has been done by other societies through celibate religious orders or lives based on companionship among adults rather than between adults and children. Once it is recognized that the world needs educated and committed individuals, each person can ask whether the best possible contribution he or she can make is by devoting a large proportion of time to parenthood. With our sights once more lifted to national and international ventures that are deeply worthwhile, people need not regard the begetting of several children as the only form of the good life— a form that leaves many with a meaningless future at the midpoint of their lives.

Each individual can ask: "Should I marry? Am I interested in devoting myself permanently to another person, or in letting another person devote himself wholly to me?" Once this question has been answered, the next can be: "Should I have children?" The mere capacity to bear children is no reason for having them. In a world in which fewer children, all of them well reared, are needed, each woman can ask: "Granted I would like to marry and devote myself to my husband, and granted I have every reason to expect to bear a healthy child, do I myself want to devote years to bringing up small children? Under present conditions, even if we have the money, is there a chance I could actually get the help required by present standards of child care? If not, have I the duty or the right to have children?"

The phrasing of such questions can also be reversed. A woman who has great talent as an artist, a scientist, or a professional worker can ask: "If I marry and take over full responsibility for another person's life, will the quality of the work I do in my profession be better or less good? If my husband's career takes him someplace where I can't do my work, will I follow him? If following him means giving up my work, will I punish him for this? How much of my own work will I be able to do if I have children? What am I having children for? Are the exercise of my husband's talents and skills and the exercise of my talents and skills compatible with having children? How many? When?"

The immense increase in population along with modern techniques of contraception force us to raise questions about the present ethic in which a continuous sexual relationship is permitted if it is legalized and in which parenthood is considered to be a necessary part of marriage. This ethic, based on an outmoded social need for more children, need not be perpetuated. A continuing insistence that most men and women marry and have children will inevitably mean also that there will be more failures, more divorces, more heartbreak, and more confused children who will grow up to become confused parents. Or all individuals can be permitted more choice, with the expectation that many people will forego marriage or parenthood.

Every good home would benefit greatly by the presence of a lively circle of childless aunts, uncles, and friends who would enjoy and help bring up the children. Intelligent, educated people, engrossed in their own work, people who would perish if they were left alone with children for a month, can easily enjoy caring for a child for a night or over a weekend. They would replace the now necessary, but all too carelessly chosen baby sitter. Fewer homes with children, more adults to every child, more people free to teach, nurse, and succor would help to redress the present imbalance of population. For such a solution, the style of family living would have to be altered very little. The women rearing families would be those who loved caring for individuals; after their own children were grown, they would be eager grandparents or older caring relatives. And it may be found, as more children are reared from infancy by both parents, that a preference for a life related to other individuals is not a characteristic of one sex only. Some men may rear children and be supportive husbands just as capably as women can care for children and be supportive wives. With wider choice, greater leisure, and more variety in styles of life, some men may elect to become the major, homemaking parent or may enjoy developing a supportive role in relation to a wife's talents. Or the idea of two life phases for women may be further developed—marriage and motherhood for young women and an independent career when the children are grown.

WOMEN'S RIGHT TO CHOOSE THEIR LIVES

Whatever direction is taken, women's right to work must be underwritten with all necessary public help and facilitation. Beyond that, society must also support fully women's right to remain unmarried, their right to a personal life without children, to a career alone or to a life of devotion to a small circle of others.

Burdened as women have been for hundreds of thousands of years with childbearing and the tasks of homemaking, what their special capabilities may be is hardly known. The changing prospects for American women may enlarge our knowledge. It is known that in societies in which maternal principles are honored, there is greater peace and balance. It is possible that women's traditional experience in relating to others, which underlies what is called "feminine intuition," may promise great advances in the human sciences. It may be hoped that women in public affairs will stress an attitude of cooperation with nature rather than the ruthless and exploitive mastery of nature. And we may wonder what women, as the sex that has not handled weapons, will be able to make of a peaceful world.

Now America needs skilled womanpower. The climate of opinion is turning against the idea that homemaking is the only form of feminine achievement. But the pendulum must not swing too far, forcing out of the home women whose major creative life is grounded in motherhood and wifehood. Finally, women can only be given real opportunity by being offered real choices, each one underwritten by fair laws and fair practice and a social climate that ensure that each life pattern will be considered a feasible and dignified one.

APPENDIXES
AND INDEX

Executive Order 10980

Establishing the President's Commission on the Status of Women

WHEREAS prejudices and outmoded customs act as barriers to the full realization of women's basic rights which should be respected and fostered as part of our nation's commitment to human dignity, freedom, and democracy; and

WHEREAS measures that contribute to family security and strengthen home life will advance the general welfare; and

WHEREAS it is in the national interest to promote the economy, security, and national defense through the most efficient and effective utilization of the skills of all persons; and

WHEREAS in every period of national emergency women have served with distinction in widely varied capacities but thereafter have been subject to treatment as a marginal group whose skills have been inadequately utilized; and

WHEREAS women should be assured the opportunity to develop their capacities and fulfill their aspirations on a continuing basis irrespective of national exigencies; and

WHEREAS a governmental commission should be charged with the responsibility for developing recommendations for overcoming discriminations in government and private employment on the basis of sex and for developing recommendations for services which will enable women to continue their role as wives and mothers while making a maximum contribution to the world around them:

Now, THEREFORE, by virtue of the authority vested in me as President of the United States by the Constitution and statutes of the United States, it is ordered as follows:

PART I—ESTABLISHMENT OF THE PRESIDENT'S COMMISSION ON THE STATUS OF WOMEN

Sec. 101. There is hereby established the President's Commission on the Status of Women, referred to herein as the "Commission." The Commission shall terminate not later than October 1, 1963.

Sec. 102. The Commission shall be composed of twenty members appointed by the President from among persons with a competency in the area of public affairs and women's activities. In addition, the Secretary of Labor, the Attorney General, the Secretary of Health, Education and Welfare, the Secretary of Commerce, the Secretary of Agriculture, and the Chairman of the Civil Service Commission shall also serve as members of the Commission. The President shall designate from among the membership a Chairman, a Vice-Chairman, and an Executive Vice-Chairman.

Sec. 103. In conformity with the Act of May 3, 1945 (59 Stat. 134, 31 U.S.C. 691), necessary facilitating assistance, including the provision of suitable office space by the Department of Labor, shall be furnished the Commission by the federal agencies whose chief officials are members thereof. An Executive Secretary shall be detailed by the Secretary of Labor to serve the Commission.

Sec. 104. The Commission shall meet at the call of the Chairman.

Sec. 105. The Commission is authorized to use the services of consultants and experts as may be found necessary and as may be otherwise authorized by law.

PART II—DUTIES OF THE PRESIDENT'S COMMISSION ON THE STATUS OF WOMEN

Sec. 201. The Commission shall review progress and make recommendations as needed for constructive action in the following areas:

(*a*) Employment policies and practices, including those on wages, under federal contracts.

(*b*) Federal social insurance and tax laws as they affect the net earnings and other income of women.

(*c*) Federal and state labor laws dealing with such matters as hours, night work, and wages, to determine whether they are accomplishing the purposes for which they were established and whether they should be adapted to changing technological, economic, and social conditions.

(*d*) Differences in legal treatment of men and women in regard to political and civil rights, property rights, and family relations.

(*e*) New and expanded services that may be required for women as wives, mothers, and workers, including education, counseling, training, home services, and arrangements for care of children during the working day.

208

(*f*) The employment policies and practices of the government of the United States, with reference to additional affirmative steps which should be taken through legislation, executive or administrative action to assure nondiscrimination on the basis of sex and to enhance constructive employment opportunities for women.

Sec. 202. The Commission shall submit a final report of its recommendations to the President by October 1, 1963.

Sec. 203. All executive departments and agencies of the federal government are directed to cooperate with the Commission in the performance of its duties.

PART III—REMUNERATION AND EXPENSES

Sec. 301. Members of the Commission, except those receiving other compensation from the United States, shall receive such compensation as the President shall hereafter fix in a manner to be hereafter determined.

John F. Kennedy

The White House,
    December 14, 1961.

Recommendations of the President's Commission on the Status of Women

EDUCATION AND COUNSELING

Means of acquiring or continuing education must be available to every adult at whatever point he or she broke off traditional formal schooling. The structure of adult education must be drastically revised. It must provide practicable and accessible opportunities, developed with regard for the needs of women, to complete elementary and secondary school and to continue education beyond high school. Vocational training, adapted to the nation's growing requirement for skilled and highly educated manpower, should be included at all of these educational levels. Where needed and appropriate, financial support should be provided by local, state, and federal governments and by private groups and foundations.

In a democracy offering broad and everchanging choices, where ultimate decisions are made by individuals, skilled counseling is an essential part of education. Public and private agencies should join in strengthening counseling resources. States and school districts should raise their standards for state employment service counselors and school guidance counselors. Institutions offering counseling education should provide both course content and ample supervised experience in the counseling of females as well as males, adults as well as adolescents.

The education of girls and women for their responsibilities in home and community should be thoroughly re-examined with a view to discovering more effective approaches, with experimentation in content and timing, and under auspices including school systems, private organizations, and the mass media.

210

HOME AND COMMUNITY

For the benefit of children, mothers, and society, child-care services should be available for children of families at all economic levels. Proper standards of child care must be maintained, whether services are in homes or in centers. Costs should be met by fees scaled to parents' ability to pay, contributions from voluntary agencies, and public appropriations.

Tax deductions for child-care expenses of working mothers should be kept commensurate with the median income of couples when both husband and wife are engaged in substantial employment. The present limitation on their joint income, above which deductions are not allowable, should be raised. Additional deductions, of lesser amounts, should be allowed for children beyond the first. The 11-year age limit for child-care deductions should be raised.

Family services under public and private auspices to help families avoid or overcome breakdown or dependency and establish a soundly based homelife, and professionally supervised homemaker services to meet emergency or other special needs should be strengthened, extended, or established where lacking.

Community programs under public and private auspices should make comprehensive provisions for health and rehabilitation services, including easily accessible maternal and child health services, accompanied by education to encourage their use.

Volunteers' services should be made more effective through coordinated and imaginative planning among agencies and organizations for recruitment, training, placement, and supervision, and their numbers augmented through tapping the large reservoir of additional potential among youth, retired people, members of minority groups, and women not now in volunteer activities.

WOMEN IN EMPLOYMENT

Equal opportunity for women in hiring, training, and promotion should be the governing principle in private employment. An Executive order should state this principle and advance its application to work done under federal contracts.

At present, federal systems of manpower utilization discourage part-time employment. Many able women, including highly trained professionals, who are not free for full-time employment, can work part time. The Civil Service Commission and the Bureau of the Budget should facilitate the imaginative and prudent use of such personnel throughout the government service.

LABOR STANDARDS

The federal Fair Labor Standards Act, including premium pay for overtime, should be extended to employment subject to federal jurisdiction but now uncovered, such as work in hotels, motels, restaurants, and laundries, in additional retail establishments, in agriculture, and in nonprofit organizations.

State legislation, applicable to both men and women, should be enacted, or strengthened and extended to all types of employment, to provide minimum-wage levels approximating the minimum under federal law and to require premium pay at the rate of at least time and a half for overtime.

The normal workday and workweek at this moment of history should be not more than 8 hours a day and 40 hours a week. The best way to discourage excessive hours for all workers is by broad and effective minimum-wage coverage, both federal and state, providing overtime of at least time and a half the regular rate for all hours in excess of 8 a day or 40 a week.

Until such time as this goal is attained, state legislation limiting maximum hours of work for women should be maintained, strengthened, and expanded. Provisions for flexibility under proper safeguards should allow additional hours of work when there is a demonstrated need. During this interim period, efforts should continuously and simultaneously be made to require premium rates of pay for all hours in excess of 8 a day or 40 a week.

State laws should establish the principle of equal pay for comparable work.

State laws should protect the right of all workers to join unions of their own choosing and to bargain collectively.

SECURITY OF BASIC INCOME

A widow's benefit under the federal old-age insurance system should be equal to the amount that her husband would have received at the same age had he lived. This objective should be approached as rapidly as may be financially feasible.

The coverage of the unemployment-insurance system should be extended. Small establishments and nonprofit organizations should be covered now through federal action, and state and local government employees through state action. Practicable means of covering at least some household workers and agricultural workers should be actively explored.

Paid maternity leave or comparable insurance benefits should be provided for women workers; employers, unions, and governments should explore the best means of accomplishing this purpose.

WOMEN UNDER THE LAW

Early and definitive court pronouncement, particularly by the United States Supreme Court, is urgently needed with regard to the validity under the Fifth and Fourteenth Amendments of laws and official practices discriminating against women, to the end that the principle of equality become firmly established in constitutional doctrine.

Accordingly, interested groups should give high priority to bringing under court review cases involving laws and practices which discriminate against women.

The United States should assert leadership, particularly in the United Nations, in securing equality of rights for women as part of the effort to define and assure human rights; should participate actively in the formulation of international declarations, principles, and conventions to improve the status of women throughout the world; and should demonstrate its sincere concern for women's equal rights by becoming a party to appropriate conventions.

Appropriate action, including enactment of legislation where necessary, should be taken to achieve equal jury service in the states.

State legislatures, and other groups concerned with the improvement of state statutes affecting family law and personal and property rights of married women, including the National Conference of Commissioners on Uniform State Laws, the Council of Sate Governments, the American Law Institue, and state Commissions on the Status of Women, should move to eliminate laws which impose legal disabilities on women.

WOMEN AS CITIZENS

Women should be encouraged to seek elective and appointive posts at local, state, and national levels and in all three branches of government.

Public office should be held according to ability, experience, and effort, without special preferences or discriminations based on sex. Increasing consideration should continually be given to the appointment of women of demonstrated ability and political sensitivity to policy-making positions.

CONTINUING LEADERSHIP

To further the objectives proposed in this report, an Executive order should:

1. Designate a Cabinet officer to be responsible for assuring that the resources and activities of the federal government bearing upon the Commission's recommendations are directed to carrying them out, and for making periodic progress reports to the President.

2. Designate the heads of other agencies involved in those activities to serve, under the chairmanship of the designated Cabinet officer, as an interdepartmental committee to assure proper coordination and action.

3. Establish a citizens committee, advisory to the interdepartmental committee and with its secretariat from the designated Cabinet officer, to meet periodically to evaluate progress made, provide counsel, and serve as a means for suggesting and stimulating action.

213

Two Consultations Sponsored by the Commission

Portrayal of Women by the Mass Media
MARCH 19, 1963

The President's Commission on the Status of Women, at a consultation on March 19, 1963, asked representatives of the communications industry for advice on the following:

1. Actual portrayal of women by the mass media.
2. What new needs of American women the media can help meet.
3. How well women are achieving full occupational opportunity in communications—broadcasting, the press, magazines, and films.

The meeting, attended by 29 mass-media representatives, was chaired by Margaret Hickey, a Commission Member and editor with the *Ladies Home Journal*. Facilities for the consultation were provided by the New School for Social Research, New York City, through its president, Dr. Henry David, who is also a member of the Commission.

Discussion opened on the charge by the Chairman that the mass media are "projecting, intentionally or unintentionally, an image [of women] that contains old myths, misconceptions, and even distortions, of a true image."

TODAY'S PORTRAYAL OF WOMEN
BY THE MASS MEDIA

Bennett Korn (with an independent television company using dramatic shows produced in Hollywood studios) noted that women are presented in an "unrealistic way. They seem to be typically in the middle-income groups, subservient to the male who earns the money." Women never are portrayed as "a serious partner or breadwinner. You never see creative women in politics or as working mothers. So I know there is a big distortion from reality." He reported difficulty, however, in obtaining women specialists for serious discussions, because "women as intellectual leaders and experts, who think as people rather than from a feminine viewpoint, are rare indeed."

Lorraine Hansberry (playwright) added that the image of women frequently portrayed is "the glorification of the courtesan, the notion of women as object and very little else." The uniform, shallow, even grotesque image in the commercials, she felt, undoubtedly plays a part in determining standards of womanhood for men of the younger generation.

Marya Mannes (writer), while agreeing with the point, took exception to the word "courtesan." She felt it was the "bunny" and the entire "Playboy" psychology that were degrading to women.

Al Capp (cartoonist), in defending the woman in the commercial as an ideal, cited the value to American women of having as an ideal "an impossibly attractive, charming, cultured woman, and all girls in the country trying to be like her. There's not a woman in this room who hasn't been influenced by this means." He pointed out that in family comedies, the woman comes out ahead of her husband; he is portrayed as a fool while she keeps the house "like a glowing jewel," is a great cook, and generally is able to cope with situations."

Margaret Culkin Banning (writer) noted the marked contrast in the stamp put on women over the past 40 years; the stamp of the present decade—a search for glamor—tends to demote women, even though advertisements have greatly improved the appearance of women; the stamp of the 1920's and 1930's was due to a minority of women interested in women's rights and suffrage who were great leaders.

In the film field, Arthur Mayer (writer) sounded an optimistic note: "I think there are signs of genuine improvement in the offing. The success of newer pictures indicates we're reaching a place where soon we can show women in more favorable aspects of their activities than we have in the past."

215

A fairly sharp division was evident between those who felt the mass women's magazines were, in Betty Friedan's (writer) words, "not projecting a new horizon for women," as they did 30 years ago, and those who felt they were raising the standards of living and taste.

Herbert R. Mayes (magazine) spoke of the value of the service features of mass magazines on food, fashion, child care, beauty, and home decorating, but acknowledged that the "weak spot in all mass magazines is fiction—not nonfiction nor the service area." He and Morton Hunt (writer) felt that its influence was so minimal, however, as to be of little concern, since fiction was escape and entertainment. In Miss Mannes' opinion, on the other hand, it was "precisely in the area of entertainment that the false image . . . has the most subtle subcutaneous impact."

Gerri Major reported that her magazine (*Ebony*) attempted to give an honest picture of the Negro woman's aspirations, activities, and progress. Louis Cowan (mass-media research) deplored that this story was not presented in the whole of the nation's press. Curtiss Anderson (magazine) added: "We are bringing up a whole generation of little Negro girls who think being glamorous means being white. I think the whole ghetto atmosphere is one of our great, great shortcomings. We don't hear enough about, by, and for Negro women in the general media. The race issue is the only really important issue of our time."

POSSIBILITIES FOR NEW SERVICES

Stockton Helffrich (broadcasters association) joined Mr. Korn in suggesting that the Commission bring its findings to the attention of various groups in the broadcasting industry to help modify existing stereotypes and present a more pluralistic and varied portrayal of women. He said: "It takes a conscious tabulation of what we ought to be doing and the dissemination of that to the people who create the programs. If the activities of this Commission move in that direction, they will be most constructive—as similar efforts have been in fields of mental health and racial minorities."

Polly Cowan (radio) reported on a month-old experiment—a joint venture of New York City radio station WMCA and a group of trained women volunteers who provide a telephone service to direct public inquiries about serious housing violations and problems to the proper city department. Its continued success could constitute a prototype for projects harnessing the mass media to social needs in other cities.

Hartford Gunn (television) pointed out the growing recognition by educational television of a serious lack in daytime educational programs for women. He encouraged the Commission to support efforts already being made to increase such programing, possibly related to local political and welfare campaigns such as WMCA's. Mr. Mayes also stressed continuing education for women: "One major problem all of us in our field are confronted with is providing women with the means for living fuller lives after their children are grown."

Kathleen McLaughlin (newspaper) saw a need for more attention to the problems of the younger generation rather than the average American housewife and mother, and Betsy Talbot Blackwell (magazine) was concerned with dropouts from colleges and high schools.

Many felt the Commission should underline the importance of counseling to make young women aware of the need to plan their lives on a long-range basis. Dr. Richard A. Lester (Commission member) told how the Commission's Subcommittee on Counseling became aware that counselors, in working with children who have acquired stereotyped images from the mass media, feel ineffectual in countering the trends toward early marriage and away from self-development.

Mrs. Friedan suggested that magazines could project new images with which, perhaps, only a minority of women could identify, but "it would give a sense of possibility. The women's magazines did that 30 or 40 years ago, but they don't do it much today. We need more heroines in fiction as well as nonfiction. They exist in real life and should be projected by the media to give women the image of a heroine who is using herself to the fullest for some purpose or goal."

Margaret Twyman (motion picture association) and Ethel J. Alpenfels (anthropologist) agreed that the mass media have not done a good enough job of interpreting the importance of the mother's influence on her young children.

JOB OPPORTUNITIES FOR WOMEN IN COMMUNICATIONS

Lisa Howard (broadcasting) mentioned the onus on a career woman, particularly if she becomes a success in a field considered to be a man's. "She is made to feel guilty or unfeminine. She is called aggressive, brash, and pushy. A lot of women don't want to fight that kind of psychological barrier."

Mr. Cowan and Mr. Korn cited the need "to change the frame of reference of the employer so that he looks at women in a dispassionate way as functioning work units. The stigma attached to the working mother should be changed, so that she is a proud possession in the family rather than a problem person."

Wallace W. Elton (advertising) noted the importance for women of being prepared for competition. The majority of women in his agency seemed to have been prepared in home and school for competition as brides and housewives. "The training must be in the school or home, not with the mass media, which are simply catering to what we have been taught."

George Heinemann (broadcasting) stated that women in broadcasting could make a greater contribution by educating themselves with "honest-to-goodness courses in sociology so that they would understand the basic roots of our country and the needs of people at home."

SUMMARY

Many of the participants stated a willingness to cooperate with the Commission, both by supplying further information and by implementing Commission recommendations, particularly those relating to education and social welfare. Others spoke of a new awareness which, they felt, if made more widely known to policy makers in the communications industry, would result in tangible changes. The Commission was asked to identify present limitations of the mass media in showing pluralistic images of women and to relate the effect of a limited image to such problems as women's aspirations, motivations, standards of performance, interest in lifelong education and career planning, and attitudes of employers.

ADDENDUM

Subsequent to the meeting, letters from participants in the consultation expressed additional thoughts. To quote briefly:

Stockton Helffrich: ". . . a rundown of true and false premises, properly disseminated to the key personnel at networks and creative broadcast sources, would move . . . [the implementation of attitudes now crystallizing on the actual needs of women] in the right direction. Further conferences and seminars, mailings, and general publicity are doubtless likewise in order and certainly not in conflict."

Marya Mannes: "To a certain degree they [mass media] do reflect the conditions and goals of a majority of women as embodied in the middle-

218

class homebound housewife with children. To a much greater—and uncondonable—degree they neglect very large minorities of women; among them [are] the full-time working wife, the wife who supports the family, the single working woman, the career woman with husband and family, the professional intellectual, the Negro woman. . . ."

Arthur Mayer: "Nonetheless, if . . . films dealing candidly and sincerely with the political or economic inequities to which women are still subject or the unromantic aspects of their lives—any more than pictures dealing with equal candor and sincerity with the Negro situation or the perils of nuclear annihilation—are to be produced, I am fearful that we cannot leave this wholly to the initiative of high-minded, low-budgeted picturemakers."

Perrin Stryker (formerly magazine): "I concurred completely with . . . remarks about the need to focus on diverse groups of women; this is allied to my unspoken suggestion that the Commission decide what groups of women are most deserving of study. Personally, the . . . women who are working full-time would get my vote for concentrated attention."

Problems of Negro Women
APRIL 19, 1963

The purpose of the consultation on the Problems of Negro Women was stated by Esther Peterson, Executive Vice Chairman of the President's Commission on the Status of Women, in her greeting: To obtain advice and information from experts on the problems and aspirations of Negro women because they are the largest minority group in the United States; the suggestions received will be of help to the Commission as it develops recommendations in the areas assigned it by the President's Executive Order 10980.

Miss Dorothy Height, president of the National Council of Negro Women and a Commission member, served as chairman of the consultation at the request of the Commission.

According to the chairman, the Commission has been dealing in a fresh way with the whole concept of equality; it was thinking less of women as a cause and more of the extent to which women, as part of the whole society, are free to participate as persons and take their place as they themselves choose in the home, in the community, and in the wider society. The commission thought of equailty as not meaning "the same" but equality of treatment with respect to rights, obligations, opportunity.

At the outset, there was consensus that the problem of race discrimination permeates the whole life picture of the Negro—in housing, education, employment opportunities, interpersonal relations, and so forth—and that approaches to the problems of the Negro woman should be based on this premise. Moreover, the American public is not consciously aware of the vast differences between opportunities for individuals in minority groups and for others and of the manpower resources that are not being fully utilized. Therefore, there must be concern for helping all women, since this in turn would bring about the development and use of abilities and skills of all persons to the economy.

NEGRO FAMILY PATTERNS

Discussion centered first on the patterns of Negro family life and how they affect parent and child.

EFFECTS ON PARENTS. It generally was agreed that, traditionally, Negro families have been more matriarchal than white families. The tendency has continued because of the inability of many Negro men to get a decent job and earn a sufficient wage to carry the responsibilities of family life. Thus the Negro wife is forced into the labor market where she often earns more than her husband and sometimes becomes the only earner for the family. Therefore, not by choice, she may become the head of the household.

Because of the barriers to education and better-paying jobs encountered by men, the Negro woman frequently has had to assume additional social and economic burdens. The Negro woman also faces discrimination in the labor market. She usually is employed in jobs paying low wages, and if she is in domestic service, as many are, she works long hours. A long working day complicates her responsibilities in childbearing and prevents her active participation in community affairs where she might work for better conditions both for herself and her family.

A study of Negro women by Dr. Jeanne L. Noble of Teachers College, Columbia University, showed that Negro women generally based their educational choice on vocational opportunity. If a Negro girl felt she had a chance to become a teacher, she majored in education. But if she then found that being a teacher was threatening the status of her mate, she tended not to go on to advanced study because the preservation of the marriage relationship was more important. Thus, the progress of the Negro woman—her personal advancement and that of the whole family—is inextricably bound to the improvement of opportunities for the Negro male.

This study also pointed out how difficult it is for the Negro male to assume the expected masculine role of defender, protector, and provider of the family when he is confronted with constant rebuff—a demoralizing experience—when seeking employment.

More Negro women have attended college and hold college degrees than Negro males. This has created an awkward and serious problem for the college-educated Negro girl, who, unable to meet a wide group of educated men, frequently marries below her educational standard. When she earns more than her husband, his resulting insecurity and jealousy may dissolve the family and thus continue the matriarchal family pattern.

The group felt that greater effort should be made to convince more Negro males of the importance both to themselves and to their families that they take advantage of the greater opportunities open to them if they go to college.

EFFECTS ON THE CHILDREN. The matriarchal-type family presents problems to Negro children, both boys and girls, in developing their masculine or feminine roles. Lack of a strong male model for boys, especially in slum areas where success models too often are people "beating the game," places a heavy burden on the Negro family in trying to transmit values. Is it any wonder that a child may find the man who is "beating the game" a more tempting model to follow than a hard-working parent stuck in a low-paid job?

The children of many Negro mothers who must work are not cared for properly during their mothers' working hours. Consultants expressed a strong hope for Commission advocacy of more community child-care facilities, public, cooperative, and private, open to children of all economic levels. However, several participants stated that establishment of additional child-care services should not be part of a program to try to force mothers of young children into the labor market by taking away public assistance.

Hope was expressed that public-assistance legislation would be further improved to strengthen family life. Formerly, under Aid to Dependent Children legislation, if the father was present in the home and employable, the family, regardless of need, was automatically ineligible for assistance involving federal funds. Amendments passed in 1961 provide federal funds on a matching basis to states whose laws permit Aid to Families with Dependent Children based on need, regardless of whether there is an employable male in the household. Less than ⅓ of our states, however, have accepted this new aid program designed to maintain and strengthen family life during periods of economic dislocation. In many jurisdictions, the unemployed father is, in effect, encouraged to desert his family to make it eligible for public aid.

Forging stronger family relationships is of particular concern to the Negro woman if the pressures now upon her are to be eased. It was suggested that greater emphasis in public education curricula on the rich history and culture of the Negro would be of particular help in the strengthening of Negro family relationships.

EMPLOYMENT OPPORTUNITIES

Problems related to employment opportunities have a great impact on the Negro woman and her family. The group emphasized the importance of recognizing the special difficulties of women who are at the bottom of the economic ladder, particularly those in household employment, but was equally concerned with the importance of considering those at all employment levels.

WHITE-COLLAR, SEMIPROFESSIONAL, AND PROFESSIONAL OPPORTUNITIES. The need for greater vocational-training opportunities, especially for middle-range jobs, and the dilemma in many areas where Negroes are not trained for particular jobs because the jobs are not open to them were stressed. Negro women often find that jobs are available only at the lowest economic level or at the professional level: sales and clerical jobs and many skilled

222

jobs are closed to them. For example, a major means of entering the secretarial field is through graduation from a recognized business or secretarial school. Many of these schools, however, do not admit Negroes. Yet they are granted licenses to operate and have such advantages as tax exemption and indirect federal funds through veterans' programs. Training for new jobs must go hand in hand with efforts to open up new job opportunities. Not only should job opportunities be found for Negroes already trained, but vocational training also should be stimulated for jobs which currently are not open to them.

Entrance to new types of job opportunity has been hampered by vocational legislation which has not kept up with the kind of work skills needed and by an absence of training of youths, Negroes in particular, for the new jobs.

Generally, educational standards in high schools and in commercial schools should be raised, and preparation for specific professional work should be improved in the colleges. That efficiency in job training and performance is the key to opening new job opportunities should be stressed among young people. The Manpower Training and Development Act would become a stronger vehicle for the preparation and placement of Negro women workers if its programs for training and retraining were broadened and expanded.

Efforts should be made also to overcome the limitations and evasions which bar Negroes from employment and training for employment in higher-paying jobs. Training and apprenticeship programs, which are avenues to such jobs, should be accessible to all citizens, regardless of race or sex.

HOUSEHOLD WORKERS. Some participants emphasized the widespread desire among Negro household workers to move upward out of what they consider to be an undesirable occupation. Others said that since many Negroes undoubtedly will continue to be in household work, upgrading of its skills and improvements in employment conditions were desirable. In this period of social change, the occupation should be re-evaluated to determine what kinds of household workers are needed now, what kinds of new skills are required to handle modern laborsaving devices, and what means will assure better pay and job satisfaction for those employed in this type of work.

Training centers to prepare household workers were considered. Where household training is not provided by schools, certified training programs could increase the career household worker's skills. It was also brought out that household occupations have within them many possibilities for the development of skills and technical knowledge which are closely enough allied to occupations in service industries to offer opportunities for advancement.

In a discussion of the basic need for broadening opportunities for those in household employment, two additional approaches were suggested: (1) unionization of household workers to establish decent wages and hours and standards of working conditions and (2) facilities to help those who are qualified or desire further training to move to better employment opportunities.

All such efforts could lead to greater interest and incentive on the job and increase the sense of dignity necessary to good job performance.

It was pointed out that Negro women employed in household service frequently do not receive social security coverage, partly because many employers fail to pay contributions to old-age, survivors, and disability insurance. The group urged that the federal government take further steps to enforce compliance with the law requiring contributions to social security for these women and to educate the Negro household worker on her rights and benefits under this program.

VOCATIONAL GUIDANCE

A key issue of discussion was the type of guidance given to Negro youth which, it was felt, limited their view and realization of job opportunities open to them. The following underlying reasons were given:

On the high school level, many guidance counselors themselves need to broaden their concepts of realistic opportunities for the young Negro woman who wants to go to college or who is weighing that possibility. This is particularly true in newly integrated high schools, where guidance for Negro youth often is based on misconception of the individual's capacities and abilities, and a lack of knowledge of the accomplishments of Negro women and of probable social change.

The attitude of expectancy toward obtaining an education or working in certain occupations is crucial. When families and children have limited hopes as to future vocational possibilities, counselors also may believe that a girl or a boy has no chance for a particular type of job.

The aspirations of parents and children should be supported and, if necessary, raised so they can foresee that new opportunities will be available if prepared for. Negro parents often fail to encourage their children to stay in school or seek higher education because they see no job opportunities at the "end of the road." Such a pattern is self-defeating for self-improvement. "Why should I go to school?" the child asks. "I will get a low-status job like my father's." Here is where the guidance teacher needs to stress upward mobility and provide inspiration toward higher goals. It was suggested that the Commission could help greatly by making known the availability of resources. The Negro girl needs role models even more than does the white girl. Counselors should have specially prepared films and handbooks to inform themselves and their students of present-day work possibilities open to Negro youth.

COMMUNITY SERVICES AND PARTICIPATION

How women of minority groups could participate more effectively in community activities and in planning for community needs was considered.

BROADER PARTICIPATION. Our democratic system of government and way of life depend on wide citizen participation in governmental and community activities. Improved cooperation among various types of community organizations would broaden and strengthen community programs. Recognition by voluntary organizations of the great untapped resources among working women, particularly among minority groups, would provide a new reservoir of participation. But community activities should be scheduled more realistically to attract greater participation by working people; for example, women in lower socioeconomic levels, unavailable for daytime meetings, could attend meetings at night or on weekends. Voluntary organizations should consider all the cultural nuances of the group they want to have participate. Women of lower economic levels cannot be expected to take part in situations where they are socially uncomfortable.

POLICY-MAKING BOARDS. More Negroes from various economic levels should be involved in community policy planning and decision making because of the benefit to them and the future of their children. Such participation could be useful both to the agency and to the individual. Boards of education, for example, and PTA boards could benefit from views and knowledge of the Negro woman regarding education programs and problems. It was recognized, however, that the Negro woman has been slow to participate in meetings she *was* able to attend because lack of opportunity sometimes prevented the development of confidence. But it was emphasized that Negro women need to know they *can* participate.

Although she may feel she lacks experience for service on voluntary or community-planning boards, the Negro woman's knowledge derived from experience can be advantageous to civic bodies and planning agencies. It is particularly important for the Negro to serve on decision-making bodies in behalf of the community and its needs where many members of the community are Negroes or where the needs of a large minority have been overlooked. If the Negro woman serves on boards, she should, indeed, be qualified to do so, but she also should have opportunities to obtain training and experience. Some organizations provide their members and officers with leadership training. Because many white children have seen Negroes only as domestic workers and because few white adults have been in a peer relationship with Negroes, a false image of Negroes is prevalent and needs to be overcome.

AVAILABILITY OF FEDERAL SERVICES. Because of local control, federal programs in many areas do not reach people they were designed to aid. The problem here is twofold: (1) to see that federal programs are made available to all persons regardless of race and (2) to help Negroes learn that resources are available.

A major block preventing federal funds from flowing smoothly and quickly to the local level is the necessity for matching funds by state and local governments. Few programs operate with only federal money in the local community.

The importance of effectively administering a program at the local level in accordance with its purpose was stressed. It was emphasized that there should be more Negroes with necessary qualifications in policy-making jobs in regional offices administering federal programs. Technical people representing an agency in a particular locality should not be subject to political influences and control that often hamper an agency's work because of conflict with local interests.

COMMUNICATION. Because the Negro is not aware of available services, he often does not benefit from public programs. A proposed method of improving communications was to establish centers in cities and counties where individuals and families could get information from one source about available services at federal, state, and city levels. Such centers would be manned by federal and state or city representatives and would be prepared to provide information on legislation, education, social security, juvenile delinquency, urban renewal, etc. In view of the mobility of our population, and particularly of the Negro movement from the South and from rural to urban centers, such centers would be most useful. They would help close the gap between local administration of services and federal provisions.

Participants agreed that voting and intelligent political participation are essential to achieve many of these goals, and that it was imperative that voting rights be secured and exercised by *all* American citizens throughout the country.

ADULT EDUCATION

An area of particular concern to the Negro woman is the expansion of adult education and training programs. Educational facilities available to the Negro still lag greatly. Of the 3.8 million women in the United States who are functional illiterates, a great many are Negroes. There is much need for additional adult education and training programs tailored particularly to the requirements of those with low literacy.

The work of a Philadelphia minister whose community included many unemployed was cited. The pastor's initiative led to the building of a factory to manufacture vestments and choral gowns for gospel singers and to the training of women to cut material and operate power sewing machines. The business has been successful; its profits have been used to finance adult education classes for men and women.

SUMMARY

In summarizing the discussion, Miss Height said that problems of the Negro woman cannot be dismissed by saying, "Well, all women have those problems.

"Negro women have the same problems and hopes as other women, but they cannot take even the same things for granted," she continued, adding, "If the Negro woman has a major underlying concern, it is the status of the Negro man and his position in the community and his need for feeling himself an important person, free and able to make his contribution in the whole society in order that he may strengthen his home."

She reiterated that all problems facing the Negro woman are interrelated and cannot be isolated. The group discussion had centered on Negro women not only because they are the largest ethnic minority but also because many of their problems bear on problems of women in all minority groups.

Miss Height emphasized that the conference tried to fulfill its assignment from the perspective of all American women and the way in which the Negro woman fits into the total picture; that the group had dealt with important problems that must be faced realistically if the total society in the United States is to improve family life, provide better futures for young people, and achieve a sense of equitable participation by all citizens.

Eight Tables Showing Comparative State Positions on the Status of American Women

TABLE 5 · EXTENT OF PROTECTION UNDER STATE

STATE OR OTHER JURISDICTION	COMPULSORY LAW	FARM EMPLOYMENT COVERED	NO NUMERICAL EXEMPTION	FULL COVERAGE OF OCCUPATIONAL DISEASES	FULL MEDICAL CARE FOR ACCIDENTAL INJURIES
Alabama	a				
Alaska	X	X	X	X	X
Arizona	X				X
Arkansas	X			X	X
California	X	X	X	X	X
Colorado					
Connecticut	X	X		X	X
Delaware	X			X	X
District of Columbia	X		X	X	X
Florida				X	X
Georgia	a				
Hawaii	X	X	X	X	X
Idaho	X		X		X
Illinois	X		X	X	X
Indiana			X	X	X
Iowa			X		X
Kansas	a				
Kentucky				X	X
Louisiana			X		
Maine					X
Maryland	X		X	X	X
Massachusetts	X	X		X	X
Michigan	X			X	X
Minnesota	X		X	X	X
Mississippi	X				X
Missouri				X	X
Montana			X		
Nebraska			X	X	X
Nevada	X			X	X
New Hampshire	X				X
New Jersey		X	X	X	X
New Mexico					
New York	X		X	X	X
North Carolina					X
North Dakota	X		X	X	X
Ohio	X	X		X	X
Oklahoma	X				X
Oregon			X	X	X
Pennsylvania			X	X	X
Rhode Island	X			X	X
South Carolina				X	X
South Dakota			X		
Tennessee	a				
Texas					X
Utah	X		X	X	X
Vermont		X			X
Virginia	X			X	
Washington	X		X	X	X
West Virginia			X	X	
Wisconsin	X	X		X	X
Wyoming	X		X		X

a Workmen's compensation laws in effect do not meet any recommended standards.

WORKMEN'S COMPENSATION LAWS AS OF DECEMBER, 1964

FULL MEDICAL CARE FOR OCCUPATIONAL DISEASES	MAINTENANCE BENEFITS DURING PERIOD OF REHABILITATION	COMPENSATION FOR TEMPORARY TOTAL DISABILITY NOT LESS THAN 66⅔ PER CENT OF AVERAGE WAGES	COMPENSATION FOR PERMANENT TOTAL DISABILITY FOR LIFE OR PERIOD OF DISABILITY	DEATH BENEFITS TO WIDOW UNTIL HER DEATH OR REMARRIAGE
X	X	X	X	X
	X	X	X	X
	X			
X			X	
			X	
X	X		X	X
X			X	
X	X	X	X	X
X			X	
X	X	X	X	
X			X	
			X	
X			X	
X				
X			X	X
	X			
X				
X	X	X	X	
X			X	
X	X		X	
X	X			
X	X		X	
	X			
X			X	
			X	X
X				
X			X	
X				
X	X		X	X
X	X		X	X
X	X		X	
X				
X	X		X	X
X			X	
X			X	
X				
	X		X	
X			X	X
	X		X	X
X	X		X	

TABLE 6 · SELECTED PROVISIONS OF STATE UNEMPLOYMENT

STATE OR OTHER JURISDICTION	WAGE OR EMPLOYMENT QUALIFICATIONS (NUMBER IS REQUIRED MULTIPLE OF WBA, WEEKLY BENEFIT AMOUNT, UNLESS OTHERWISE INDICATED) b	WEEKLY BENEFIT AMOUNT FOR TOTAL UNEMPLOYMENT c (IN DOLLARS)	
		MINIMUM	MAXIMUM
Alabama	1½ times high-quarter wages; with $221 in 1 quarter	9	32
Alaska	1¼ times high-quarter wages, but not less than $500	10–15 c	45–70 c
Arizona	30, and wages in 2 quarters	10	43
Arkansas	30, and wages in 2 quarters	15	36
California	$600; if more than 75% paid in 1 quarter, wages of at least $630 in base period and $458 in high quarter	25	55
Colorado	30	14	50
Connecticut	$300, and wages in 2 quarters	10–14	45–67
Delaware	30	7	50
District of Columbia	1½ times high-quarter wages, but not less than $276; with $130 in 1 quarter	8–9	53
Florida	20 weeks of employment at average of $20 or more	10	33
Georgia	36; with $175 in 1 quarter and wages in 2 quarters	8	35
Hawaii	30, and 14 weeks of employment	5	55

a Consult the state law and state employment security agency for authoritative information.

b Earnings or employment required in a 1-year period; "high-quarter" is that calendar quarter of the period in which wages were highest.

c Amount related to individual's past earnings. When two amounts are given, higher includes dependents' allowances; no maximum augmented payment shown for Massachusetts, since such amount is limited only by the claimant's average weekly wage. In Alaska, no dependents' allowances are paid to interstate claimants, and the maximum amount is $20. In Ohio and Wyoming, maximum amount for interstate claimants may be less than that shown.

d For claimants with minimum qualifying wages and minimum weekly benefit amount. The sign + indicates that minimum annual benefits are not evenly divisible by minimum

DURATION IN 52-WEEK PERIOD (WEEKS OF BENEFITS FOR TOTAL UNEMPLOYMENT)		SIZE OF FIRM COVERED (MINIMUM NUMBER OF EMPLOYEES AND/OR SIZE OF PAYROLL)	SPECIAL DISQUALIFICATIONS *e* UNEMPLOYMENT DUE TO:		TEMPORARY DISABILITY INSURANCE *f*
MINIMUM *d*	MAXIMUM		PREGNANCY	MARITAL OBLIGATION	
12+	26	4 in 20 weeks			
15	26	1 at any time	X	X	
10	26	3 in 20 weeks			
10	26	1 in 10 days	X	X	
12 *g*	26 *g*	1 and over $100 in any quarter		X	X
10	26	4 in 20 weeks	X	X	
10–12 *d, g*	26 *g*	3 in 13 weeks	X		
11+	26	1 in 20 weeks	X		
17+	34	1 at any time	X		
10	26	4 in 20 weeks, or 4 in 8 weeks and over $6,000 in any quarter			
9	26	4 in 20 weeks	X		
26 *g*	26 *g*	1 at any time	X	X	

wba. In states noted, range of duration applies to claimants with minimum qualifying wages in base period; the longer duration applies with the minimum weekly benefit amount; the shorter duration applies with maximum possible concentration of wages in high quarter and, therefore, wba higher than the minimum.

e All states deny benefits to claimants for weeks when they are not able to work and available for work. All states disqualify work-ers who leave their jobs voluntarily without good cause; in 23 states, good cause is limited to causes related to the work. In the states checked in these columns, however, a person who left a job for the indicated reason is subject to a disqualification without regard to actual ability to work, or availability for work.

f These 4 states have comprehensive programs of cash benefits related to wage loss caused by sickness or accident not covered by workmen's compensation.

TABLE 6 · SELECTED PROVISIONS OF STATE UNEMPLOYMENT

STATE OR OTHER JURISDICTION	WAGE OR EMPLOYMENT QUALIFICATIONS (NUMBER REQUIRED IS MULTIPLE OF WBA, WEEKLY BENEFIT AMOUNT, UNLESS OTHERWISE INDICATED)	WEEKLY BENEFIT AMOUNT FOR TOTAL EMPLOYMENT (IN DOLLARS)	
		MINIMUM	MAXIMUM
Idaho	33+ − 38+ but not less than $572; with $365 in 1 quarter and wages in 2 quarters	17	45
Illinois	$750; with $175 outside high quarter	10	38–59
Indiana	$250; with $150 in last 2 quarters	10	36
Iowa	$300; with $200 in 1 quarter and $100 in another quarter	10	30–44
Kansas	30	10	47
Kentucky	1⅜ times high-quarter wages; with 8 times wba in last 2 quarters and $250 in 1 quarter	12	40
Louisiana	30	10	40
Maine	$400	9	34
Maryland	1½ times high-quarter wages; with $192.01 in 1 quarter and wages in 2 quarters	10–12	46
Massachusetts	$700	10–16	45 c
Michigan	14 weeks of employment at $15.01 or more	10–12	33–60
Minnesota	$520	12	38
Mississippi	36; with $130.01 in 1 quarter and wages in 2 quarters	8	30
Missouri	17 weeks of employment at $15 or more	3	40

g Benefits are extended when unemployment in state reaches specific levels.

h One in 20 weeks applies in corporate limits of cities of 10,000 or more population.

INSURANCE LAWS, AS OF JANUARY 1965

DURATION IN 52-WEEK PERIOD (WEEKS OF BENEFITS FOR TOTAL UNEMPLOYMENT)		SIZE OF FIRM COVERED (MINIMUM NUMBER OF EMPLOYEES AND/OR SIZE OF PAYROLL)	SPECIAL DISQUALIFICATIONS UNEMPLOYMENT DUE TO:		TEMPORARY DISABILITY INSURANCE
MINIMUM	MAXIMUM		PREGNANCY	MARITAL OBLIGATION	
10 g	26 g	1 and $150 in any quarter	X	X	
10–26 d, g	26 g	4 in 20 weeks	X	X	
6+	26	4 in 20 weeks	X	X	
10	26	4 in 20 weeks			
10	26	4 in 20 weeks, or 25 in 1 week	X	X	
15	26	4 in 20 weeks, or 4 in 3 quarters of preceding year and $50 per quarter for each worker		X	
12	28	4 in 20 weeks	X		
26	26	4 in 20 weeks	X	X	
26	26	1 at any time	X		
8+ – 25+ d	30	1 in 13 weeks	X		
9+	26	4 in 20 weeks	X		
18	26	1 in 20 weeks, or 4 in 20 weeks h	X	X	
12	26	4 in 20 weeks	X	X	
10+ – 26 d	26	4 in 20 weeks	X		

i Or 15 weeks in last year and 40 weeks in last 2 years at average weekly wage of $15 or more (New York); or 14 weeks in last year and 55 weeks in last 2 years at average of $16 or more (Wisconsin).

TABLE 6 · SELECTED PROVISIONS OF STATE UNEMPLOYMENT

STATE OR OTHER JURISDICTION	WAGE OR EMPLOYMENT QUALIFICATIONS (NUMBER REQUIRED IS MULTIPLE OF WBA, WEEKLY BENEFIT AMOUNT, UNLESS OTHERWISE INDICATED)	WEEKLY BENEFIT AMOUNT FOR TOTAL EMPLOYMENT (IN DOLLARS)	
		MINIMUM	MAXIMUM
Montana	1½ times high-quarter wages; with $285 in 1 quarter	15	34
Nebraska	$600; with $200 in each of 2 quarters	12	38
Nevada	30	8–12	37.50–57.50
New Hampshire	$600; with $100 in each of 2 quarters	13	45
New Jersey	17 weeks of employment at $15 or more	10	50
New Mexico	27+ – 30; with $156 in 1 quarter	10	36
New York	20 weeks of employment at average of $15 or more *i*	10	50
North Carolina	$550, and wages in 2 quarters	12	35
North Dakota	40, and wages in 2 quarters	15	44
Ohio	20 weeks of employment at $20 or more	10–15 *c*	42–53 *c*
Oklahoma	1½ times high-quarter wages, but not less than $300; or $3,000	10	32
Oregon	20 weeks of employment at average of $20 or more, but not less than $700	20	44
Pennsylvania	30; with $120 in 1 quarter and 20% of wages in another quarter	10	45

INSURANCE LAWS, AS OF JANUARY 1965

DURATION IN 52-WEEK PERIOD (WEEKS OF BENEFITS FOR TOTAL UNEMPLOYMENT)		SIZE OF FIRM COVERED (MINIMUM NUMBER OF EMPLOYEES AND/OR SIZE OF PAYROLL)	SPECIAL DISQUALIFICATIONS UNEMPLOYMENT DUE TO:		TEMPORARY DISABILITY INSURANCE
MINIMUM	MAXIMUM		PREGNANCY	MARITAL OBLIGATION	
13	26	1 in 20 weeks, or over $500 in a year	X	X	
11	26	4 in 20 weeks, or $10,000 in any quarter	X		
10	26	1, and $225 in any quarter	X	X	
26	26	4 in 20 weeks	X		
12+	26	4 in 20 weeks	X		X
18	30	1, and $450 in any quarter, or 2 in 13 weeks			
26	26	1, and $300 in any quarter		X	X
26 g	26 g	4 in 20 weeks	X		
18	26	4 in 20 weeks	X	X	
20	26	3 at any time	X	X	
10	39	4 in 20 weeks	X	X	
11+	26	1, and $225 in any quarter	X	X	
18	30	1 at any time	X	X	

TABLE 6 · SELECTED PROVISIONS OF STATE UNEMPLOYMENT

STATE OR OTHER JURISDICTION	WAGE OR EMPLOYMENT QUALIFICATIONS (NUMBER REQUIRED IS MULTIPLE OF WBA, WEEKLY BENEFIT AMOUNT, UNLESS OTHERWISE INDICATED)	WEEKLY BENEFIT AMOUNT FOR TOTAL UNEMPLOYMENT (IN DOLLARS)	
		MINIMUM	MAXIMUM
Rhode Island	20 weeks of employment at $20 or more; or $1200	10–13	36–48
South Carolina	1½ times high-quarter wages, but not less than $300; with $180 in 1 quarter	10	38
South Dakota	1½ times high-quarter wages; with $250 in 1 quarter, and $600 in base period	12	34
Tennessee	36; with $286.01 in 1 quarter	12	36
Texas	$375; with $250 in 1 quarter and $125 in another; or $450 with $50 in each of 3 quarters; or $1,000 in 1 quarter	10	37
Utah	19 weeks of employment at $20 or more, but not less than $700	10	47
Vermont	20 weeks of employment at $20 or more	10	43
Virginia	46	15	36
Washington	$800	17	42
West Virginia	$700	12	35
Wisconsin	18 weeks of employment at average of $16 or more *i*	11	55
Wyoming	26 weeks of employment with 24 hours and $18 in each week plus 1½ times high-quarter wages; with $250 in 1 quarter	10	46 *c*

DURATION IN 52-WEEK PERIOD (WEEKS OF BENEFITS FOR TOTAL UNEMPLOYMENT)		SIZE OF FIRM COVERED (MINIMUM NUMBER OF EMPLOYEES AND/OR SIZE OF PAYROLL)	SPECIAL DISQUALIFICATIONS UNEMPLOYMENT DUE TO:		TEMPORARY DISABILITY INSURANCE
MINIMUM	MAXIMUM		PREGNANCY	MARITAL OBLIGATION	
12	26	1 at any time			X
10	22	4 in 20 weeks	X		
16	24	4 in 20 weeks, or $24,000 in a year	X		
12	26	4 in 20 weeks	X		
10+	26	4 in 20 weeks			
10–22 d	36	1, and $140 in any quarter	X	X	
26 g	26 g	3 in 20 weeks	X		
12	26	4 in 20 weeks			
15+	30	1 at any time	X	X	
26	26	4 in 20 weeks; or 10 in 3 weeks; or 4 in any quarter and $5,000; or $20,000 in any year	X	X	
12+	34	4 in 20 weeks; or $10,000 in any quarter; or $6,000 in any year	X	X	
11–15 d	26	1, and $500 in any year			

TABLE 7 · STATE LABOR LAWS FOR WOMEN, AS OF JANUARY 1965

STATE OR OTHER JURISDICTION	HOURS				MINIMUM WAGE		EQUAL PAY	INDUSTRIAL HOMEWORK	EMPLOYMENT BEFORE AND AFTER CHILDBIRTH	OCCUPATIONAL LIMITATIONS	WORKING CONDITIONS		FACILITIES		
	MAXIMUM DAILY—WEEKLY a	DAY OF REST	MEAL AND/OR REST PERIOD	NIGHT WORK PROHIBITED AND/OR REGULATED	STATUTORY RATE	WAGE BOARD PROVISIONS					SEATING	WEIGHT LIFTING	LUNCH ROOM	DRESSING, REST ROOMS	WASHROOM TOILETS
Alabama	b									X	X				X
Alaska	c				X d		X			X	X	X	X	X	X
Arizona	8–48	X	X	X e		X	X			X	X			X	X
Arkansas	8	X	X		X		X			X			X		X
California	8–48	X d	X	X		X	X	X		X	X	X		X	X
Colorado	8–48	X	X			X	X	X		X	X			X	X
Connecticut	8–48	X	X	X	X d	X d	X	X	X	X	X			X	X
Delaware	10–55	X	X	X						X e	X		X		X
Dist. of Columbia	8–48	X	X	X e		X					X				X
Florida	b									X e	X				
Georgia	10–60 d									X	X	X			X
Hawaii	c				X d		X	X							
Idaho	8–48 f	X d	X		X d			X			X				
Illinois	8–48	X	X	X		X	X	X		X	X		X	X	X
Indiana			X					X		X	X			X	X
Iowa										X e	X				X
Kansas	8–48	X	X	X		X				X	X		X	X	X
Kentucky	10–60	g	X			X				X	X			X	X
Louisiana	8–48	X	X			X					X			X	
Maine	9–50		X		X d		X			X e	X				X
Maryland	10–60	b	X	X			X	X		X		X		X	X
Massachusetts	9–48	X d	X	X	X d	X d	X	X	X	X	X	X	X	X	X
Michigan	9–54				X	X	X	X		X		X		X	X
Minnesota	54	b			X	X				X		X	X	X	X
Mississippi	10–60	b											X	X	X
Missouri	9–54	b					X	X	X	X	X			X	X

State	Basic hour standard									
Montana	8-48 d					X		X e	X	X	X
Nebraska	9-54	b	X	X			X	X		X	X
Nevada	8-48	X	X					X			X
New Hampshire	10-48	X d	X	X			X	X			X
New Jersey	10-54	X	X d	X	h	X	X e	X	X	X	X
New Mexico	8-48	X	X d				X e	X			
New York	8-48	X d	X	X d	X	X	X	X	X	X	X
North Carolina	9-48	X	X d				X e	X			X
North Dakota	8½-48	X	X			X		X	X	X	X
Ohio	8-48	X	X			X	X	X	X	X	X
Oklahoma	9-54		X				X	X			X
Oregon	8-44	X	X			X	X	X	X	X	X
Pennsylvania	10-48	X	X d		X	X	X	X	X	X	X
Rhode Island	9-48	g	X d	X	h	X	X e	X	X	X	X
South Carolina	10-55 d	X	X			X	X e	X			X
South Dakota	10-54		X		X			X	X	X	X
Tennessee	10-50				X			X	X	X	X
Texas	9-54				X		X e	X	X	X	X
Utah	8-48	X	X			X	X	X	X	X	X
Vermont	9-50		X d		X		X	X			X
Virginia	9-48	b					X	X		X	X
Washington	8	X	X d		X	X	X	X	X	X	X
West Virginia		b	X			X	X e	X			X
Wisconsin	9-50	X d	X		X	X	X	X	X	X	X
Wyoming	8-49 i	X d	X		X	X	X	X	X	X	X

a Highest standard established, applicable to one or more industries or occupations.

b No law limiting the workweek to 6 days; however, law, applicable to both men and women, prohibits employment on Sunday, with specified exceptions.

c Wage and hour law requires payment of premium rates to both men and women for time worked over specified hours.

d Law also covers men.

e Law applicable only to employees under 21 years of age.

f Females may not be employed over 8 hours a day or 48 hours a week without payment of 1½ times the rate for hours worked in excess of 8 a day or 48 a week.

g Law requires payment of overtime rates to both men and women for work on seventh day or on Sunday.

h Provision for compensation only (under Temporary Disability Insurance Act).

i Law permits employment of females over 8 hours a day, provided time and one-half is paid for each hour worked over 8 a day in a 12-hour period.

TABLE 8 · STATE LAWS WITH RESPECT TO JURY SERVICE BY WOMEN, AS OF JANUARY 1965

STATE OR OTHER JURISDICTION	WOMEN SERVE ON SAME BASIS AS MEN	WOMEN MAY CLAIM EXEMPTION ON BASIS OF:		WOMEN MAY SERVE ONLY IF REGISTERED WITH CLERK	WOMEN MAY NOT SERVE
		SEX	CHILD CARE OR FAMILY RESPONSIBILITIES a		
Alabama					X
Alaska		X			
Arizona	X				
Arkansas		X			
California	X		b		
Colorado	X		b		
Connecticut			X		
Delaware	X				
District of Columbia		X			
Florida				X	
Georgia		X	X		
Hawaii	X				
Idaho	X				
Illinois	X				
Indiana	X				
Iowa	X				
Kansas		X			
Kentucky	X				
Louisiana				X	
Maine	X				
Maryland	19 c	4 c			
Massachusetts		d	X		
Michigan	X		b		
Minnesota		X			
Mississippi					X
Missouri		X			
Montana	X		b		
Nebraska		d, e	X		
Nevada		X			
New Hampshire				X	
New Jersey	X		b		
New Mexico	X				
New York		X			
North Carolina			X		
North Dakota		X			
Ohio	X				
Oklahoma			X		
Oregon	X				
Pennsylvania	X				
Rhode Island		X e			
South Carolina					X
South Dakota	X				
Tennessee		X			
Texas			X		
Utah			X		
Vermont	X				
Virginia		X			
Washington		X			
West Virginia	X				
Wisconsin		X			
Wyoming			X		

a Other than general excuse for hardship. d Not required to serve in trials involving certain crimes.
b Exemption allowed to either sex. e Women included when courthouse facilities permit.
c Number of counties.

TABLE 9 · STATE LAWS GOVERNING DOMICILE OF MARRIED WOMEN, AS OF JANUARY 1965

STATE OR OTHER JURISDICTION	SEPARATE DOMICILE FOR ALL PURPOSES			SEPARATE DOMICILE FOR:				
	WITHOUT LIMITATION	WIFE LIVING APART FROM HUSBAND		VOTING	JURY DUTY	PUBLIC OFFICE	PROBATE	TAXA-TION
		WITH HIS CONSENT OR ACQUIESCENCE	FOR CAUSE					
ALL STATES	4	22	43	15	5	6	5	7
Alabama								X
Alaska			X					
Arizona		X	X	X				
Arkansas	X	X	X					
California			X	X				
Colorado								
Connecticut		X	X	X				
Delaware	X	X	X					
District of Columbia		X	X					
Florida			X				X	
Georgia		X	X					
Hawaii	X	X	X					
Idaho			X					
Illinois		X	X					
Indiana		X	X					
Iowa			X					
Kansas			X					
Kentucky		X	X	X				X
Louisiana			X					
Maine			X	X	X	X		
Maryland			X					
Massachusetts			X	X				
Michigan			X			X		
Minnesota			X					
Mississippi								
Missouri		X	X					
Montana			X					
Nebraska			X					
Nevada		X	X	X	X	X	X	X
New Hampshire	X	X	X					
New Jersey		X	X	X	X	X	X	X
New Mexico								
New York		X	X	X	X	X	X	X
North Carolina			X	X				
North Dakota			X					
Ohio		X	X	X				X
Oklahoma								
Oregon		X	X					
Pennsylvania			X					
Rhode Island			X					
South Carolina		X	X					
South Dakota			X					
Tennessee		X	X					
Texas			X					
Utah								
Vermont			X	X				
Virginia		X	X	X				X
Washington		X	X				X	
West Virginia		X	X					
Wisconsin			X	X	X	X		
Wyoming								

TABLE 10 · STATE MARRIAGE LAWS, AS OF JANUARY 1965

STATE OR OTHER JURISDICTION	AGE AT WHICH MARRIAGE CAN BE CONTRACTED WITH PARENTAL CONSENT		AGE BELOW WHICH PARENTAL CONSENT IS REQUIRED	
	MALE	FEMALE	MALE	FEMALE
Alabama	17 *a*	14 *a*	21	18
Alaska	18 *d*	16 *d*	21	18
Arizona	18 *d*	16 *d*	21	18
Arkansas	18 *d*	16 *d*	21	18
California	18 *a, e*	16 *a, e*	21	18
Colorado	16 *e*	16 *e*	21	18
Connecticut	16 *e*	16 *e*	21	21
Delaware	18 *d*	16 *d*	21	18
District of Columbia	18 *a*	16 *a*	21	18
Florida	18 *a, d*	16 *a, d*	21	21
Georgia	18 *d, g*	16 *d, g*	21 *g*	21 *g*
Hawaii	18	16 *e*	20	20
Idaho	15	15 *e*	18	18
Illinois	18	16	21	18
Indiana	18 *d*	16 *d*	21	18
Iowa	18 *d*	16 *d*	21	18
Kansas	18 *e*	16 *e*	21	18
Kentucky	18 *a, d*	16 *a, d*	21	21
Louisiana	18 *e*	16 *e*	21	21
Maine	16 *e*	16 *e*	21	18
Maryland	18 *d*	16 *d*	21	18
Massachusetts	18 *e*	16 *e*	21	18
Michigan	*j*	16 *d*	18	18
Minnesota	18 *a*	16 *k*	21	18

a Parental consent is not required if minor was previously married.
b Indicates common-law marriage recognized.
c Venereal diseases.
d Statute establishes procedure whereby younger parties may obtain license in case of pregnancy or birth of a child.
e In special circumstances statute establishes procedure whereby younger parties may obtain license.

f Residents, 24 hours; nonresidents, 96 hours.
g If parties are under 21, notice must be posted unless parent of female consents in person, but if female is under 18, consent of parent is required.
h Unless parties are 21 years or more, or female is pregnant.
i Feeblemindedness.
j No provision in law for parental consent for males.

244

TABLE 10 · CONTINUED

| COMMON-LAW MARRIAGE RECOGNIZED | PHYSICAL EXAMINATION AND BLOOD TEST FOR MALE AND FEMALE | | WAITING PERIOD | |
	MAXIMUM PERIOD BETWEEN EXAMINATION AND ISSUANCE OF MARRIAGE LICENSE	SCOPE OF MEDICAL EXAMINATION	BEFORE ISSUANCE OF LICENSE	AFTER ISSUANCE OF LICENSE
b	30 days	c		
	30 days	c	3 days	
	30 days	c		
	30 days	c	3 days	
	30 days	c		
b	30 days	c		
	40 days	c	4 days	
	30 days	c		f
b			3 days	
b	30 days	c	3 days	
b	30 days	c	3 days h	
	30 days	c	3 days	
b	30 days	c		
	15 days	c		
	30 days	c	3 days	
b	20 days	c	3 days	
b	30 days	c, i	3 days	
	15 days	c	3 days	
	10 days	c		72 hours
	30 days	c	5 days	
			48 hours	
	30 days	c	3 days	
	30 days	c	3 days	
			5 days	

k Parental consent and permission of judge required.

l Below age of consent parties need parental consent and permission of judge.

m Marriage may not be solemnized within 3 days from date on which specimen for serological test was taken.

n Subject to uncontrolled epileptic attacks, idiocy, imbecility, mental defectiveness, unsound mind, infectious tuberculosis, and venereal diseases.

o 48 hours if both are nonresidents.

p Feeblemindedness, imbecility, insanity, chronic alcoholism, and venereal diseases. (Also in Washington, advanced tuberculosis, and, if male, contageous venereal disease.)

q 3 days if one or both parties are below the age for marriage without parental consent.

r Time limit between examination and expiration of marriage license.

TABLE 10 · STATE MARRIAGE LAWS, AS OF JANUARY 1965

STATE OR OTHER JURISDICTION	AGE AT WHICH MARRIAGE CAN BE CONTRACTED WITH PARENTAL CONSENT		AGE BELOW WHICH PARENTAL CONSENT IS REQUIRED	
	MALE	FEMALE	MALE	FEMALE
Mississippi	17 e	15 e	21	21
Missouri	15 e	15 e	21	18
Montana	18 e	16 e	21	18
Nebraska	18 d	16 d	21	21
Nevada	18 a, e	16 a, e	21	18
New Hampshire	l	l	20	18
New Jersey	18 e	16 e	21	18
New Mexico	18 d	16 d	21	18
New York	16	16 e	21	18
North Carolina	16	16 d	18	18
North Dakota	18	15	21	18
Ohio	18 d	16 d	21	21
Oklahoma	18 d	15 d	21	18
Oregon	18	15	21	18
Pennsylvania	16 e	16 e	21	21
Rhode Island	18 e	16 e	21	21
South Carolina	16 d	14 d	18	18
South Dakota	18 d	16 d	21	18
Tennessee	16 e	16 e	21	21
Texas	16	14	21	18
Utah	16 a	14 a	21	18
Vermont	18 e	16 e	21	18
Virginia	18 a, d	16 a, d	21	21
Washington	17 e	17 e	21	18
West Virginia	18 a	16 a	21	21
Wisconsin	18	16	21	18
Wyoming	18	16	21	21

s Venereal diseases, feeblemindedness, mental illness, drug addiction and chronic alcoholism.

t Infectious tuberculosis and venereal diseases.

TABLE 10 · CONTINUED

COMMON-LAW MARRIAGE RECOGNIZED	PHYSICAL EXAMINATION AND BLOOD TEST FOR MALE AND FEMALE		WAITING PERIOD	
	MAXIMUM PERIOD BETWEEN EXAMINATION AND ISSUANCE OF MARRIAGE LICENSE	SCOPE OF MEDICAL EXAMINATION	BEFORE ISSUANCE OF LICENSE	AFTER ISSUANCE OF LICENSE
	30 days	c	3 days	
	15 days	c	3 days	
b	20 days	c	5 days	
	30 days	c		
		c		
	30 days	c	5 days	
	30 days	c	72 hours	
	30 days	c		
	30 days	c		24 hours m
	30 days	n	o	
	30 days	p		
b	30 days	c	5 days	
b	30 days	c	q	
	30 days r	s	7 days	
b	30 days	c	3 days	
b	40 days	t		u
b			24 hours	
	20 days	c		
	30 days	c	3 days v	
b	15 days	c	q	
	30 days	c		
	30 days	c		5 days
	30 days	c		
		p	3 days	
	30 days	c	3 days	
	20 days	c	5 days	
	30 days	c		

u If female is nonresident, must complete and sign license 5 days prior to marriage.

v Does not apply when parties are over 21 years of age.

TABLE 11 · STATE DIVORCE LAWS, AS OF JANUARY 1965

STATE OR OTHER JURISDICTION	REQUIRED RESIDENCE BEFORE FILING SUIT FOR DIVORCE	ADULTERY	MENTAL AND/OR PHYSICAL CRUELTY	DESERTION	ALCOHOLISM	IMPOTENCY	NON-SUPPORT	INSANITY	PREGNANCY AT MARRIAGE	BIGAMY
				GROUNDS FOR ABSOLUTE DIVORCE						
Alabama	b	a	a	1 yr.	a	a	a, c	5 yrs.	a	
Alaska	1 yr.	a	a	1 yr.	a	a	a	18 mos.		
Arizona	1 yr.	a	a	1 yr.	a	a	a		a	
Arkansas	2 mos.	a	a	1 yr.	a	a	a, i	3 yrs.		a
California	1 yr.	a	a	1 yr.	a		a	3 yrs.		
Colorado	1 yr. k	a	a	1 yr.	a	a	a	3 yrs.		
Connecticut	3 yrs. k	a	a	3 yrs.	a			5 yrs.		
Delaware	2 yrs. k	a	a	2 yrs.	a		a	5 yrs.		a
District of Columbia	2 yrs. k	a		2 yrs.						
Florida	6 mos.	a	a	1 yr.	a	a				a
Georgia	6 mos.	a	a	1 yr.	a	a		2 yrs.	a	
Hawaii	2 yrs.	a	a	6 mos.	a		a	3 yrs.		
Idaho	6 wks.	a	a	1 yr.	a		a	3 yrs.		
Illinois	1 yr. k	a	a	1 yr.	a	a				a
Indiana	1 yr. s	a	a	2 yrs.	a	a	a	5 yrs.		
Iowa	1 yr.	a	a	2 yrs.	a				a, v	
Kansas	1 yr. w	a	a	1 yr.	a	a	a	5 yrs.	a	a
Kentucky	1 yr.	a	a	1 yr.	a, x	a		5 yrs.	a	
Louisiana	aa	a								
Maine	6 mos. k	a	a	3 yrs.	a	a	a			
Maryland	1 yr. ad	a		18 mos.		a		3 yrs.		
Massachusetts	5 yrs. k	a	a	3 yrs.	a	a	a			
Michigan	1 yr. k	a	a	2 yrs.	a	a	a			

a Indicates ground for absolute divorce
b No specific period, except 1 year when ground is desertion or defendant is nonresident, or 2 years if wife sues husband for nonsupport.
c To wife, living separate and apart from husband, as resident of the state for 2 years before suit, and without support from him during such time.
d May be enlarged into an absolute divorce after expiration of 4 years. *Connecticut:* any time after decree of separation; *Hawaii:* 2 years after decree for separate maintenance or from bed and board.
e Crime against nature.
f Except to each other.
g Incompatibility.
h Crime before marriage.
i Also to husband in certain circumstances.

j Final decree is not entered until 1 year after interlocutory decree.
k Under certain circumstances a lesser period of time may be required.
l Female under 16, male under 18, complaining party under age of consent at time of marriage has not confirmed the marriage after reaching such age.
m In the discretion of the court.
n Habitual violent and ungovernable temper.
o Defendant obtained divorce from plaintiff in another state.
p Mental incapacity.
q Under decree of separate maintenance.
r Loathsome disease.
s Five years if on ground of insanity.
t Two years where service on defendant is only by publication.

TABLE 11 · CONTINUED

SEPARATION OR ABSENCE	FELONY CONVICTION OR IMPRISONMENT	DRUG ADDICTION	FRAUD, FORCE, OR DURESS	INFAMOUS CRIME	RELATIONSHIP WITHIN PROHIBITED DEGREES	PRIOR DECREE OF LIMITED DIVORCE	OTHER	PERIOD BEFORE PARTIES MAY REMARRY AFTER FINAL DECREE — PLAINTIFF	DEFENDANT	DIVORCE GRANTED ON SAME GROUNDS FOR MEN AND WOMEN
	a	a				d	e	60 days f	60 days f	
	a	a					g			
5 yrs.	a			a			h	1 yr.	1 yr.	
3 yrs.	a			a						X
	a							j	j	
3 yrs.	a	a								
7 yrs.	a		a	a		d				X
3 yrs.	a						l	3 mos. m	3 mos. m	
5 yrs.	a						u	6 mos.	6 mos.	X
		a			a		n, o			X
	a			a		a	p	m	m	
2 yrs. q	a	a				d				
5 yrs.	a									
	a			a			r			X
				a			t			
	a							1 yr. f, m	1 yr. f, m	
	a	a						6 mos.	6 mos.	
5 yrs.	a			a			r,y,z			
2 yrs.	a						ab	wife, 10 mos.	wife, 10 mos. ac	X
	a									
18 mos.	a						ae			X
	a	a							2 yrs.	
	a						o	af		

u Limited divorce may be enlarged into absolute divorce after 2 years.

v Unless at time of marriage husband had an illegitimate child living which fact was not known to wife.

w Five years if on ground of insanity and insane spouse is in out-of-state institution.

x If on part of the husband, accompanied by wasting of husband's estate to the detriment of the wife and children.

y Joining religious sect disbelieving in marriage.

z Unchaste behavior on part of wife after marriage.

aa No statutory requirement for adultery or felony conviction; 2 years when ground is separation.

ab Limited divorce may be enlarged into absolute divorce after 1 year for innocent spouse, and after 1 year and 60 days for guilty spouse.

ac When divorce is granted on ground of adultry, guilty party cannot marry the accomplice in adultery, during lifetime of former spouse.

ad No specific period required except 1 year if cause occurred out of state, and 2 years if on ground of insanity.

ae Any cause which renders marriage null and void ab initio.

af Not more than 2 years in court's discretion.

ag Limited divorce may be enlarged into absolute divorce after 5 years.

ah When divorce is granted on ground of adultery, court may prohibit remarriage. After 1 year court may remove disability upon satisfactory evidence of reformation.

ai Husband a vagrant.

TABLE 11 · STATE DIVORCE LAWS, AS OF JANUARY 1965

STATE OR OTHER JURISDICTION	REQUIRED RESIDENCE BEFORE FILING SUIT FOR DIVORCE	GROUNDS FOR ABSOLUTE DIVORCE								
		ADULTERY	MENTAL AND/OR PHYSICAL CRUELTY	DESERTION	ALCOHOLISM	IMPOTENCY	NON-SUPPORT	INSANITY	PREGNANCY AT MARRIAGE	BIGAMY
Minnesota	1 yr. *k*	*a*	*a*	1 yr.	*a*	*a*		5 yrs.		
Mississippi	1 yr.	*a*	*a*	1 yr.	*a*	*a*		3 yrs.	*a*	*a*
Missouri	1 yr. *k*	*a*	*a*	1 yr.	*a*	*a*			*a*	*a*
Montana	1 yr.	*a*	*a*	1 yr.	*a*		*a*	5 yrs.		
Nebraska	2 yrs. *k*	*a*	*a*	2 yrs.	*a*	*a*	*a*	5 yrs.		
Nevada	6 wks. *k*	*a*	*a*	1 yr.	*a*	*a*	*a*	2 yrs.		
New Hampshire	1 yr. *k*	*a*	*a*	2 yrs.	*a*	*a*	*a*			
New Jersey	2 yrs. *k*	*a*	*a*	2 yrs.						
New Mexico	1 yr.	*a*	*a*	*a*	*a*	*a*	*a*	5 yrs.	*a*	
New York	*ak*	*a*								
North Carolina	6 mos.	*a*				*a*		5 yrs.	*a*	
North Dakota	1 yr. *s*	*a*	*a*	1 yr.	*a*		*a, i*	5 yrs.		
Ohio	1 yr.	*a*	*a*		*a*	*a*	*a*			*a*
Oklahoma	6 mos. *w*	*a*	*a*	1 yr.	*a*	*a*	*q*	5 yrs.	*a*	
Oregon	1 yr.	*a*	*a*	1 yr.	*a*	*a*		3 yrs.		
Pennsylvania	1 yr.	*a*	*a*	2 yrs.		*a*				*a*
Rhode Island	2 yrs.	*a*	*a*	5 yrs.*ao*	*a*	*a*	*a*			
South Carolina	1 yr.	*a*	*a*	1 yr.	*a*					
South Dakota	1 yr. *k*	*a*	*a*	1 yr.	*a*		*a*	5 yrs.		
Tennessee	1 yr.	*a*	*a*	1 yr.	*a*	*a*	*a*		*a*	*a*
Texas	12 mos.	*a*	*a*	3 yrs.				5 yrs.		
Utah	3 mos.	*a*	*a*	1 yr.	*a*	*a*	*a*	*a*		
Vermont	6 mos. *au*	*a*		3 yrs.			*a*	5 yrs.		
Virginia	1 yr.	*a*		1 yr.		*a*			*a*	
Washington	1 yr.	*a*	*a*	1 yr.	*a*	*a*	*a*	2 yrs.		
West Virginia	2 yrs. *k*	*a*	*a*	1 yr.	*a*					
Wisconsin	2 yrs.	*a*	*a*	1 yr.	*a*		*a*			
Wyoming	60 days *k*	*a*	*a*	1 yr.	*a*	*a*	*a*	2 yrs.	*a*	

aj Wife's absence out of state for 10 years without husband's consent.

ak No time specified. Parties must be residents when offense committed; or married in state; or plaintiff resident when offense committed and action commenced; or offense committed in state and injured party resident when action commenced.

al Defendant is prohibited from remarrying unless after 3 years court removes disability upon satisfactory evidence of reformation.

am When husband is entitled to a divorce and alimony or child support from husband is granted, the decree may be delayed until security is entered for payment.

an Incapable of procreation.

ao Or a lesser time in court's discretion.

ap Void or voidable marriage.

aq Gross misbehavior or wickedness. Loss of citizenship rights of one party due to crime; presumption of death.

ar When divorce is for adultery, guilty party cannot remarry except to the innocent person, until the death of the other.

as To husband for wife's refusal to move with him to this state without reasonable cause, and

TABLE 11 · CONTINUED

SEPARATION OR ABSENCE	FELONY CONVICTION OR IMPRISONMENT	DRUG ADDICTION	FRAUD, FORCE, OR DURESS	INFAMOUS CRIME	RELATIONSHIP WITHIN PROHIBITED DEGREES	PRIOR DECREE OF LIMITED DIVORCE	OTHER	PERIOD BEFORE PARTIES MAY REMARRY AFTER FINAL DECREE		DIVORCE GRANTED ON SAME GROUNDS FOR MEN AND WOMEN
GROUNDS FOR ABSOLUTE DIVORCE								PLAINTIFF	DEFENDANT	
2 yrs. q	a					ag		6 mos.	6 mos.	X
	a	a			a		p		ah	
	a			a			h, ai			
	a							6 mos.	6 mos.	
	a							6 mos.	6 mos.	
3 yrs.	a			a						
2 yrs.	a						y, aj			
								3 mos. m	3 mos. m	X
	a						g			
									al	X
2 yrs.	a						e			
	a	a				d		m	m	X
1 yr.	a		a				o	am		
	a		a				g, o	6 mos.	6 mos.	
	a							6 mos.	6 mos.	X
	a		a		a		an		ac	X
10 yrs.		a					ap,aq	6 mos.	6 mos.	
		a								X
	a								ar	
2 yrs. as	a			a			an		ac	
7 yrs.	a							at	at	X
3 yrs. q	a							3 mos. m	3 mos. m	
3 yrs.	a						av	6 mos. m	2 yrs. m	
2 yrs.	a			a		aw	e, ax	ay	ay	
5 yrs.	a		a				az	6 mos.	6 mos.	
	a	a						60 days	60 days aaa	X
5 yrs.	a					aab		1 yr.	1 yr.	
2 yrs.	a			a			h, ai			

willfully absenting herself from him for 2 years.
at When divorce is granted on ground of cruelty, neither party may remarry for 12 months except each other.
au One year before final hearing, and 2 years if on ground of insanity.
av Intolerable severity.
aw A limited divorce granted on the ground of cruelty or desertion may be merged with an absolute divorce after one year.
ax Two years fugitive from justice; wife a prostitute prior to marriage.

ay When divorce is granted on ground of adultery, court may decree the guilty party cannot remarry. After 6 months the court may remove disability for good cause. Remarriage of either party forbidden pending appeal.
az Want of legal age or sufficient understanding.
aaa In court's discretion, guilty party may be prohibited from remarrying for a period not to exceed 1 year.
aab Living entirely apart for 5 years pursuant to a judgment of legal separation.

TABLE 12 · ADDITIONAL FACTS ABOUT

STATE OR OTHER JURISDICTION	FEMALE POPULATION 14 YEARS AND OVER			AVERAGE SCHOOL LEAVING AGE *a*	MEDIAN YEARS OF SCHOOL COMPLETED, WOMEN 25 AND OVER	
	TOTAL	WHITE	NONWHITE		WHITE	NONWHITE
Alabama	1,157,899	828,533	329,366	16	10.4	7.0
Alaska	60,024	46,629	5,563	16	12.4	6.5
Arizona	436,091	398,413	37,678	16	12.0	7.2
Arkansas	643,013	515,321	127,692	16	9.8	7.1
California	5,659,129	5,250,791	408,338	16	12.1	10.8
Colorado	616,843	599,500	17,343	16	12.1	11.4
Connecticut	943,664	906,004	37,660	16	11.4	9.5
Delaware	158,088	137,796	20,292	16	11.8	8.7
District of Columbia	313,301	162,387	150,914	16	12.4	10.2
Florida	1,829,192	1,539,010	290,182	16	11.8	7.6
Georgia	1,397,951	1,018,671	379,280	16	10.6	6.7
Hawaii	194,788	59,809	134,979	16	12.4	10.4
Idaho	221,598	218,795	2,803	16	12.1	9.5
Illinois	3,723,281	3,357,257	366,024	16	10.8	9.3
Indiana	1,671,516	1,579,865	91,651	16	11.1	9.4
Iowa	998,595	988,595	10,000	16	12.0	9.9
Kansas	784,183	751,023	33,160	16	12.0	10.1
Kentucky	1,074,244	997,314	76,930	16	8.8	8.5
Louisiana	1,127,057	783,884	343,173	16	10.7	6.5
Maine	349,329	347,632	1,697	16	11.5	10.6
Maryland	1,101,782	927,645	171,390	16	11.1	8.5
Massachusetts	1,972,462	1,929,470	42,992	16	11.8	10.5
Michigan	2,729,762	2,486,544	243,218	16	11.3	9.6
Minnesota	1,196,494	1,183,635	12,859	16	11.6	10.2
Mississippi	746,005	453,895	292,110		11.3	6.7
Missouri	1,621,490	1,482,473	139,017	16	10.1	8.9
Montana	224,898	218,227	6,671	16	12.1	8.7
Nebraska	508,115	496,516	11,599	16	12.1	10.0
Nevada	96,984	90,403	6,581	17	12.2	9.2
New Hampshire	223,604	222,874	730	16	11.3	12.1
New Jersey	2,280,584	2,093,630	186,924	16	10.8	9.1
New Mexico	301,779	280,161	21,618	17	11.8	7.2
New York	6,506,505	5,936,487	570,018	16	10.9	9.6
North Carolina	1,600,721	1,230,147	370,574	16	10.3	7.5
North Dakota	208,196	204,786	3,390	16	10.8	8.6
Ohio	3,501,539	3,230,650	270,889	18	11.3	9.5
Oklahoma	856,366	782,650	73,716	18	11.0	8.8
Oregon	634,732	623,466	11,266	18	12.1	10.3
Pennsylvania	4,272,191	3,961,648	310,543	17	10.5	9.3
Rhode Island	324,077	317,875	6,202	16	10.1	9.6
South Carolina	810,800	548,453	262,347		10.7	6.4
South Dakota	229,673	221,708	7,965	16	11.7	8.7
Tennessee	1,300,500	1,098,246	202,254	17	9.4	8.0
Texas	3,352,809	2,944,773	408,036	16	11.0	8.5
Utah	290,046	285,358	4,688	18	12.2	10.1
Vermont	141,398	141,128	270	16	11.6	9.4
Virginia	1,392,549	1,121,750	268,194		11.4	7.6
Washington	1,002,319	972,678	29,641	16	12.1	10.9
West Virginia	668,074	636,732	31,342	16	9.0	8.8
Wisconsin	1,396,001	1,368,382	27,619	16	11.0	9.4
Wyoming	109,013	107,121	1,892	17	12.2	9.2

a Although the age given is the upper compulsory age for school attendance, children may leave school earlier under certain conditions. In different states acceptable reasons include completion of high school, completion of the eighth grade, entering employment, economic need, or physical or mental

FEMALE HEADS OF FAMILIES		FAMILIES WITH INCOME UNDER $3,000		FEMALE LABOR FORCE AS PERCENTAGE OF FEMALE POPULATION			
WHITE	NONWHITE	TOTAL IN THOUSANDS	PER CENT WITH FEMALE HEAD	ALL WOMEN	SINGLE WOMEN	MARRIED WOMEN, HUSBANDS PRESENT	WOMEN OF OTHER MARITAL STATUS
47,458	44,508	309	21	32	30	31	38
1,304	985	7	17	32	36	29	40
12,440	1,265	66	22	40	45	36	53
27,949	15,422	216	15	29	27	28	33
320,918	46,572	563	28	36	42	32	42
32,292	1,909	80	20	35	43	31	39
51,884	5,216	64	28	39	52	34	39
7,250	2,759	18	26	36	43	32	42
13,178	19,106	30	39	52	59	46	54
5,626	2,260	368	20	35	36	32	42
61,480	52,346	338	22	38	35	37	41
4,300	7,542	17	35	40	40	40	37
9,474	235	35	15	32	35	31	36
179,894	51,676	389	24	36	49	31	40
79,628	10,608	215	19	34	41	30	39
45,919	1,258	180	13	32	43	28	34
34,886	3,819	127	16	32	41	29	36
62,180	10,519	286	16	27	31	25	31
46,061	46,763	275	23	30	31	27	36
21,214	161	55	20	34	41	31	35
51,296	21,241	116	28	36	41	33	42
134,122	6,179	160	30	38	54	32	36
119,855	29,693	305	23	33	44	28	39
59,462	1,549	179	14	34	51	29	35
25,605	35,896	259	18	33	27	33	38
81,861	20,096	305	18	33	42	30	36
10,357	658	33	16	33	41	29	39
22,893	1,554	95	12	33	46	29	36
4,842	591	9	23	41	41	38	54
13,112	35	23	23	40	48	38	38
117,668	23,617	180	27	36	49	30	39
16,259	2,024	54	21	30	35	27	39
365,436	82,119	600	28	37	52	30	40
72,809	47,381	406	20	37	32	39	39
8,755	337	43	11	30	41	26	32
8,411	1,456	386	23	33	44	28	39
42,532	11,017	190	18	30	32	29	34
30,488	1,143	78	19	34	39	32	39
245,892	43,336	488	26	33	47	28	36
23,875	1,008	37	31	38	51	34	33
33,642	36,226	214	23	38	34	40	39
9,654	851	56	10	31	42	28	34
68,771	25,864	342	18	33	33	32	37
161,113	52,369	688	19	33	35	30	42
13,308	346	31	21	32	40	29	37
8,210	10	22	18	34	41	31	36
72,509	32,888	266	24	34	36	32	38
50,031	2,889	111	22	34	40	32	38
45,193	3,728	151	21	24	29	21	30
67,719	3,476	172	17	34	47	30	35
4,750	173	14	18	34	41	31	43

disability. In over half the states, children may leave school if they have completed the eighth grade and are employed, or if they are 14 years of age and employed, or if they are 14 and have completed the eighth grade regardless of employment.

Acknowledgments and References of the President's Commission

The President's Commission on the Status of Women desires to recognize the service rendered by the many individuals and organizations that associated themselves with its work in one phase or another. We regret that even our extensive lists do not include them all. We owe a particular debt to individuals in virtually every federal agency, and especially in the Women's Bureau of the United States Department of Labor. We owe a comparable debt to the Congress, whose support and appropriations made our work possible and permitted publication in this form.

The seven Committees that explored in depth the areas indicated in the Executive order establishing the Commission worked intensively for over a year in the areas of their specialization; their findings, and their suggestions for recommendations, were of inestimable help to the Commission in reaching its own conclusions. Technical secretaries assigned to each Committee provided continuing staff work and, together with Committee members, drafted their final reports.

The final reports of the Committees, which give substantiation for the recommendations of the Commissions, have been published by the Commission as separate documents for ready reference by individuals and groups working in particular fields. These reports contain recommendations and analysis in broader areas than could be included in the Commission's report. Each Committee's conclusions are its own, reflecting its concerns and beliefs; these were developed prior to the taking of final decisions by the Commission.

The Commission is also publishing, in a single document, summaries of what was said at four consultations on the subject of "Private Employment Opportunities," "New Patterns in Volunteer Work," "Portrayal of Women by the Mass Media," and "Problems of Negro Women."

These publications may be obtained from the Women's Bureau, United States Department of Labor, or from the Superintendent of Documents, Washington, D. C., 20402.

During the sessions of the Committees, many materials—studies, briefs, statements in support of various viewpoints—were presented by individuals, organizations, and agencies, and their contents considered by the Committees as they reached their conclusions. These materials have been deposited with the Women's Bureau, United States Department of Labor, where interested persons may consult them; specific references are contained in the Committee reports. Limited numbers of some of them are available for free distribution in mimeographed form.

Special acknowledgment should be made of a general background memorandum on *Women Today: Trends and Issues* prepared by Dr. Caroline F. Ware at Commission request. Initially available in mimeographed form under Commission imprint, it was republished by the National Board of the Young Women's Christian Association of the United States of America.

Below are listed the seven working committees, the names and affiliations of their members at the time of their appointment, and the names of their technical secretaries.

COMMITTEE ON CIVIL AND POLITICAL RIGHTS

Honorable Edith Green, *Chairman and Commission Member*
Miss Marguerite Rawalt, *Co-chairman and Commission Member*
Mrs. Harper Andrews, Former President, Illinois League of Women Voters, Kewanee, Ill.
Mrs. Angela Bambace, Manager, Upper South Department, and Vice President, International Ladies' Garment Workers Union
James B. Carey, President, International Union of Electrical, Radio and Machine Workers
Miss Gladys Everett, Attorney, Portland, Ore.
Mrs. Yarnall Jacobs, President, National Council of Women of the United States, Inc.
John M. Kernochan, Director, Legislative Drafting Research Fund, Columbia University
Judge Florence Kerins Murray, Associate Justice, Rhode Island Superior Court
Miss Pauli Murray, Senior Fellow, Law School, Yale University
Mrs. E. Lee Ozbirn, President, General Federation of Women's Clubs
Miss Katherine Peden, President, National Federation of Business and Professional Women's Clubs, Inc.
Mrs. Harriet F. Pilpel, Attorney, Greenbaum, Wolff and Ernest, New York
Frank E. A. Sander, Professor of Law, Law School of Harvard University
Technical Secretary, Miss Mary Eastwood

255

COMMITTEE ON EDUCATION

Dr. Mary I. Bunting, *Chairman and Commission Member*
Miss Edna P. Amidon, Director, Home Economics Education Branch, United States Office of Education
Mrs. Algie E. Ballif, Former President, Utah School Board Association
Mrs. John D. Briscoe, Board of Directors, League of Women Voters of the United States
Mrs. Opal D. David, Former Director, Commission on the Education of Women, American Council on Education
Dr. Elizabeth M. Drews, Professor, College of Education, Michigan State University
Dr. Seymour M. Farber, Assistant Dean for Continuing Education in Health Sciences, University of California, San Francisco Medical Center
Mrs. Raymond Harvey, Dean, School of Nursing, Tuskegee Institute
Mrs. Agnes E. Meyer, Washington, D. C.
Dr. Kenneth E. Oberholtzer, Superintendent, Denver Public Schools
Dr. Esther Raushenbush, Director, Center of Continuing Education, Sarah Lawrence College
Lawrence Rogin, Director of Education, AFL–CIO
Miss Helen B. Schleman, Dean of Women, Purdue University
Dr. Virginia L. Senders, Lecturer, Former Coordinator of Minnesota Plan, Lincoln, Mass.
Dr. Pauline Tompkins, General Director, American Association of University Women
Technical Secretary, Mrs. Antonia H. Chayes

COMMITTEE ON FEDERAL EMPLOYMENT

Miss Margaret Hickey, *Chairman and Commission Member*
E. C. Hallbeck, Chairman, Government Employes Council, AFL–CIO
Judge Lucy Somerville Howorth, Former General Counsel, War Claims Commission, Cleveland, Miss.
Honorable Stephen S. Jackson, Deputy Assistant Secretary of Defense for Manpower, United States Department of Defense
Mrs. Esther Johnson, Secretary-Treasurer, American Federation of Government Employees
Honorable Roger W. Jones, Bureau of the Budget
Dr. Esther Lloyd-Jones, Head, Department of Guidance and Student Personnel Administration, Columbia University
Honorable John W. Macy, Jr., *Commission Member*
Dr. Jeanne L. Noble, President, Delta Sigma Theta, and Assistant Professor, Center for Human Relations Studies, New York University
Dr. Peter H. Rossi, Director, National Opinion Research Center, Chicago
Honorable Kathryn H. Stone, Virginia House of Delegates, and Director, Human Resources Program, Washington Center for Metropolitan Studies
Honorable Tyler Thompson, Director General of the Foreign Service, United States Department of State
Dr. Kenneth O. Warner, Director, Public Personnel Association
Technical Secretary, Mrs. Catherine S. East

COMMITTEE ON HOME AND COMMUNITY

Dr. Cynthia C. Wedel, *Chairman and Commission Member*
Mrs. Marguerite H. Coleman, Supervisor of Special Placement Services, New York
    State Division of Employment
Dr. Rosa L. Gragg, President, National Association of Colored Women's Clubs, Inc.
Mrs. Randolph Guggenheimer, President, National Committee for Day Care of
    Children, Inc.
Mrs. Viola H. Hymes, *Commission Member*
Mrs. Emerson Hynes, Arlington, Va.
Maurice Lazarus, President, Wm. Filene's Sons Co., Boston
Mrs. Martha Reynolds, United Community Services, AFL–CIO, Grand Rapids
Charles I. Schottland, Dean of Faculty, Brandeis University
Miss Ella V. Stonsby, Dean of College of Nursing, Rutgers University
Dr. Caroline F. Ware, *Commission Member*
Dr. Esther M. Westervelt, Instructor, Guidance and Personnel Administration,
    Teachers College, Columbia University
Technical Secretaries, Miss Ella C. Ketchin and Mrs. Margaret M. Morris

COMMITTEE ON PRIVATE EMPLOYMENT

Dr. Richard A. Lester, *Chairman and Commission Member*
Jacob Clayman, Administrative Director, Industrial Union Department, AFL–CIO
Miss Caroline Davis, Director, Women's Department, United Automobile, Aero-
    space and Agricultural Implement Workers of America
Miss Muriel Ferris, Legislative Assistant to Honorable Philip A. Hart, United States
    Senate
Charles W. Gasque, Jr., Assistant Commissioner for Procurement Policy, General
    Services Administration
Miss Dorothy Height, *Commission Member*
Joseph D. Keenan, Secretary, International Brotherhood of Electrical Workers
Norman E. Nicholson, *Commission Member*
Frank Pace, Jr., General Dynamics Corp., New York
Mrs. Ogden Reid, Former President, Board Chairman, *New York Herald Tribune*
John A. Roosevelt, Bache and Co., New York
Samuel Silver, Industrial Relations Adviser, Office of Assistant Secretary of De-
    fense for Manpower, United States Department of Defense
Technical Secretary, Sam A. Morgenstein

COMMITTEE ON PROTECTIVE LABOR LEGISLATION

Miss Margaret J. Mealey, *Chairman and Commission Member*
Mrs. Margaret F. Ackroyd, Chief, Division of Women and Children, Rhode Island
    State Department of Labor
Dr. Doris Boyle, Professor of Economics, Loyola College, Baltimore, Md.
Mrs. Mary E. Callahan, *Commission Member*
Dr. Henry David, *Commission Member*
Mrs. Bessie Hillman, Vice President, Amalgamated Clothing Workers of America
Mrs. Paul McClellan Jones, Vice President, National Board, Young Women's Chris-
    tian Association of the United States of America

Mrs. Mary Dublin Keyserling, Associate Director, Conference on Economic Progress

Carl A. McPeak, Special Representative on State Legislation, AFL–CIO

Clarence R. Thornbrough, Commissioner, Arkansas State Department of Labor

S. A. Wesolowski, Assistant to President, Brookshire Knitting Mills, Inc., Manchester, N.H.

Mrs. Addie Wyatt, Field Representative, United Packinghouse, Food and Allied Workers

Technical Secretary, Miss Ella C. Ketchin

COMMITTEE ON SOCIAL INSURANCE AND TAXES

Honorable Maurine B. Neuberger, *Chairman and Commission Member*

Honorable Jessica M. Weis, *Associate Chairman and Commission Member* (*deceased*)

Dr. Eveline M. Burns, Professor of Social Work, New York School of Social Work, Columbia University

Mrs. Margaret B. Dolan, Chairman, Department of Public Health Nursing, University of North Carolina

Dean Fedele F. Fauri, School of Social Work, University of Michigan

Dr. Richard B. Goode, Brookings Institution

Miss Fannie Hardy, Executive Assistant, Arkansas State Insurance Commissioner

Miss Nina Miglionico, Attorney, Birmingham, Ala.

J. Wade Miller, Vice President, W. R. Grace & Co., Cambridge, Mass.

Dr. Raymond Munts, Assistant Director, Social Security Department, AFL–CIO

Mrs. Richard B. Persinger, Chairman, National Public Affairs Committee, Young Women's Christian Association of the United States of America

Technical Secretary, Dr. Merrill G. Murray

CONTRIBUTORS TO COMMISSION MEETINGS

In addition to the members of the Commission and the Committees, the following persons attended meetings of the Commission at various times, either to represent their principals or to make special presentations.

Bess Furman Armstrong, Writer

Hyman H. Bookbinder, Special Assistant to the Secretary of Commerce, United States Department of Commerce

Harvey E. Brazer, Deputy Assistant Secretary of the Treasury, United States Department of the Treasury

Ugo Carusi, Office of United States Senator George D. Aiken

Wilbur J. Cohen, Assistant Secretary of Health, Education, and Welfare (for Legislation), United States Department of Health, Education, and Welfare

Anne Draper, Research Associate, AFL–CIO

Evelyn Harrison, Deputy Director, Bureau of Programs and Standards, United States Civil Service Commission

Grace Hewell, Program Coordination Officer, United State Department of Health, Education, and Welfare

Dorothy H. Jacobson, Assistant to the Secretary of Agriculture, United States Department of Agriculture

Nicholas de B. Katzenbach, Deputy Attorney General, United States Department of Justice

Katie Louchheim, Deputy Assistant Secretary, Bureau of Public Affairs, United States Department of State

Ivan A. Nestingen, Under Secretary, United States Department of Health, Education, and Welfare

John Nolan, Administrative Assistant to the Attorney General, United States Department of Justice

Mrs. Donald Quarles, Chairman, Defense Advisory Committee on Women in the Services

Carlisle P. Runge, Assistant Secretary for Manpower, United States Department of Defense

Norbert Schlei, Assistant Attorney General, Office of Legal Counsel, United States Department of Justice

John F. Skillman, Special Assistant to the Secretary of Commerce, United States Department of Commerce

John S. Stillman, Deputy to the Secretary for Congressional Relations, United States Department of Commerce

Gladys A. Tillett, United States Representative to the United Nations Commission on the Status of Women

Anita Wells, Fiscal Economist, United States Department of the Treasury

Ellen Winston, Commissioner of Welfare, United States Department of Health, Education, and Welfare

FOUR CONSULTATIONS

Attendance at the consultations organized by the Committees and the Commission indicated the widespread interest that has existed in the Commission's work. The document which presents the summaries of what was said at these meetings contains full lists of the attendance at each. The lists below give the names of the individuals, other than members of the Commission and the Committees and federal officials, who took part.

NEW PATTERNS IN VOLUNTEER WORK

Gretchen Abbott, Washington, D. C.
Miriam Albert, B'nai B'rith Women
Eunice P. Baker, National Association of Colored Women's Clubs, Inc.
A. June Bricker, American Home Economics Association
Wilda Camery, American Nurses' Association, Inc.
Sarah W. Coleman, National Association of Colored Women's Clubs, Inc.
Marjorie Collins, New York
Leora Conner, Zonta International
George Dooley, AFL–CIO
Mrs. Robert Egan, National Council of Catholic Women
Etta Engles, American Association of University Women
Mrs. A. G. Gaston, National Council of Negro Women, Inc.
Mrs. Arthur J. Goldberg, Washington, D. C.
Mrs. Maurice Goldberg, B'nai B'rith Women
Mrs. Edward Gudeman, Washington, D. C.

Margaret W. Harlan, Bethesda, Md.

Benjamin Henley, Urban Service Corps, District of Columbia Public Schools

Hulda Hubbell, Volunteer Service Committee, Health and Welfare Council of National Capital Area

T. Margaret Jamer, School Volunteers, New York

Ollie L. Koger, American Legion Auxiliary

Ruth O. Lana, American Association of Retired Persons–National Retired Teachers Association

Margaret Lipchik, Urban Service Corps, District of Columbia Public Schools

Florence W. Low, American Home Economics Association

Edith E. Lowry, National Council on Agricultural Life and Labor

Ruth T. Lucas, Cleveland City Welfare Federation

Lillian T. Majally, National Federation of Business and Professional Women's Clubs, Inc.

Marie McGuire, Public Housing Administration

Mrs. Abbot L. Mills, American National Red Cross

Ernestine C. Milner, Altrusa International, Inc.

Mrs. Stephen J. Nicholas, General Federation of Women's Clubs

Mrs. Alexander S. Parr, Association of the Junior Leagues of America, Inc.

Barbara Phinney, Girl Scouts of the United States of America

Betty Queen, District of Columbia Department of Public Welfare

Mildred Reel, Future Homemakers of America

Edith H. Sherrard, American Association of University Women

Constance Smith, Radcliffe Institute for Independent Study

Mansfield Smith, Experiment in International Living

Hilda Torrop, National Council of Women of the United States, Inc.

Mrs. Arthur E. Whittemore, League of Women Voters of the United States

Mrs. Joseph Willen, National Council of Jewish Women, Inc.

Mrs. J. Skelly Wright, National Association for Mental Health

Emily H. Ziegler, Soroptimist Federation of the Americas, Inc.

PRIVATE EMPLOYMENT OPPORTUNITIES

Eileen Ahern, Continental Can Co.

Charles B. Bailey, Brotherhood of Railway and Steamship Clerks, Freight Handlers, Express and Station Employes

Ethel Beall, Boston University

Mrs. Robert Bishop, Wellesley College

Louise Q. Blodgett, National Consumers League

Irving Bluestone, United Automobile, Aerospace and Agricultural Implement Workers of America

H. T. Brooks, General Dynamics Corp.

E. B. Bruner, American Telephone and Telegraph Co.

William C. Bullard, Kelly Girls Service, Inc.

R. P. Carlson, The Martin Co.

John M. Convery, National Association of Manufacturers

Wesley W. Cook, Textile Workers Union of America

Mrs. C. E. Cortner, Girl Scouts of the United States of America

J. Curtis Counts, Douglas Aircraft Co., Inc.

Lucinda Daniel, National Council of Negro Women, Inc.

Marie Daniels, Rhode Island Department of Employment Security

Mary M. Dewey, Connecticut State Department of Labor
Anne Draper, AFL–CIO
Charles E. Engelbrecht, Insurance Workers International Union
Gerald B. Fadden, Philco Corp.
Walter R. Farrel, Kaiser Industries Corp.
M. Irene Frost, Trenton Trust Co.
G. Roy Fugal, General Electric Co.
Sherman L. Gillespie, Hughes Aircraft Co.
Stephen Habbe, National Industrial Conference Board
Doris Hartman, New Jersey Division of Employment Security
Miriam Healey, Girl Scouts of the United States of America
S. P. Herbert, General Precision Equipment Corp.
Fred Z. Hetzel, United States Employment Service for the District of Columbia
Cernoria D. Johnson, National Urban League
Elizabeth S. Johnson, Pennsylvania Department of Labor and Industry
Gloria Johnson, International Union of Electrical, Radio and Machine Workers
Lowell F. Johnson, American Home Products Corp.
Dan A. Kimball, Aerojet-General Corp.
Paul A. King, Scholastic Magazines, Inc.
Elizabeth J. Kuck, International Harvester Co.
Sarah Leichter, United Hatters, Cap and Millinery Workers International Union
P. B. Lewis, E. I du Pont de Nemours & Co.
Kenneth MacHarg, Sperry Gyroscope Co.
Olya Margolin, National Council of Jewish Women, Inc.
R. W. Markly, Jr., Ford Motor Co.
Betty Martin, Institute of Life Insurance
F. F. McCabe, International Telephone and Telegraph Corp.
F. L. McClure, Radio Corp. of America
Ralph E. McGruther, Bendix Corp.
Eleanor McMillan, The Fashion Group, Inc.
Charles C. McPherson, Stanley Home Products, Inc.
Mrs. G. G. Michelson, Macy's
Minnie C. Miles, National Federation of Business and Professional Women's Clubs, Inc.
Frieda Miller, Easton, Pa.
Eileen Millin, Lobsenz & Co., Inc.
Mrs. C. B. Morgan, General Federation of Women's Clubs
Corma A. Mowrey, National Education Association
Ann Roe, Harvard University
Joseph S. Schieferly, Standard Oil Co. of New Jersey
Mary E. Tobin, New York State Department of Commerce
S. W. Towle, Northrop Corp.
R. A. Whitehorne, International Business Machines Corp.
Paul F. Wold, Campbell Soup Co.

PORTRAYAL OF WOMEN BY THE MASS MEDIA

Ethel J. Alpenfels, Professor of Anthropology, New York University
Curtiss Anderson, Editor, Ladies' Home Journal
Margaret Culkin Banning, Writer
Betsy Talbot Blackwell, Editor, Mademoiselle

Al Capp, Cartoonist
Louis Cowan, Communication Research Center, Brandeis University
Polly Cowan, Station WMCA: Call for Action
Wallace W. Elton, Senior Vice President, J. Walter Thompson Co.
Betty Friedan, Writer
Hartford Gunn, General Manager, Station WGBH
Lorraine Hansberry, Playwright
George Heinemann, Public Affairs, National Broadcasting Co.
Stockton Helffrich, National Association of Broadcasters
Lisa Howard, American Broadcasting Co.
Morton Hunt, Writer
Joseph Klapper, Research Department, Columbia Broadcasting System
Bennett Korn, President, Metropolitan Broadcasting, New York
Gerri Major, Johnson Publications
Marya Mannes, Writer
Rosalind Massow, Women's Editor, Parade
Arthur Mayer, Writer
Herbert R. Mayes, President, McCall Corp.
Kathleen McLaughlin, New York Times
Joy Miller, Women's Editor, Associated Press
Jane Ostrowska, Cowles Publications
Marion K. Sanders, Editor, Harper's Magazine
Perrin Stryker, New York
Margaret Twyman, Community Relations, Motion Picture Association of America
Helen Winston, Producer, Columbia Pictures

PROBLEMS OF NEGRO WOMEN

Walter Davis, Assistant Director, Civil Rights Department, AFL–CIO
Hilda Fortune, New York Urban League
Maude Gadsen, Beauty Owners Association
Cernoria D. Johnson, National Urban League
Lewis Wade Jones, Consultant, Fisk University
John R. Larkins, North Carolina State Department of Public Welfare
Inabel Lindsay, Howard University
Gerri Major, Johnson Publications
Paul Rilling, Executive Dirctor, District of Columbia Council on Human Relations
Ruth Whaley, Secretary, New York City Board of Estimates
Deborah Partridge Wolfe, Chief of Education, Committee on Education and Labor, United States House of Representatives

THE SECRETARIAT

The work of the Commission would not have been possible without the support of the central secretariat. The persons listed below worked for the Commission for varying lengths of time. A number were made available by agencies represented on the Commission.

The editorial committee in charge of preparation of the report consisted of the following Commission members: Margaret Hickey, chairman, Richard A. Lester, John W. Macy, Jr., and Esther Peterson.

The report was drafted by Helen Hill Miller; its format was designed by Frank A. Guaragna of the United States Department of Labor.

Executive Secretary, Katherine P. Ellickson
Special Assistant, Mary N. Hilton

PROFESSIONAL	SECRETARIAL	ADMINISTRATIVE
Antonia H. Chayes	Marguerite H. Adams	Colonel Irene Galloway
Catherine S. East	Marjorie P. Brown	(*deceased*)
Mary Eastwood	Paul W. Gibbs	Jean M. Wittman
Ruth K. Holstein	Jeanne L. Greene	
Frances B. Kaplan	Marie C. Hansom	
Ella C. Ketchin	Edith M. Holland	
Diana T. Michaelis	June Mace	
Sam A. Morgenstein	Caroline Mode	
Margaret M. Morris	Ruth Morris	
Merrill G. Murray	Marilyn D. Necessary	
Ruth T. Prokop	Rose Pistolesi	
Irene B. Reedy	Olga Redman	
Roger Sheldon	Marlon E. Seward	
	Bertha H. Whittaker	

COOPERATING ORGANIZATIONS

The following organizations assisted in one phase or another of the Commission's work; a number of them made substantial contributions through the preparation of special papers for Committe consideration.

Alliance of Unitarian Women
Altrusa International, Inc.
American Association of University Women
American Bar Association, Family Law Section
American Civil Liberties Union
American Federation of Labor and Congress of Industrial Organizations
American Home Economics Association
American Legion Auxiliary
American Medical Women's Association, Inc.
American Newspaper Women's Club, Inc.
American Nurses' Association, Inc.
American Personnel and Guidance Association, Inc.
American Society of Women Accountants
American Women in Radio and Television, Inc.
Association of the Junior Leagues of America, Inc.
B'nai B'rith Women
Camp Fire Girls, Inc.
Council of State Governments
Defense Advisory Committee on Women in the Services
Delta Sigma Theta
The Fashion Group, Inc.
General Federation of Women's Clubs

Girl Scouts of the United States of America
Hadassah, The Women's Zionist Organization of America, Inc.
International Association of Governmental Labor Officials
International Union of Electrical, Radio and Machine Workers
League of Women Voters of the United States
The Lucy Stone League, Inc.
National Association of Colored Women's Clubs, Inc.
National Association of Women Lawyers
National Consumers League
National Council of Catholic Women
National Council of Jewish Women, Inc.
National Council of Negro Women, Inc.
National Council of Women of the United States, Inc.
National Federation of Business and Professional Women's Clubs, Inc.
National League for Nursing, Inc.
National Office Management Association
National Woman's Party
Phi Chi Theta
Public Personnel Association
Quota International, Inc.
Soroptimist Federation of the Americas, Inc.
Theta Sigma Phi
United Church Women
Women's Division of Christian Service of the Board of Missions of the Methodist
    Church
Women's International League for Peace and Freedom
Women's National Press Club
Young Women's Christian Association of the United States of America
Zonta International

MEMBERS OF THE COMMISSION

The names of the men and women appointed to the Commission, and the posts they occupied at the time of their appointment, were:

Mrs. Eleanor Roosevelt, *Chairman (deceased)*
Mrs. Esther Peterson, *Executive Vice Chairman,* Assistant Secretary of Labor
Dr. Richard A. Lester, *Vice Chairman,* Chairman, Department of Economics,
    Princeton University
The Attorney General, Honorable Robert F. Kennedy
The Secretary of Agriculture, Honorable Orville L. Freeman
The Secretary of Commerce, Honorable Luther H. Hodges
The Secretary of Labor, Honorable Arthur J. Goldberg, Honorable W. Willard
    Wirtz
The Secretary of Health, Education, and Welfare, Honorable Abraham A. Ribicoff,
    Honorable Anthony L. Celebrezze
Honorable George D. Aiken, United States Senate
Honorable Maurine B. Neuberger, United States Senate
Honorable Edith Green, United States House of Representatives
Honorable Jessica M. Weis *(deceased),* United States House of Representatives
The Chairman of the Civil Service Commission, Honorable John W. Macy, Jr.

Mrs. Macon Boddy, Henrietta, Tex.
Dr. Mary I. Bunting, President, Radcliffe College
Mrs. Mary E. Callahan, Member, Executive Board, International Union of Electrical, Radio and Machine Workers
Dr. Henry David, President, New School for Social Research
Miss Dorothy Height, President, National Council of Negro Women, Inc.
Miss Margaret Hickey, Public Affairs Editor, *Ladies' Home Journal*
Mrs. Viola H. Hymes, President, National Council of Jewish Women, Inc.
Miss Margaret J. Mealey, Executive Director, National Council of Catholic Women
Mr. Norman E. Nicholson, Administrative Assistant, Kaiser Industries Corp., Oakland, Calif.
Miss Marguerite Rawalt, Attorney; past president: Federal Bar Association, National Association of Women Lawyers, National Federation of Business and Professional Women's Clubs, Inc.
Mr. William F. Schnitzler, Secretary-Treasurer, American Federation of Labor and Congress of Industrial Organizations
Dr. Caroline F. Ware, Vienna, Va.
Dr. Cynthia C. Wedel, Assistant General Secretary for Program, National Council of the Churches of Christ in the United States of America

CHART SOURCES

Chart 1. For 1900–1955, *Historical Statistics of the United States, Colonial Times to 1957* (United States Bureau of the Census, 1960), Series B 19–30, p. 23, and B 129–142, p. 27; for 1960–61, *Monthly Vital Statistics Reports* (United States Department of Health, Education, and Welfare, Public Health Service, National Office of Vital Statistics), annual summary, those years; for 1962–80, *Interim Revised Projections of the Population of the United States, by Age and Sex: 1975 and 1980* (United States Bureau of the Census, Current Population Reports), Series P–25, No. 251.

Chart 2. *Income of Families and Persons in the United States: 1961* (United States Bureau of the Census, Current Population Reports), Series P–60, No. 39, tables 2, 7, and 18, pp. 16, 19, and 26.

Chart 3. *U. S. Census of Population: 1960, U. S. Summary, Detailed Characteristics* (United States Bureau of the Census), PC(1)–1D, 1963, table 177, p. 436.

Chart 4. For 1920–30, *Historical Statistics of the United States, op. cit.*, Series D 13–25, p. 71; for 1940–60, *U. S. Census of Population: U. S. Summary, General Social and Economic Characteristics* (United States Bureau of the Census), PC(1)–1C, 1962, table 84, p. 214.

Chart 5. Denis F. Johnston, *Educational Attainment of Workers, 1962* (United States Department of Labor, Bureau of Labor Statistics), Special Labor Force Report No. 30.

Chart 6. *Ibid.*

Chart 7. *U. S. Census of Population: 1960, U. S. Summary, Detailed Charac-teristics, op. cit.*, tables 159, 194, 200, pp. 361, 487, and 519.

Chart 8. Jacob Schiffman, *Marital and Family Characteristics of Workers, March 1962* (United States Department of Labor, Bureau of Labor Statistics), Special Labor Force Report No. 26, table K, p. A–15.

Chart 9. *Children of Working Mothers* (United States Department of Health, Education, and Welfare, Children's Bureau, 1960), Bulletin 382.

Chart 10. For 1920–30, *Historical Statistics of the United States, op. cit.*, Series D 13–25, p. 71; for 1940–60, *U. S. Census of Population: 1960, U. S. Summary, General Social and Economic Characteristics, op. cit.*, table 84, p. 214; for 1970, Sophie Cooper, *Interim Revised Projections of U. S. Labor Force, 1965–75* (United States Department of Labor, Bureau of Labor Statistics), Special Labor Force Report No. 24, table 2, p. 4.

Chart 11. For 1920–40, *U. S. Census of Population: 1940, The Labor Force, U. S. Summary* (United States Bureau of the Census), vol. III, pt. 1, table 9, p. 26; for 1960, *U. S. Census of Population: 1960, U. S. Summary, Detailed Characteristics, op. cit.*, table 196, p. 501; for March 1962, Jacob Schiffman, Special Labor Force Report No. 26, *op. cit.*, table A, p. A–8.

Chart 12. *Federal Employment Statistics Bulletin* (United States Civil Service Commission), April 1962.

Chart 13. For 1945, *Income of Families and Persons in the United States*, Series P–60, *op. cit.*, No. 25, table 35, p. 50; for 1947–61, *ibid.*, No. 39, table 39, p. 42.

Chart 14. *Employee Earnings in Retail Trade, June 1961* (United States Department of Labor, Bureau of Labor Statistics, 1963), Bulletin 1338–8, table 3, p. 19.

Chart 15. Data prepared by United States Department of Health, Education, and Welfare, Social Security Administration, Division of the Actuary.

Chart 16. Data compiled by United States Department of Labor, Women's Bureau, May 23, 1963.

Chart 17. For population data, *U. S. Census of Population: 1960, U. S. Summary, General Population Characteristics, New York, PC(1)–34B, 1961, Pennsylvania, PC(1)–40B, 1961, Wisconsin, PC(1)–51B, 1961* (United States Bureau of the Census); for registered voters, *Legislative*

Manual, State of New York, 1961–62 (New York Secretary of State), and *Pennsylvania Manual, 1961–62* (Pennsylvania Department of Property and Supplies); for voters in Milwaukee, from the Board of Election Commissioners, City of Milwaukee.

Chart 18. For 1960, *U. S. Census of Population: 1960, U. S. Summary, General Social and Economic Characteristics, op. cit.,* table 83, p. 214; for 1980, *Interim Revised Projections of the Population of the United States, by Age and Sex: 1975 and 1980, op. cit.*

Chart 19. United States Department of Health, Education, and Welfare, Public Health Service, National Office of Vital Statistics: for 1900–1940, *Vital Statistics Rates in the United States, 1900–1940;* for 1950, *Vital Statistics of the United States,* Vol. I; for 1955 and 1960–61, *Monthly Vital Statistics Reports,* annual summaries, those years.

Chart 20. *Income of Families and Persons in the United States,* Series P–60, *op. cit.,* table 27, p. 32.

Chart 21. *Employment Projections, by Industry and Occupation, 1960–75* (United States Department of Labor, Bureau of Labor Statistics), Special Labor Force Report No. 28, table 2, p. 244.

SOURCES OF NEW TABULAR MATERIAL

Table 1. *Education Directory 1963–64, Part 3: Higher Education.* United States Department of Health, Education and Welfare, Office of Education.

2. Interdepartmental Committee on the Status of Women, United States Department of Labor. (Based on surveys by the Civil Service Commission.)

3. United States Department of Health, Education, and Welfare, Social Security Administration, Division of the Actuary.

4. Interdepartmental Committee on the Status of Women, United States Department of Labor.

5. Bureau of Labor Standards, United States Department of Labor.

6. Bureau of Employment Security, United States Department of Labor.

7–11. Women's Bureau, United States Department of Labor.

12. United States Department of Commerce, Bureau of the Census, 1960 Census of Population.

INDEX

About the Editors

Margaret Mead has long been interested in women's changing role in contemporary society. She is the author of *Male and Female,* the well-known study that deals with masculine and feminine personality in various primitive cultures as well as our own.

Dr. Mead received her B.A. from Barnard College and her M.A. and Ph.D. from Columbia University. Her first field expedition took her to Samoa in 1925–26; her by now classic book on adolescent girls in Samoa came out of this research. Dr. Mead is Curator of Ethnology at The American Museum of Natural History, New York, and Adjunct Professor of Anthropology at Columbia University. Internationally famous as a teacher and lecturer, she has done field work on seven Pacific cultures in New Guinea, the Admiralty Islands, Bali, and Samoa.

A fellow in many scholarly societies, she has been given numerous awards and honorary degrees in recognition of her work. Dr. Mead is the author of volumes of interest to both professional and lay readers; among them are *Coming of Age in Samoa, Growing Up in New Guinea, Sex and Temperament in Three Primitive Societies, New Lives for Old,* and, most recently, *Continuities in Cultural Evolution.*

Frances Balgley Kaplan's career has centered around the presentation of information significant to American women and their families. During the work of the President's Commission on the Status of Women, she served as Consultant on Public Information. Prior to that, she served successively as a specialist in the Public Information Programs of the Public Health Service, the Children's Bureau, and the Office of Education.

Mrs. Kaplan graduated from Hunter College, and received an M.A. from Columbia University. She now lives with her husband and two daughters in Chevy Chase, Maryland, where she works as a free-lance writer. Her principal interest lies in interpreting specialized or technical information for the general reader.